COLOSSAL CRACKS

Other titles in the Stackpole Military History Series

THE AMERICAN CIVIL WAR
Cavalry Raids of the Civil War
Pickett's Charge
Witness to Gettysburg

WORLD WAR II
Armor Battles of the Waffen-SS, 1943–45
Australian Commandos
The B-24 in China
Backwater War
Beyond the Beachhead
The Brandenburger Commandos
Bringing the Thunder
Coast Watching in World War II
Colossal Cracks
D-Day to Berlin
Exit Rommel
Fist from the Sky
Flying American Combat Aircraft of World War II
Forging the Thunderbolt
The German Defeat in the East, 1944–45
Germany's Panzer Arm in World War II
Grenadiers
Infantry Aces
Iron Arm
Luftwaffe Aces
Messerschmitts over Sicily
Michael Wittmann, Volume One
Michael Wittmann, Volume Two
The Nazi Rocketeers
On the Canal
Packs On!
Panzer Aces
Panzer Aces II
The Panzer Legions
Retreat to the Reich
The Savage Sky
A Soldier in the Cockpit
Surviving Bataan and Beyond
The 12th SS, Volume One
The 12th SS, Volume Two
Tigers in the Mud

THE COLD WAR / VIETNAM
Flying American Combat Aircraft: The Cold War
Land with No Sun
Street without Joy

WARS OF THE MIDDLE EAST
Never-Ending Conflict

OTHER
Desert Battles

COLOSSAL CRACKS

Montgomery's 21st Army Group
in Northwest Europe,
1944–45

Stephen Ashley Hart

STACKPOLE
BOOKS

Published in paperback in 2007 by
STACKPOLE BOOKS
5067 Ritter Road
Mechanicsburg, PA 17055
www.stackpolebooks.com

MONTGOMERY AND "COLOSSAL CRACKS": THE 21ST ARMY GROUP IN
NORTHWEST EUROPE, 1944–45, by Stephen Ashley Hart, was originally published
in hard cover by Greenwood Press, an imprint of Greenwood Publishing Group, Inc.,
Westport, CT. Copyright (c) 2000 by Stephen Ashley Hart. Paperback edition by
arrangement with Greenwood Publishing Group, Inc. All rights reserved.Paperback
edition by arrangement with Greenwood Publishing Group, Inc. All rights reserved.

Cover design by Tracy Patterson

Printed in the United States of America

10 9 8 7 6 5 4 3 2 1

FIRST EDITION

Library of Congress Cataloging-in-Publication Data

Hart, S. (Stephen), 1968–
  [Montgomery and "colossal cracks"]
  Colossal cracks : Montgomery's 21st Army Group in Northwest Europe,
1944–45 / Stephen Ashley Hart. — 1st ed.
      p. cm. — (Stackpole military history series)
  Originally published: Westport, Ct. : Praeger, 2000, under the title: Montgomery
and "colossal cracks.".
  Includes bibliographical references and index.
  ISBN-13: 978-0-8117-3383-0
  ISBN-10 0-8117-3383-1
    1. World War, 1939–1945—Campaigns—Western Front.   2. Allied Forces.
Army Group, 21st. 3. Montgomery of Alamein, Bernard Law Montgomery,
Viscount, 1887–1976. I. Title.

D756.3.H37 2007
940.54'1241—dc22
                                                          2006024171

Table of Contents

Acknowledgments

The author would like to express his gratitude to the following for their help in the process of bringing this book to completion. To the staffs of the following institutions I owe a debt of gratitude for their assistance: to Patricia Methven and Kate O'Brien at the Liddell Hart Centre for Military Archives, King's College, London; to the staffs of the Public Record Office, the Churchill College Cambridge Archive, and the Imperial War Museum; to Major Bob Caldwell and the staff of the Directorate of History, Canadian National Defense Headquarters, Ottawa; to the staff of the National Archives of Canada, Ottawa; and last, to the helpful staff at the Central Library, the Royal Military Academy Sandhurst.

I am indebted to the following for their comments and suggestions on this work: Professor Michael Dockrill, Lieutenant-Colonel Dr. John English, Professor David French, Allison Gough, Professor Dominick Graham, Dr. Tim Harrison Place, Dr. Russell Hart, Gary Huckle, Dr. Matthew Hughes, Dr. Chris Mann, Dr. Tim Moreman, Chris Packham, John Peaty, Professor Ed Spiers, and my colleagues at the Department of War Studies, the Royal Military Academy Sandhurst. For their help with the maps and final layouts, I must thank Dr. Niall Barr, Keith Chaffer, and Aryk Nusbacher. My parents and sister have all been generous in their support. I am grateful also for the help and cooperation of Lieutenant-General W. A. B. Anderson, Brigadier G. E. Beament, and Major-General N. Elliot Rodger who kindly agreed to be interviewed.

I would like to state my appreciation for the financial support awarded me by the Economic and Social Research Council, without which this work would not have been possible, and also that by the Department of War Studies, King's College London.

I also owe a vital debt of gratitude to the sagacious comments and advice of Dr. Brian Holden Reid of the War Studies Department, King's College London. Dr. Heather Ruland Staines, Nicole Cournoyer and the staff at Praeger also merit my gratitude for their patience and professionalism. Notwithstanding all the help I have received, any errors of fact or interpretation that remain are solely the responsibility of the author. And finally, let me take this opportunity to dedicate this book to Gill Watson, without whose support this study would not have been completed.

Copyright Acknowledgments

Abbreviations

IBC; IBAbC	I (British) Corps; I British Airborne Corps
ICC	I Canadian Corps
2CC	II Canadian Corps
2ORS	No. 2 Operational Research Section
2KRRC	2nd Battalion, King's Royal Rifle Corps
2CID	2nd Canadian Infantry Division
2TAF	2nd Tactical Air Force
3CID	3rd Canadian Infantry Division
3USA	The Third United States Army
6DWR	6th Battalion, Duke of Wellington's Regiment
8A	The Eighth Army
8C	VIII Corps
9USA	The Ninth United States Army
12C	XII Corps
12USAG	The 12th United States Army Group
15AG	The 15th Army Group
21AG	The 21st Army Group
30C	XXX Corps
83 Grp; 84 Grp	83rd and 84th Groups, 2nd Tactical Air Force
A	Adjutant-General's Branch
ACIGS	Assistant Chief of the Imperial General Staff
ACM	Air Chief Marshal
AD (or Armd Div)	Armored Division
Addrs	Address
Adm	Administration; Administrative
AEAF	Allied Expeditionary Air Forces
AGRA	Army Group, Royal Artillery (plural AGsRA)
AIR#	(Royal) Air Force Papers (at PRO)
AL	Archivist and Librarian File Number (at PRO)
AOC (-in-C)	Air Officer Commanding (-in-Chief)
AORG	Army Operational Research Group
AP/	Field Marshal Alanbrooke Papers (at LHCMA)

APC	Armored Personnel Carrier
Apprcn	Appreciation
App[s]	Appendix [Appendices]
AQ	Adjutant- and Quarter-Master General's Branch
AVM	Air Vice Marshal
AVRE	Armored Vehicle, Royal Engineer (plural AVsRE)
BAOR	British Army of the Rhine
Bde	Brigade
BGS	Brigadier, General Staff
BLA	British Liberation Army (name for the 21st Army Group)
BLM	Field Marshal, Viscount Bernard Montgomery of Alamein
BLM/	Papers of Field Marshal Montgomery (at IWM)
Bn	Battalion
Brig	Brigadier
BT	Battlefield Tour
CAB	Canadian Armored Brigade
CAB#	Cabinet Papers (at PRO)
CAC	Canadian Armored Corps
CAD	Canadian Armored Division
CAO	Chief Administrative Officer
CCA	Churchill College Archive, Cambridge
CCGS	Chief of the Canadian General Staff
CCRA	Corps Commander, Royal Artillery (plural CCsRA)
CCS	Combined Chiefs of Staff
Cdn	Canadian
CG	Commanding General (American Army)
CiC (or C-in-C)	Commander-in-Chief (Army Group Commander)
CID	Canadian Infantry Division
CIGS	Chief of the Imperial General Staff
CMHQ	Canadian Military Headquarters, London
CO[s]	Commanding Officer[s]
Col	Colonel
Coll	College (as in Staff College)
Comd	Commander
Conf	Conference
Conv	Conversation
Corr	correspondence
CoS	Chief of Staff
COSSAC	Chief of Staff to the Supreme Allied Commander
Coy	Company
CP/	Papers of General Henry D. G. Crerar (at NAC)

CPS	Canadian Planning Staff
CRA	Commander, Royal Artillery
CWP	Papers of Chester Wilmot (at LHCMA)
DA&QMG	Deputy Adjutant- and Quarter-Master General
DAAG	Deputy Assistant Adjutant-General
DAQMG	Deputy Assistant Quarter-Master General
DCIGS	Deputy Chief of the Imperial General Staff
DEFE#	Ministry of Defense Papers (at PRO)
DGP/	Papers of Major-General F. W. de Guingand (at LHCMA)
DHist	Directorate of History, Canadian National Defense HQ
Dir	Directive
Diss	Dissertation
Div	Division
DMO	Director of Military Operations, War Office
DMT	Director of Military Training, War Office
DO	Demi-Official
Doc(s)	document(s)
DRA	Director, Royal Artillery, War Office
DRAC	Director, Royal Armored Corps, War Office
DSD	Director, Staff Duties, War Office
f[s]	folio[s]
FAJ	Field Artillery Journal
FCA	The First Canadian Army
Fld Rtn	Offcrs Field Return of Officers
FM	Field Marshal
FR	Final Report
FSR	Field Service Regulations
FUSA	The First United States Army
FUSAG	The 1st United States Army Group
G(Air); G(Int)	General Staff, Air Branch; Intelligence Branch
G(L); G(Ops)	General Staff, Liaison Branch; Operations Branch
G(Pl); G(SD)	General Staff, Plans Section; Staff Duties Branch
GAD	Guards Armored Division
Gen	(Full) General
GHQ	General Headquarters
GOC	General Officer Commanding (a Division or Corps)
GOCiC	General Officer Commanding-in-Chief (Army Commander)
GS (or G)	General Staff
GSO1; GS02; 3	General Staff officer, Grade 1; Grade 2; Grade 3
GS(R)	General Staff, Deception Section

HF	(United Kingdom) Home Forces
HQ	Headquarters
IB	Infantry Brigade
IBn	Infantry Battalion
Inf	Infantry
Infm	Information
IR (or Imd Rpt)	Immediate Report
IS (or Int Sum)	Intelligence Summary
IWM	Department of Documents, Imperial War Museum
Jnl	Journal
J.Mil.H	Journal of Military History
JNP/	Papers of Major John North (at LHCMA)
JRA	Journal of the Royal Artillery
LHP	Papers of Captain B. H. Liddell Hart
LHCMA	Liddell Hart Centre for Military Archives
LO	Liaison Officer
Lt-Col	Lieutenant-Colonel
Lt-Gen	Lieutenant-General
Ltr[s]	Letter[s]
MA	Military Assistant
Maj-Gen	Major-General
MEF	Middle Eastern Forces
Memo	Memorandum
Mess	Message
mf[s]	microfilm folio[s]
MGA	Major-General, Administration
MGRA	Major-General, Royal Artillery
MGRAC	Major-General, Royal Armored Corps
MHQ	Main Headquarters
Min Nat Def	(Canadian) Minister of National Defense
MIRS	Military Intelligence Research Section
Mnpwr	Manpower
MORU	Military Operational Research Unit
MSC/	Montgomery-Simpson Correspondence (IWM)
Mtng	Meeting
MTP	Military Training Pamphlets
n.[ns.]	Note number[s]
NAC	National Archives of Canada, Ottawa
NAM	National Army Museum, London
narr	narrative (typically a section of a War Diary)
NWE	Northwest Europe

OCP/	Papers of General Sir Richard O'Connor (LHCMA)
OI	Operation Instruction
OO	Operation Order
OP	Operational Plan
Opn; Opl	Operation; Operational
Ops	Operations Branch, General Staff; Operations
Orgn	Organization
ORS	Operational Research Section
"Ovld"	Operation "Overlord"
PAD	Polish Armored Division
Para	Paragraph
Pers Min	Personal Minute
Plng	Planning
PM	Prime Minister
PREM#	Prime Minister's Papers (at PRO)
PRO	Government Records, Public Record Office, Kew
Pz	Panzer
PzGr	Panzer Grenadier
Q	Quarter-Master General's Branch
RA	Royal Artillery
RAC	Royal Armored Corps
RAF	Royal Air Force
RCA	Royal Canadian Artillery
RCAF	Royal Canadian Air Force
Regt	Regiment
RPGPD	Rounds per Gun per Day
RLEW/	Papers of Ronald Lewin (at CCA)
Rpt	Report
RTR	Royal Tank Regiment
SASO	Senior Air Staff Officer
SBA	The Second (British) Army
SCAEF	Supreme Commander, Allied Expeditionary Forces
Sect	Section
SHAEF	Supreme Headquarters, Allied Expeditionary Forces
Snr	Senior
SoS War	Secretary of State for War
Stf	Staff
"Swbk"	Operation "Switchback"
THQ (or Tac HQ)	Tactical Headquarters
TOO	Time of Origin
TOR	Time of Receipt

"Tot"	Operation "Totalize"
Univ	University
V(s) (or Vol(s))	Volume(s)
VCIGS	Vice Chief of the Imperial General Staff
"Verit"	Operation "Veritable"
WD	War Diary
WO	War Office, London
WO#	War Office Papers (at PRO)

CHAPTER 1

Introduction

This study examines the manner in which the 21st Army Group conducted the Northwest Europe campaign of 6 June 1944–8 May 1945.[1] This army group formed the combined Anglo-Canadian contribution to the Allied forces that landed on the Normandy coast on D-Day in Operation "Overlord" and successfully advanced into the heart of Germany by VE-Day. The British General (from 1 September 1944, Field Marshal) Bernard Law Montgomery ("Monty") commanded the 21st Army Group.[2] This work argues that the 21st Army Group conducted this campaign more effectively than some scholars have argued previously and that the generalship of Montgomery and his two subordinate army commanders was both appropriate and competent.

The date 1 September 1944 marks an important chronological divide within the campaign. Before this, during the battles fought for Normandy, Montgomery not only commanded the Anglo-Canadian 21st Army Group but, as temporary Land Forces Commander, controlled all Allied troops in the theater irrespective of their nationality. In Normandy, Montgomery held his dual operational and strategic responsibilities under the overarching authority of the theater Supreme Allied Commander, the American General Dwight ("Ike") Eisenhower. However, after 1 September 1944, in accordance with the pre-"Overlord" planning, Montgomery ceased to act as Land Forces Commander. Instead he became solely an army group commander in a theater in which the Americans now also deployed two national army groups.[3] From this date, all three army group commanders came under the direct operational command of Eisenhower, who now assumed the role of Land Forces Commander in addition to his responsibility as Supreme Allied Commander.[4]

This changing command structure is crucial to understanding both the campaign and Montgomery's handling of the 21st Army Group. Here, one should make a distinction between theater strategy and operations, between the decisions made at the level of the theater concerning the development of an entire campaign, and the individual decisions ordering action in pursuance of that strategy. Prior to 1 September 1944, there existed a unity between theater strategy and operations since the same commander, Montgomery, not only controlled both but also believed fervently in the need for such a unity. After 1 September, however, Eisenhower developed a theater strategy that balanced the conflicting demands of his three army group commanders, but it was the latter who enacted operations to fulfill this strategy; thus, after this date a disjuncture existed between strategy and operations.[5] The focus of this study on the way in which the 21st Army Group conducted the campaign requires a definition of the operational level of war. It will suffice here to define this briefly as the "area between strategy and tactics which denotes the fighting of battles in a given theater of operations in pursuit of the political objective of the war,"[6] and as the "gray zone once called Grand Tactics, the tactics of large formations," such as army groups, armies, and corps.[7] This concept is examined in more detail later.

This analysis of the operational technique utilized by the 21st Army Group in Northwest Europe is based on a systematic examination of the individual characteristics that comprised its overall operational approach. It is not a narrative of the part that the 21st Army Group played in the wider Allied campaign in Northwest Europe.[8] This formation's operational technique closely reflected British army doctrine—the body of corporate knowledge that was either "officially approved to be taught" or used in practice on the battlefield.[9] Doctrine is critical because it "is the substance that binds" together the correct organizing, equipping, and training of military forces.[10] The first section of this study, chapters 2 through 5, examines Montgomery's operational methods, and demonstrates that he made a crucial contribution to the manner in which the 21st Army Group conducted the campaign. Montgomery's operational technique is encapsulated by his phrase "Colossal Cracks," which is used here as a generic name for his approach.[11]

The second part of this work extends the investigation of how the 21st Army Group conducted the campaign beyond Montgomery to the army level. This section examines the methods utilized by Montgomery's subordinate army commanders, Lieutenant-Generals Miles Dempsey, commanding the Second (British) Army, and Henry Crerar, commanding the First Canadian Army.[12] It demonstrates the degree of consensus on operational technique that existed between Montgomery and his two subordinate army commanders. Although not examined in this study, the evidence demonstrates that Montgomery's six original corps commanders—Gerard Bucknall, John Crocker, Brian Horrocks, Richard O'Connor, Neil Ritchie, and Guy Simonds—utilized the same methods as their 21st Army Group superiors.[13]

Within the above framework, this book argues that the 21st Army Group conducted the campaign more effectively than some scholars have suggested previously. This assertion combines two interconnected subarguments: first, that Montgomery handled the 21st Army Group more appropriately than some of the existing literature has recognized;[14] and second, that historians can fully appreciate how the 21st Army Group conducted the campaign only by examining its two highest command echelons rather than by focusing solely on Montgomery. The re-evaluation presented in the first subargument, however, is a measured one that falls short of the overly favorable view of the Field Marshal portrayed by his eulogizers.[15] Some early narrative-based British works favorable to Montgomery, heavily reliant on his own biased accounts, used the fact of ultimate Allied victory as evidence of the extent of Montgomery's achievement, instead of presenting sustained critical analysis.[16] This indiscriminate praise of Montgomery has obscured appreciation by historians of his real abilities and achievements—as has the excessive criticism made by his detractors. A systematic and balanced analysis needs to explain in what ways Montgomery effectively handled the 21st Army Group, because the ultimate Allied victory is not evidence in itself that Montgomery conducted the campaign well. This study presents a balanced assessment of Montgomery that appropriately combines criticism and credit; such an analysis produces an opinion that falls marginally closer to the views presented by the Field Marshal's hagiographers than those offered by his critics.

The second subargument asserts that historians can only fully comprehend the way in which the 21st Army Group conducted the campaign through an analysis of how the formation's two highest command echelons interacted, rather than through one that focuses solely on Montgomery. Scholars only can obtain a full picture by examining the methods utilized by this formation's army commanders, as well as their command relationships with Montgomery and with one another. The two subarguments this study develops are complementary, because exploration of the second assertion reveals the extent of the consensus that existed within the 21st Army Group concerning operational techniques. The existence of this consensus reinforces the argument that historians critical of Montgomery have blamed him unfairly for methods shared by his senior subordinates.

This reassertion both of Montgomery's operational abilities, and of the 21st Army Group's conduct of the campaign, reflects the author's conviction that, to date, historians have not produced an entirely satisfactory comprehensive analysis of these two interconnected aspects. The following six interconnected weaknesses evident in historians' works on this campaign explain why this body of literature still lacks such an entirely satisfactory analysis: that they have overemphasized Montgomery's unpleasant personality and the significance of his role within the campaign; that they have focused excessively on theater strategic disputes rather than on the operational level; that they have not systematically analyzed Montgomery's operational technique; that they have given insufficient regard to the actual situation facing the 1944 British army; that they have underestimated the appropriateness of

Montgomery's methods to British war aims; and that they have criticized Montgomery personally both for methods shared by his subordinates and for failures as attributable to the latter as to himself. Appreciation of these features has prompted this reappraisal of the campaign.

First, the excessive focus placed by historians on Montgomery's distasteful personality has obfuscated a proper appreciation of his operational abilities. Any historical analysis of this campaign must consider Montgomery's personality, but some historians' assessments of Montgomery's operational technique have been clouded by the excessive emphasis they place on this aspect. Only in certain—yet important—areas did the Field Marshal's personality impinge on operations, particularly in the case of inter-Allied cooperation. Furthermore, some historians, overly influenced by Montgomery's manifest egotism, have interpreted his military actions as reflecting principally his personal ambition and vanity; yet the Field Marshal was too intensely a professional soldier for such factors to be more than modest influences on his conduct of the campaign. Consequently, some historians have understated the extent to which Montgomery's pursuit of a British agenda within the Allied effort in Northwest Europe influenced his conduct of the campaign.[17] Together, these factors have obscured an accurate appreciation of Montgomery's true abilities. Finally, this excessive focus on Montgomery also has heightened the underestimation of the contribution made by his subordinate army commanders.

Second, this study asserts that a satisfactory analysis of the campaign needs to focus firmly on the operational level. Instead, historical literature on the campaign has focused excessively on the disputes over theater strategy that arose between Montgomery and Eisenhower after late August 1944 over the "broad front versus narrow thrust" controversy.[18] Even though this dispute is significant, it does not merit the vast attention paid to it by scholars.[19] The emphasis historians have placed on this debate has fueled historiographical confusions based on the lingering repercussions of wartime inter-Allied tensions; unfortunately, nationalistic undertones have permeated too many studies of the campaign.[20] Furthermore, this historical debate also has reinforced some historians' assumptions that theater strategic decisions determined success or failure in this campaign, rather than the combination of these with operational decisions. Some historians have discussed whether the Allies would have won the war earlier if they had advanced on a narrow front after September 1944 with negligible consideration of whether this strategic decision was compatible with current operational techniques. Indeed, many accounts of this inter-Allied dispute fail to distinguish clearly between theater strategy and operations. Much of the literature on this campaign has not focused sufficiently on the operational level when considering how the 21st Army Group conducted the campaign.

Third, this study argues that some analyses have criticized aspects of Montgomery's generalship, such as his caution and reliance on firepower, without giving due regard to the other facets that comprised his operational approach.[21] For historians can fully appreciate each element of Montgomery's operational technique only in the light of all the other components of his approach: historians can understand each individual facet only as part of the whole. Such a comprehensive analysis, however, demonstrates that Montgomery's caution and predilection for firepower were more justified than many historians have acknowledged.

Fourth, this analysis asserts that some historical works have understated the difficulties facing the British army during summer 1944. The retrospective knowledge of both ultimate Allied success and overwhelming superiority in matériel suggests an inevitability to victory not perceived by participants at the time; to the British population of mid-1944 the success of "Overlord" remained as uncertain as the vast risks involved were clear. Many historians have underestimated not only the extent of Britain's war weariness by D-Day after four years of war but also the practical difficulties faced by the British army in prosecuting this campaign.[22] By June 1944 Britain was in the grip of a chronic manpower shortage, and the British army would not be able to replace all the casualties it would sustain in the liberation of Europe; the 21st Army Group could be nothing other than a wasting asset.

This force, moreover, represented Britain's last substantial field army, and if this was lost, the British could only make a modest contribution to any eventual Allied success. Montgomery realized the necessity to avoid incurring heavy casualties in Northwest Europe. This manpower shortage also placed a premium on getting the best out of the relatively limited personnel resources at Montgomery's disposal through sustaining their morale. However, the morale of the civilian conscript soldiers that served in the 21st Army Group proved rather more fragile than that of the determined and resilient *Wehrmacht*. Montgomery's concern about how well his troops would "stand up when they had to play in the big league" constantly influenced his operational behavior.[23] He recognized both that simple weight of matériel was not enough in itself to assure victory, and that such numerical superiority in equipment did not obviate the need to nurture high morale within his Anglo-Canadian troops. Montgomery's appreciation that the morale of his forces represented a key to victory reflected his accurate perception of the strategic and operational situation facing the 21st Army Group in mid-1944.

Historians have often underemphasized these two features of Montgomery's operational methods, which might be termed casualty conservation and the maintenance of morale. Yet these two factors influenced Montgomery's conduct of the campaign more than any other consideration. All senior commanders within the 21st Army Group strove to conduct this campaign in a manner that both sustained the morale of their troops and avoided heavy casualties. These two concerns remained interconnected: Avoiding heavy casualties bolstered the morale of these soldiers, and high morale facilitated a superior battlefield performance that contributed to reducing casualties.

Though some of the campaign's historical literature has given modest attention to these influences, no work has accorded them the attention justified by their significance.[24] Historians have not fully recognized the influence these two factors exerted on the other characteristics of Montgomery's operational technique. Scholars can only understand his utilization of cautious, firepower-laden methods in the light of these twin concerns. This work, after giving due consideration to these two influences, concludes that Montgomery's utilization of his "Colossal Cracks" operational technique was appropriate to the circumstances facing the 21st Army Group in mid-1944. This reinforces the argument that in 1944 Montgomery, despite operational flaws such as his inability to master exploitation, was one of the most competent British generals in Europe. One particular quality was his perceptive appreciation of the art of what was practicable operationally in the longer term given the wider politico-strategic situation facing him.

Fifth, this work argues that some works critical of Montgomery have not appreciated the appropriateness of his methods to achieving British war aims given the relative capabilities of the 1944 British and German armies; indeed, some analyses have not grasped fully the essence of British war aims in Northwest Europe. Though "Colossal Cracks" was crude and methodical, it was still an appropriate way of achieving Britain's objectives given this balance of relative capabilities. These war aims did not seek simply to remove the Nazi canker, but rather to obtain victory over Germany within a larger Allied effort with tolerable casualties and yet, paradoxically, with a high military profile. This high profile would ensure Britain a strong influence in the political reconstruction of postwar Europe; protection of this influence had contributed to Britain's decision to go to war in 1939.[25] To accomplish these specific war aims, Montgomery correctly sought to nurture his limited, fragile resources through an adequate, but sustained, combat performance that would, as part of a larger Allied effort, slowly grind the enemy into submission by the inexorable logic of an attritional war of industrial production, of matériel. As Professor Michael Howard observed, Montgomery's conduct of the campaign was "determined by his perception of the limited capabilities" of his troops. The 1939–45 British army "was not very good" as "the British High Command was very aware," and Montgomery "did not regard his troops as capable of any higher performance" than a set-piece battle style of fighting.[26] In this context, Montgomery's utilization of such attritional, firepower-laden techniques represented an appropriate use of the resources available to him. The Allies rightly fought the sort of war that gave them the best chance of eventual victory, irrespective of how crude or mechanistic was this style of warfare. This campaign, therefore, represents a military situation where warfare involving strong attritional elements represented the most appropriate method; as such, this study serves to counter the possible inference from modern British army doctrine that any strategic or operational technique other than maneuver warfare must be misguided.[27]

Not only was the 21st Army Group unlikely to produce a magnificent combat performance against the Germans, but such an achievement also was unnecessary for the attainment of British war aims. The relatively unimpressive combat performance of the 21st Army Group in Northwest Europe has prompted some historians to criticize Montgomery's generalship. Though an element of this criticism is justified, much of it is excessive because it assumes that the British army ought to have striven to compete tactically with the *Wehrmacht*. The great strength of the 1939–45 German army lay at the tactical level, and its forces typically produced fine tactical combat performances even in highly unfavorable battlefield situations. Yet it was neither necessary nor appropriate for the British forces, a civilian mass conscript army, to try to compete with the more ideologically motivated, professional, and tactically experienced enemy on the latter's terms. "Far sighted" British commanders "realized that they could never turn these wartime [conscript] soldiers into professionals" in either "their own image" nor in that of the enemy.[28] In summer 1944, therefore, what the British army needed to do in Northwest Europe to achieve victory was simply to do what it did best. This meant that the 21st Army Group had to fight a protracted series of set-piece battles based on copious matériel, during which it would both sustain troop morale by avoiding defeats and prevent excessive casualties. Through this operational approach Montgomery's forces would grind the enemy down by attrition based on massive firepower until the battlefield situation became so favorable that the Allies could undertake mobile operations that would complete the defeat of the German army in the West (the *Westheer*).

Hence, the Allies would achieve victory over the *Westheer* through crude techniques and competent generalship at the operational and tactical levels rather than through tactical excellence. Moreover, the availability of massive firepower to Montgomery's forces inadvertently created a tactical crutch that inhibited their effective use of initiative. This crutch limited the potential improvement that more realistic training might have had on the tactical performance of these troops; "Colossal Cracks" was not immune from significant inherent flaws.

The operational approach utilized by Montgomery and his senior subordinates offered the 21st Army Group the best chance, as part of a larger Allied effort, to achieve victory in the long term at reasonable cost in casualties. Montgomery's task was not one of winning battles but of winning the entire campaign. That the Allies achieved victory mattered more than the manner in which they accomplished this success. Only in the sphere of maintaining its high profile within the Allied camp did it matter to Britain how the campaign had been won. But Britain could pursue its war aim of securing this high profile in avenues other than the battlefield glory bought by the sacrifice of the bulk of Britain's last field army. One such avenue was for Montgomery to remain as Land Forces Commander after 1 September 1944, with authority over all Allied troops in theater. Any glory won by the troops (irrespective of nationality) would reflect on the Land Forces Commander, and if Montgomery held this position, this would benefit Britain and her postwar ambitions.[29]

Montgomery's methods also appropriately utilized the strengths of the British army, notably the artillery arm. His methodical, attritional approach limited the opportunities for the Germans to exploit either their tactical strengths or British weaknesses. By utilizing these methods, the 21st Army Group reduced opportunities for the Germans to exercise their tactical initiative and speed of reaction against exposed Allied troops who had advanced beyond the range of the massive firepower they could summon down on an enemy counterattack. Furthermore, "Colossal Cracks" ensured an adequate combat performance from the Anglo-Canadian soldiers by continually nurturing the latter's relatively fragile morale. The senior commanders within the 21st Army Group maintained reasonable morale among their troops by seeking to secure a continuous series of modest victories. They achieved such success by securing the best chances of victory before an attack was launched. To this end, these senior commanders would allocate in support of the troops the greatest possible cornucopia of matériel—support that helped to avoid both a setback and the sustaining of unwarranted casualties. The senior commanders of the 21st Army Group would, if humanly possible, avoid placing demands on Anglo-Canadian troops even more horrendous than those typically imposed by combat.

Sixth, this study argues that though Montgomery contributed greatly to the manner in which the 21st Army Group conducted this campaign, some historians have exaggerated his significance. The existence of so many books written directly about Montgomery, that assume that he exercised an overwhelming influence on how the 21st Army Group conducted the campaign, has fueled these exaggerations.[30] Scholars can fully appreciate Montgomery's vital role, however, only within the wider context of the senior command echelons within the 21st Army Group, particularly his army commanders. Some historians have criticized the Field Marshal personally for methods and attitudes shared by his senior subordinates. Indeed, Montgomery did not impose an alien doctrine on the 21st Army Group, which already had developed techniques similar to those of Montgomery before the latter returned to Britain in January 1944 to assume command of the formation.

Some of the Field Marshal's alleged failures, moreover, remain attributable as much to his subordinates as to himself. Sometimes, Montgomery was only "responsible" for these failings in the technical sense that, as the army group commander, he was ultimately responsible for all the activities of those serving under him irrespective of any direct culpability on his part. The spreading of this culpability among this formation's senior commanders also reinforces this reassertion of Montgomery's reputation. The extent of the consensus that existed within the army group's two senior command levels supports the argument that analysts have underestimated the appropriateness of Montgomery's technique; this issue is the subject of the latter half of this work.

The existence of these six interconnected distortions within the literature on this campaign justify a reassessment of the way in which Montgomery and the 21st Army Group conducted the Northwest Europe campaign. This study develops these twin subarguments first through an analysis of all the components of Montgomery's operational technique and then through those of his subordinate army commanders. This re-examination reveals that Montgomery was an effective general and that the 21st Army Group conducted this campaign competently.

This measured reassertion of Montgomery's abilities, however, does not argue that he was one of the "great captains" of history, as he so vainly believed; for clearly he was not. Historians should not attribute the fact that he so fervently believed this himself with more significance than it deserves. Montgomery proved no more than fully competent at the flexible, masterly, hands-on control of a battle. His greatest operational strengths lay in his perceptive grasp of the wider art of the practicable. He astutely recognized the real long-term capabilities of his forces, both man and machine, relative to that of the skilled, and resilient, *Westheer*. Moreover, Montgomery perceptively recognized what the British army had to do to defeat the Germans. He then correctly matched together these two appreciations. It is also possible that he next matched these two assessments to a private understanding of his true capabilities as a general. "Colossal Cracks" represented what the conscript 1944 British army did best; it remained a way of winning the war with tolerable casualties; and above all it was what Montgomery did best. It remains unclear whether he stuck to this approach because he believed that there was insufficient necessity or time to develop another effective technique or because he realized privately that he was incapable of effective generalship using any alternative technique.[31] Montgomery's egotism might lead

historians to dismiss the possibility that he privately appreciated his own limitations, but he was a complex personality, paradoxically capable of both
acute perception and astounding myopia.[32]

Montgomery is excluded from the ranks of the "great captains" of history by his obvious shortcomings as a military commander: his failure to
exploit ruthlessly any success gained; his deficiency in the fluid battle; and
his limited ability at adjusting his methods to changing operational situations.[33] This assumes that achieving inclusion within the ranks of the "great
captains" is historically significant, but this notion may be a chimera reflecting an overemphasis on the individual element in warfare.[34] Occasionally,
alleged "military geniuses" may have imposed their will in contradiction to
the underlying realities of the battlefield situation, but most commanders
have failed to exert any significant personal influence on military events.
Neither Rommel, Rundstedt, nor any other German senior commander in
Northwest Europe exerted any real individual influence on the course of the
campaign, which was decided more by superiority in matériel than by command capabilities.[35] Moreover, during the Second World War, widespread
competence among senior commanders arguably proved more beneficial
than isolated examples of genius. The real strength of the *Wehrmacht* was the
effectiveness of the General Staff system in "*institutionalizing* military excellence" repeatedly to produce highly competent senior commanders and staff
officers.[36] Indeed, Montgomery would oversee victory in Northwest Europe
not by military genius but by sustained competence.[37]

This work systematically examines the 1944 British army's "Colossal
Cracks" technique through a categorization of its component parts. It analyzes Montgomery's methods, and those of his subordinate army commanders, in terms of eleven fundamental characteristics together with seven lesser
ones, all of which were interconnected to varying degrees. First, this study
examines the two paramount aspects, casualty conservation and the maintenance of morale. Second, it examines the four key components of the set-
piece battle: the master plan, concentration, firepower-based attrition, and a
methodical and cautious approach. These four together with the notion of
"alternate thrusts" constituted the foundation of Montgomery's physical control of operations. This work then explores the other key features—administration, air power, the initiative, and balance. Finally, it examines seven other
ancillary characteristics: grip, surprise, flank protection, flexibility, cooperation, simplicity, and the assimilation of combat lessons.

The interconnection between these various components lies behind the
assertion that historians can fully understand the individual elements of
Montgomery's technique only in the context of the totality of this approach.
The assessment this study presents concerning the significance of each indi-

vidual aspect is based partly on the importance that Montgomery attached to it in his writings. However, what is more important in this assessment is this author's evaluation of how important each individual characteristic proved in relation to both the entire "Colossal Cracks" approach and the other individual characteristics of this approach. This author's assessment does not always concur with that of Montgomery, but then the latter remained a dedicated practitioner, not a conceptual military thinker. This, together with his tendency to simplify military problems to their essentials and his professional focus when conducting active operations, meant that he never systematically conceptualized his own methods.

Montgomery's operational technique involved massive set-piece battles based on concentration of force, massed artillery firepower (supplemented by aerial bombing when possible), and integrated use of tactical air power. Montgomery would only commence these set-piece battles after careful planning, rehearsal, preparation, and massive concentration of resources. He conducted these battles cautiously and methodically, with great regard to the logistical situation, gripping their development according to a previously conceived master plan. Operationally, the Field Marshal sought to maintain the initiative and remain balanced—respectively, to force the enemy merely to react to his moves and to have his forces so deployed that any sudden enemy move could be countered rapidly. Through "alternate thrusts"—a series of limited attacks in varying sectors of the front—Montgomery strove to force the enemy to become unbalanced before he launched a decisive offensive. "Colossal Cracks" represented an attritional method based on matériel that eschewed operational maneuver. Furthermore, the devastation inflicted on the battlefield by concentrated firepower severely limited the opportunities for tactical mobility. The British army had disseminated these methods through its ranks after Montgomery's successes in North Africa after October 1942; his January 1944 assumption of command merely reinforced the reliance on these techniques within a 21st Army Group senior command that had already assimilated many of these methods prior to his arrival.

Having examined Montgomery's operational methods, the second part of this study examines the army commanders within the 21st Army Group. This analysis reflects the second subargument that this study presents, that historians cannot fully understand how the 21st Army Group conducted this campaign merely through a study of Montgomery. The personal and institutional relationships that existed between these senior commanders constituted a key element in this formation's conduct of the campaign. This study emphasizes the role of personality in these relationships, because the following three factors made this aspect significant: the distinction between the executive power wielded by commanders and the advisory power of staffs;

that the realities of active operations in the field determined relationships between higher commands rather than abstract rules; and that the War Office could not act as a centralizing body imposing abstract relationships on local situations. In Northwest Europe during 1944–45, Montgomery's subordinates understood these realities, as Lieutenant-General Brian Horrocks, commander of the XXX Corps, made clear: "The personalities concerned" and "their relationships with each other" were of "immense significance" because "there did not, could not, exist any sort of manual setting out in precise terms the roles" of organizations "such as an army group, army or even a corps."[38]

The distortion caused by the overemphasis on Montgomery within scholarship on the campaign has prevented historians from appreciating the real contribution made by Montgomery's subordinate army commanders, Henry Crerar and Miles Dempsey. This study establishes a fuller appreciation of the contribution made by these two commanders to the conduct of the campaign. In particular, a measured reassessment of Dempsey's role is put forward. This suggests that Dempsey made a significant contribution to the campaign and, hence, was not simply the cipher that scholars have portrayed him to be. This study commences the process that reverses Dempsey's decline into an undeserved historical oblivion. This study also examines the impact that these relationships exerted on the extent to which Montgomery's operational methods were shared at army level. This work uses the same eighteen-fold categorization that was employed to analyze Montgomery's methods in this examination of the approaches of his subordinate army commanders. This analysis demonstrates both that a consensus on operational technique existed between these commanders and that Montgomery did not impose an alien doctrine on an army group that already utilized his basic methods.

To reiterate, this study demonstrates that the manner in which Montgomery and the 21st Army Group conducted the Northwest Europe campaign remained more than competent. "Colossal Cracks" represented an appropriate operational technique given both British war aims and the capabilities of the 1944 British and Canadian armies relative to that of the *Westheer*. However, there remained serious drawbacks inherent in this crude operational technique, not least the limitations on mobility and exploitation of success caused by the devastation that massed firepower inflicted on the battlefield. However, all things considered, the advantages of "Colossal Cracks" outweighed the disadvantages. This approach utilized the British army's strengths, limited German exploitation of their own advantages, accurately reflected the limited personnel resources available, and achieved British war aims. "Colossal Cracks" undoubtedly represented a winning method, even if not a flawless one; it was a double-edged and rather fragile sword. Yet it had taken heroic efforts to get the British army from its 1940 nadir to a point in 1944 where it could, using these methods as part of a larger Allied effort defeat without a bloodbath the highly efficient *Wehrmacht.* By June 1944 the British army had had insufficient time, and probably insufficient ability and experience, to overcome the weaknesses inherent in "Colossal Cracks." This technique was the most appropriate weapon the British army could develop in the circumstances, because it could not have forged a more viable alternative weapon by mid-1944. And, above all else, the "Colossal Cracks" technique would prove to be enough—albeit perhaps only just enough—both to defeat the Nazi canker and achieve British war aims.

METHODOLOGY

Having outlined the main arguments of this study, some discussion of the sources and approaches used is germane. This analysis has utilized primary source material as widely as possible—an approach made particularly necessary by the existence within the historical literature on the campaign of contradictory assertions by the senior participants. Adopting such an approach helps avoid entanglement in the nationally orientated squabbles that have rumbled on since 1945. Historians previously have examined much of this primary material, but the assertion that "the archives have been drained" is incorrect.[39] This analysis has relied heavily on substantial sources not previously consulted, notably the less obvious War Office files at the Public Record Office.

The sources this study has examined include the vast range of official British and Canadian army records at the Public Record Office, the National Archives of Canada, and the Directorate of History, Canadian National Defense Headquarters. This work also has consulted extensively the private papers of officers and historians located in London at the Imperial War Museum, the Liddell Hart Centre for Military Archives, and the National Army Museum, as well as those at the Churchill College Archive, Cambridge, and both Canadian archives.[40] Interviews and correspondence with selected senior officers has reinforced this data. Though the extent of new primary material this study introduces is not inconsiderable, its contribution to scholarship on this campaign lies more in argument than in new archival material. Moreover, though the secondary literature on the campaign is immense, this study has consulted this material as widely as practicable. Despite the misconceptions sometimes apparent in such works, familiarity with this literature helps place any particular argument within its wider context.

The Operational Level of War

The central methodological concept that this study utilizes is the operational level of war, which has only reached prominence in Western military theory in the last two decades.[41] Of course, the conceptual term *operational*, which relates to this level of war, should not be confused with the descriptive adjective "operational," which relates to military operations. In 1944–45 Anglo-American military thought recognized just the grand strategic, theater (or military) strategic, and the tactical levels of war, but included "no adequate term" for the operational level.[42] At that time, most British generals concurred with Horrocks that the defining line between strategy and tactics lay at the army/corps boundary, whereas modern commanders would describe a corps' activities as operational.[43] In contrast to the ignorance of the operational level in Western military thought, in the interwar period, Soviet military thinkers, and to a lesser extent German ones, developed sophisticated operational concepts.[44] That the British army only embraced this concept in the 1980s resulted from its traditional disinterest in doctrinal theorizing in preference to a practical, extemporized approach to combat, and from the small-scale nature of its typical battlefield activities.[45] But having ignored this concept until the 1980s, Anglo-American military thought has now embraced it with a vengeance.[46]

It is methodologically questionable for historians to use anachronistically a modern concept inapplicable to the period in question. Yet it is appropriate to use the concept of the operational level in relation to how the 21st Army Group conducted this campaign. For in 1944–45, some implicit conception, termed grand tactics—similar to what commanders now call the operational level—did exist in Western military thought. In this period, just a handful of the British army's most effective generals commanded their formations in any sort of genuine operational sense, however "vague or ephemeral."[47] The idea of grand tactics had emerged in nineteenth-century military theory, and in 1914 was defined in British thought by Major-General J. F. C. Fuller as "that part of the art of war which links strategy to fighting tactics."[48] In the interwar years, the progressive British military thinkers Fuller and Captain B. H. Liddell Hart championed these ideas.[49] By 1939, grand tactical notions had permeated to some extent the gentleman-amateur British army that was dispersed across the Empire. During the 1939–45 war, a few British commanders handled their formations in a manner that suggested some hazy grand tactical or operational understanding. During September 1944, for example, Montgomery strove to regain control over Bradley's American army group, in order to coordinate fully their respective tactical activities into an operational, theater-level whole.[50]

The modern concept of the operational level is defined as the sphere where "schemes of warfare" are undertaken "to obtain the goals set by theater strategy through suitable combinations of tactics."[51] This level, therefore, concerns the planning, preparation, and conduct of a series of coordinated, synchronized battles by large formations (ranging from army groups down to divisions) within a given theater to achieve the objective of decisive victory set by military strategy; the exercise of command or generalship at this level is termed operational art.[52] The operational level also concerns the style of operations—how large formations organize and use combinations of tactics within a continuum ranging from maneuver warfare through to attrition warfare. Attrition is a routine, methodical, and inflexible style that deploys massive firepower against easily targeted concentrations of enemy forces. Maneuver warfare involves attacking enemy cohesion—their ability to react systemically—rather than their military assets, in order to achieve swiftly a decisive victory.[53]

Military thought associates closely—but not exclusively—the operational level with the concept of maneuver warfare. According to Luttwak, in pure attrition warfare "there are only techniques and tactics" but "no action at all at the operational level." Indeed, he seems to argue that the 21st Army Group did not conduct the campaign in any operational sense, as their operations remained largely attritional. To Luttwak, operational art involves expanding operations so that they are more than just disjointed conglomerations of units fighting individual tactical battles.[54]

Yet it is a gross oversimplification to dismiss the conduct of the Northwest Europe campaign by the 21st Army Group as simply an unsophisticated, attritional campaign without activity at the operational level. First, there has never been in the history of warfare either a purely attritional or maneuverist campaign. Second, Luttwak's argument reflects a marginal overemphasis on the dichotomy between maneuver and attrition; these styles are not opposites, but complements that exist simultaneously to varying degrees at all four levels of war.[55] Some historians have exaggerated both the differences between these styles and the proximity of German Blitzkrieg and British "Colossal Cracks" to pure maneuver and attrition, respectively. But Montgomery's heavy attritional emphasis was designed to wear down the enemy to the point where the Allies could conduct successful mobile warfare with tolerable casualties against their tactically superior enemy.

Firepower-laden operational techniques, moreover, do not equate precisely or simply to attritional warfare; the modern American maneuver doctrine of AirLand Battle, for example, emphasizes the heavy application of synchronized firepower throughout the enemy's depth to swiftly destroy their cohesion.[56] Furthermore, Montgomery and the 21st Army Group did design an operational level master plan for Normandy, did strive to coordinate tactical battles within a wider campaign context, and did seek—eventually—to reach mobile operations where a decisive Allied victory would be reached. Clearly, this formation did conduct the campaign in some sort of operational fashion, however partial or hazy; and how it did this is the main focus of this study.

HISTORIOGRAPHY

This study must be set within the body of literature on the campaign because this has influenced interpretations of these events. In particular, the inter-Allied tensions extant in 1944–45 have produced ripples of mutual misunderstanding that have influenced much of this historical literature.[57] The immediate postwar period saw publication of numerous personal accounts, typically self-congratulatory and uncontroversial, and based as much on memory as on methodical research.[58] Several American works, however, augured ill for the future, because they focused on the 1944–45 inter-Allied disputes over theater strategy.[59] This controversy was fanned by the critique made by Major-General de Guingand, Montgomery's chief of staff, of his superior's single thrust proposal in an otherwise innocuous memoir.[60]

In 1947 Montgomery published an uncontroversial account that only provoked disagreement through his spurious assertion that the campaign developed precisely as he had planned.[61] His recognition of the need for effective Anglo-American cooperation against the Soviet threat prompted this atypical display of sensitivity. During the early 1950s, the Cold War influenced scholarship on the campaign in other ways: Scholars emphasized the tactical abilities the *Wehrmacht* demonstrated during 1943–45 as a paradigm applicable to NATO's successful resistance of Soviet numerical superiority; while "the need to rehabilitate West Germany as a bulwark against communism, also led Anglo-American historians to de-emphasize" the impact Nazi ideology exerted within the German military.[62] During 1946–48 a serious rift emerged between the Allied commanders after the publication of accounts by Eisenhower and his chief of staff, Beddell Smith, that mildly criticized Montgomery.[63] In 1958 Montgomery retaliated with his *Memoirs*, which slated the Americans.[64] The latent nationalist tinges to accounts by the senior commanders had become overt, as had the fixation with theater strategic arguments. During the 1950s and 1960s, a British historical school developed that sought, through operational narrative, to repudiate American criticism of Montgomery.[65]

This period also saw the publication of the relevant national Official Histories.[66] Although these works represented monumental examples of diligent historical research, they left some room for critical analysis of the campaign's more controversial issues.[67] In the 1970s another genre emerged that revealed the well-kept secret of Allied intelligence successes such as "Ultra."[68] Much of this early literature was noticeable for the limited criticism it offered or how rarely it raised searching questions. In part this reflected the 1944–45 reluctance of commanders within the 21st Army Group to question the failures of colleagues who had done their best in this monumental struggle—a reluctance illustrated by the closing of ranks after the September 1944 failure at Arnhem.[69] Both this reticence and the fact that many historians still remained too bound up with the monumental psychological experience that was the Second World War hampered objective historical analysis of the campaign. Professor Michael Howard, himself a veteran of the Italian campaign, observed that "it is understandable that military historians of my generation should not have dealt with" the weaknesses of the British army "as frankly and as openly as perhaps we should."[70]

By the 1980s a generational gap had opened between the events of 1944–45 and historians, and it was no coincidence that revisionist critiques then appeared, such as the works of D'Este (1983), Lamb (1983), Hastings (1984), and English (1991).[71] These cut through the euphemisms of the earlier works to expose the unpleasant truth of Anglo-Canadian tactical weaknesses relative to those of the enemy. By the early 1990s these works had broken the mold, and most historians accepted that Allied combat performance left much to desired. During 1994–95, the fiftieth anniversary of these events, authors published many new books that introduced untapped sources rather than presented new arguments that advanced understanding of the campaign.[72]

The campaign's historical literature may now enter a postrevisionist phase. Given that scholars have elucidated the weaknesses of the Allied performance in Northwest Europe, historians now need to produce deeper analyses of why these failings existed within the Allied forces, whether they were solvable by 1944, and to what extent Allied commanders used appropriately their available resources. The most effective analysis of these issues to date is the work by John English. He not only uses detailed operational analysis to expose the weaknesses of the Canadian army in Normandy, especially its senior command, but weaves into this an explanation of these failings based on the neglect of the interwar period.[73]

This work continues in a parallel vein; rather than dwell on the failings of the 21st Army Group, this work demonstrates that given both British war aims and the weaknesses of its resources relative to those of the enemy, this formation adopted appropriate techniques. Montgomery's handling of the 21st Army Group remained hampered by the limited tactical abilities and mercurial morale of his "basically unmilitary" soldiers, the weaknesses of his staff officers, and the poor performance of Allied matériel.[74] "Colossal Cracks" involved getting the best out of what resources were available, however unpromising these military assets were.

CHAPTER OVERVIEW

The first section of this analysis, chapters 2 to 5, examines Montgomery's methods. Chapters 2 and 3 analyze the paramount influences on Montgomery's operational approach—the maintenance of morale and casualty conservation. Chapter 2 demonstrates the following three assertions: that serious morale problems existed within the 21st Army Group during the campaign; that despite this, Montgomery's forces occupied Germany with its morale fabric still intact through using his operational methods; and last, that Montgomery's concern to nurture the fragile morale of his troops affected significantly his conduct of the campaign. Chapter 3 examines the factors behind Montgomery's desire to achieve victory with tolerable casualties; the nurture of troop morale, the manpower shortage, the legacy of the slaughter in the 1914–18 Western Front trenches, and the British war aims arising from the campaign's politico-Imperial dimension. Chapters 4 and 5 examine the main characteristics of Montgomery's "Colossal Cracks" operational technique. Chapter 4 investigates the fundamental facets of this approach—the master plan, concentration, attrition-based firepower, caution, and alternate thrusts. Chapter 5 examines the other characteristics of Montgomery's approach. This completes a comprehensive examination of his operational techniques in Northwest Europe.

The second part of the work, chapters 6 and 7, extends the analysis of the 21st Army Group beyond Montgomery to the army level of command. These chapters analyze the role and contributions of Dempsey and the Second (British) Army, and Crerar and the First Canadian Army, respectively. They explore the techniques and abilities of these two commanders, their relationships with Montgomery, and how these factors impacted the conduct of the campaign. Both chapters demonstrate the extent to which Montgomery's army commanders shared his operational approach. These chapters also examine two subsidiary issues: first, the frictions inherent in Anglo-Canadian military relations; second, the tendency for higher commands to "overcontrol"—to impinge on the freedom of activity—of subordinates.

Having outlined what this analysis covers, something ought to be said on what is omitted. Considerations of space have precluded analysis of six other valid aspects of this vast subject. First, this work does not examine the period 1919–43, during which time emerged the factors that engendered the structural weaknesses of the Second World War British army, weaknesses that led to the development of "Colossal Cracks." Second, this study omits detailed discussion of the 1944–45 inter-Allied theater strategic debates—scholars already have lavished attention on this. Third, though this work has extended analysis beyond Montgomery to the army level, an exhaustive operational analysis also steeds to explore the corps, divisional, and even brigade levels. Fourth, though this study focuses on senior command echelons, on operations, and on large-unit tactics, it scarcely touches the minor tactical level.[75] Fifth, although this work demonstrates the impact of the manpower problem, it has not been possible here to examine this issue fully. Last, this study does not compare the British and Canadian armies with the

American or German ones—a recent work that compares tactical innovation within these four armies during Normandy ably covers this issue.[76]

Scholars, therefore, should regard this study as an island of knowledge that should be related both to existing and future works. For despite the enormous extant literature on the Second World War, historians "have only begun to understand an event of such magnitude."[77] With this thought in mind, it is to a fuller understanding of the manner in which Montgomery and the 21st Army Group conducted the 1944–45 Northwest Europe campaign that this analysis now turns.

CHAPTER 2

The Maintenance of Morale

A central argument of this study is that the connected issues of the maintenance of morale and casualty conservation exerted a key influence on Montgomery's operational conduct of this campaign. Put simply, the Field Marshal conducted the campaign in a way designed both to maintain the morale of his troops and to avoid heavy casualties. These two considerations represented the key motivations behind the development of Montgomery's "Colossal Cracks" approach, the techniques of which this study examines in chapters 4 and 5. This work further argues that the other individual aspects of Montgomery's operational technique can only be understood in the light of these two factors; indeed, historians can only fully comprehend these individual techniques as but a part of the totality of all the characteristics that comprised his operational approach. The principles of the maintenance of morale and of casualty conservation inherently remained connected. For the avoidance of heavy casualties bolstered the morale of the civilian soldiers fielded by the 21st Army Group during the inevitable morale degradation caused by participation in active operations; and high morale facilitated a superior battlefield performance that contributed, *ceteris paribus*, to keeping casualties down.

Although the existing literature has recognized that these factors influenced Montgomery, historians have not demonstrated fully the extent of their impact on his conduct of the campaign. Neither have scholars elucidated clearly the degree to which these considerations permeated Montgomery's entire operational approach.[1] All army commanders are concerned with the morale of their forces and the casualties that result from the use of this force. However, the real issue for historians is how important these two considerations are in relation to the other influences on a commander's conduct of a campaign: What is their significance in relation to military objectives, relative force strengths, doctrine, and the unfolding operational situation within a campaign? In Northwest Europe, doctrinal outlook, personal factors, and the battlefield circumstances that faced the 1944 British army all combined to ensure that these two factors dominated Montgomery's handling of the 21st Army Group.

This chapter first examines the phenomenon of morale and the significance this had in Montgomery's military outlook. Next, it demonstrates that at certain periods significant morale problems existed within the 21st Army Group. Last, it analyzes the impact that Montgomery's concerns with the maintenance of morale exerted on his conduct of the campaign. This examination reveals that Montgomery's cautious, firepower-based, attritional methods reflected his desire to nurture his forces to preserve the morale fabric of the 21st Army Group. Such maintenance of fighting spirit would enable Montgomery's command to deliver an adequate, but sustained, combat performance in Northwest Europe that would eventually prove sufficient, as but one part of a larger Allied effort, to defeat the *Westheer*.

MORALE AND THE MAINTENANCE OF MORALE
Montgomery's abiding concern with the human aspects of war, with morale, and with the "maintenance of morale" formed one of the two foundations of his operational doctrine.[2] The Secretary of State for War, James Grigg, who became a close colleague of Montgomery during the campaign, observed that the Field Marshal's "technique rested" on "the supreme importance of morale in war."[3] Montgomery conducted this campaign in a manner designed to sustain the morale of his troops as far as was possible within the complex, and often contradictory, requirements of the unfolding operational situation. Hence, this study analyzes the significance of morale maintenance in relation to other operational demands.

This work needs to explore the concept of morale, however, before it examines how Montgomery sought to sustain such fighting spirit. Morale is a nebulous and highly complex phenomenon. It concerns the fighting élan, or spirit, of troops; their willingness or ability to risk death or overcome abject terror, intense trauma, excruciating pain, and utter fatigue by pressing forward in attack or by remaining staunch in defense—in both cases against a terrifying, noisy hail of lethal metal. Morale is a dynamic, rapidly changing phenomenon; individuals, small groups, units, and formations from different types of society are all variously affected by disparate morale factors at different times. Morale also remains a subjective, emotive, and controversial subject that encompasses vexed judgments such as where do the genuine limits of individual endurance end and cowardice begin? Among all these complexities historians can reach few concrete conclusions on the issue of morale.[4]

During the Second World War, Montgomery, like many other senior British officers, recognized the crucial importance of these human factors in warfare. An appreciation of the significance of morale factors in war was by no means new, because most armies have long regarded this factor as one of the "classical" principles of war.[5] However, for the 1939–45 British army, the sheer extent of Montgomery's concern with such influences proved highly significant. His lectures and writings during this war, like those of Field Marshal Slim, consistently demonstrated that he believed fervently that morale was "the big thing in war" and "one of the chief factors for success."[6] In a pamphlet Montgomery issued in 1946 that summarized the ideas with which he had fought his Second World War battles, he stated that "man is still the first weapon of war. His training is the most important consideration in the fashioning of a fighting army. All modern science is directed towards his assistance but on his efforts depends the outcome of the battle. The morale of the soldier is the most important single factor in war."[7] Furthermore, in August 1946, Montgomery, now the new Chief of the Imperial General Staff [CIGS], presided over the annual War Office doctrinal exercise, this time suggestively named "Evolution." The doctrine he espoused here underscored the extent of his concern with morale factors. "Without a high morale," he declared, "no success can be achieved in battle; however good the strategic or tactical plan, or anything else."[8] Montgomery's appreciation of the human dimension of war refutes Thompson's accusation that in Northwest Europe the Field Marshal had become nothing more than a "general manager" of a campaign reduced to the mere "ironmongery" of overwhelming weight of matériel—of machines rather than of men.[9] In reality, Montgomery believed that man and machine formed "a team," but one where "the man in the machine was what really mattered."[10]

The recognition that, with hindsight, historians have attributed more certainty to the success of the "Second Front" than that expected at the time expedites a fuller understanding of Montgomery's concern with the relative fragility of the British army's morale. For recitation of crude figures indicating numerical superiority, irrespective of other considerations, is chimerical. To those involved at the time, the success of "Overlord" remained as uncertain as the vast risks involved were clear.[11] It is not inconceivable that Britain might not have enjoyed a second chance to invade Nazi-occupied Europe if "Overlord" had failed.[12] Moreover, historians often have overlooked the extent of war weariness within Britain by 1944—a lassitude indicated by the inability of civilians on the Home Front to endure the German 1944 V-weapon onslaught with the same stoic resilience as they had the German Blitz of 1940.[13]

The campaign's literature also has underestimated the fear and foreboding with which senior Allied commanders viewed "Overlord," the culmination of three years' desperate toil. Field Marshal Alan Brooke, the CIGS, confessed to his diary on 27 May 1944 that the operation was "eating into my heart. I wish God we could start and have done with it."[14] And on the eve of

D-Day he again sought catharsis by confiding his fears to his diary: "I am very uneasy about the whole operation. At the best, it will fall so very short of the expectation of the bulk of the people, namely all those who know nothing about its difficulties. At the worst it may well be the most ghastly disaster of the whole war."[15] Recognition that simple weight of matériel was insufficient to convince senior Allied commanders that victory was certain facilitates a fuller appreciation of the appropriateness of Montgomery's belief that the morale fabric of his forces represented one of the keys to victory.[16] Though there is much validity in the portrayal of the 1939–45 War as one essentially of industrial production, it was, however, not simply this. For the Anglo-Canadian land forces of 1944, at least, what really mattered was how well their civilian conscript soldiers used this vast array of machines.

Montgomery also appreciated the interrelationship between the morale of British civilians on the Home Front and that of his troops; senior commanders also had to bolster the former to prevent the morale of their troops being dragged down by any despondency discernible in the letters they received from home. Montgomery's pre-invasion tours and addresses sought to bolster the morale of both the troops and civilians; his effectiveness in persuading the public to put their trust in his abilities was evidenced by how widely it was believed that "with him in command every battle would be won; without him most would be lost."[17]

A key issue in this examination of how Montgomery sustained the morale of his troops is what Montgomery really felt about the capabilities of his troops. Professor Michael Howard has argued persuasively that Montgomery's concern with maintaining the morale of his troops prevented him expressing his negative opinions about the real capabilities of the British soldier relative to that of the enemy. Both Howard and Hastings rightly argue that Montgomery privately remained well aware of the limitations of his own troops. Consequently, much of the praise he lavished on his troops was rhetorical.[18] One simply cannot take at face value Montgomery's statements that the "Overlord" Army was "the best army we have ever had" and that "the British soldier is the finest fighting man in the world, if properly led."[19] Indeed, Howard astutely makes the crucial point that "in the Second World War this was not true. Monty knew that this was not true, and by far the most difficult part of his job" was "to make the British army, the British public, and everyone else believe that it was [true]."[20] This statement encapsulates what the maintenance of morale meant to Montgomery.

Some historians have suggested, however, both that the Field Marshal remained genuinely proud of his troops and thus that his praise was genuine, not rhetorical.[21] However, these two views are not necessarily mutually exclusive. To suggest that Montgomery, the military professional, recognized the limitations of the British army in 1944 does not deny that he was also genuinely proud of his troops, as indeed he clearly was. That the British army had risen from its 1940 nadir to a point in 1944 where it could take on the highly effective German army and consistently win was itself a tremendous achievement, of which Montgomery and his peers were justly proud. Yet, at the same time, the Field Marshal understood that there was still far to go before the British army could defeat the enemy without the benefit of overwhelming superiority in matériel. Indeed, even though the Field Marshal's praise was both part genuine and part rhetorical, the extent of the rhetoric is indicated by the fact that all of his post-operation congratulatory messages were virtually identical in their praise, irrespective of the success or failure of the operation concerned.[22]

Even though Montgomery realized that there was a long way to go before the British army could match the enemy on equal terms, the situation facing Britain in 1943–44 provided little opportunity to make much headway toward this herculean goal. However, such a target never constituted a viable option or a stated objective for the British army. For Britain, what really mattered was that the war was won, not the military methods with which this was achieved. As Max Hastings penetratingly observed, Montgomery's purpose in Normandy was not "to demonstrate the superiority of [his] fighting men to those of Hitler, but to win the war at tolerable cost." His task in mid-1944 was to do the best with whatever weapon the war-weary British Commonwealth could muster; to somehow "persuade" his troops "to do enough—albeit, just enough—to prevail on a given battlefield," and hence secure final victory while avoiding a repetition of the slaughter of the Great War.[23] Moreover, because there would be no second chance if "Overlord" failed, Montgomery would have to nurse this weapon for as long as it took for weight of numbers to bring the enemy to collapse.[24] Leigh-Mallory, the Allied Air Commander-in-Chief, observed that success in the campaign "all boil[ed] down to a question of morale" within the 21st Army Group.[25] That Montgomery succeeded in nurturing his forces throughout the campaign represents his greatest achievement of the Second World War.[26]

Having explored the importance that Montgomery placed on morale, this study now examines the factors that he considered important to the maintenance of morale. From his earliest days in the desert, Montgomery recognized the overwhelming significance of success in battle to the maintenance of high morale. He observed that "the troops must have complete confidence in their higher commander, they must know that the battle is safe in his hands, that he will not sacrifice their lives needlessly, [and] that success will always crown their efforts." If a commander achieved these conditions, Montgomery declared, "the troops will have the highest morale," for soldiers "will always follow a successful general."[27] After the war Montgomery affirmed

this conviction when he stated that "no leader, however great, can long continue unless he wins victories."[28] The Normandy experiences of Brigadier
James Hargest, the highly regarded New Zealand army observer attached to
the XXX Corps, and a trusted friend of Lieutenant-General O'Connor, convinced him of the perspicacity of such a view.[29] The ordinary British soldier,
Hargest commented, "will accept losses without losing morale provided that
he sees some results."[30] Brigadier Richardson, the army group's Brigadier
General Staff (Plans)—BGS(Plans)—observed that when he had got to know
Montgomery better, he realized that the latter's confidence and relaxed attitude "was but an outward sign of a self-imposed regime, designed to ensure
that the Army's morale did not deteriorate."[31]

There exist other factors that the majority of commanders have long
recognized as being important in the maintenance of morale. The most
important factors appreciated by Montgomery included good leadership by
officers; that the men believed in the abilities of their officers, especially
their Commander-in-Chief; firm but fair discipline; thorough and realistic
training; comradeship, self-respect, and physical robustness; that leaders
believed in the justness of the cause for which they fought; and that the
troops enjoyed the support of the largest possible weight of matériel.[32]
Moreover, Montgomery believed that good administration and man-management, in the sense of "removing all discomforts, by eliminating every
form of unpleasantness," also remained vital.[33] In particular, this meant making every possible effort to get supplies of hot food and drink forward to the
frontline troops. Montgomery's technique aimed to ameliorate the terrible
demands that combat placed on soldiers as far as possible given the operational situation. Montgomery asserted that if British commanders combined
these elements with repeated success, it was possible to create and sustain a
high state of morale among the troops. When the British army managed to
integrate good morale with a marked numerical advantage in matériel, its
troops could take on the best troops of the *Wehrmacht*, and consistently
defeat them.

THE MORALE OF THE 21ST ARMY GROUP

Having elucidated Montgomery's great concern with the maintenance of
morale, this study now examines the morale of the forces fielded by the 21st
Army Group during the campaign. Space limitations preclude a definitive
exploration of the morale aspects of the 21st Army Group experience during
1944–45. This section merely demonstrates that serious morale problems
existed within Montgomery's command during this campaign, but that
(despite this) his forces advanced into Germany with their morale still intact.
There is evidence that in the 1939–45 War, the morale of the British army
remained fragile relative to the typically high, and surprisingly resilient,

morale of the German army. This applied equally well to the 21st Army Group against the *Westheer*. Indeed, a recent study of the campaign concluded that Montgomery fought it "with a much more 'flawed weapon' in his hand than has been realised."[34]

That this was so is not surprising, when one considers that the 1939–45 British army was characterized by the following features: It was a mass-conscripted civilian army, based on a very small peacetime cadre; many of its regular officers possessed Empire-wide experiences of peacetime soldiering and training that scarcely prepared them for a major, technologically advanced European war; its soldiers came from a society that lacked a particularly strong martial tradition; and last, many of its personnel lacked the almost suicidal fanaticism that characterized sizable numbers of the German armed forces, largely because British personnel lived in a political, economic, and sociocultural context that did little, if anything, to foster such sacrificial fanaticism.[35] Most of these characteristics also applied to the 1939–45 Canadian army, but perhaps in even more extreme forms.[36]

The fanatical resistance offered by substantial elements within the *Wehrmacht* during 1943–45 was engendered by the combined and cumulative impacts of Nazi ideology, a decade of indoctrination, previous paramilitary experience and training, a stronger martial tradition, increasingly harsh military discipline, and the desperation bred by the imminent prospect of *Götterdämmerung*—unconditional surrender, utter defeat, and inevitable Allied retribution for the Nazi regime's terrible crimes.[37] The combination of this fanaticism with sheer professionalism and success at "*institutionalizing* military excellence" made the German army the most formidable of foes.[38] This may be "an unpalatable truth" given the "odiousness" of their cause "in fighting for one of the most obnoxious regimes of all time," but it nevertheless remains a clear fact.[39] Despite this general high standard, however, historians must also acknowledge that the *Wehrmacht* encompassed a curious mix across the spectrum of performance from excellence to ineptitude.[40] Within the ranks of the Allied armies, it is clear that not inconsiderable numbers of soldiers performed acts of "suicidal" courage.[41] In general, however, although British soldiers certainly "could be relied on to do their duty" and daily to risk their lives, their commanders could not expect them to meet the sacrificial, superhuman efforts German officers frequently demanded of their troops. Put simply, British and Canadian troops in Northwest Europe were not fighting to avert the immediate prospect of utter defeat, and thus could afford the "luxury" of wanting "very much to get home alive."[42]

On D-Day itself, the British and Canadian troops clearly possessed "very high" morale.[43] This pattern generally was repeated when fresh, even inexperienced, formations initially joined combat in the theater. To some "green" troops the "Overlord" assault came as a relief as they finally commenced the monumental task for which they had trained so long and hard. However, during the first three weeks of bitter fighting in Normandy, the fighting edge of the 21st Army Group became blunted. Evidence for this blunting comes from the fact that by the end of June all the Anglo-Canadian Corps ashore had established Battle Exhaustion Centers.[44] The cumulative degradation of the fighting power of this formation continued as the desperate struggle for Normandy raged on.[45] Indeed, the bitter realities of fighting in Normandy proved a shock to many; even to Montgomery they were, if not a complete surprise, then at least an undesired and unexpected reminder of the horrible truths learned by bitter experience in North Africa and Italy.

The blunting of this well-conditioned weapon was the result of a combination of the natural degradation inherent in bitter combat and of features unique to the Normandy battles. In terms of the latter, the aggregation of the following factors caused this morale degradation: The constant hard fighting and the limited British opportunities to remove frontline divisions for rest or to absorb replacements; the determined and skilled resistance offered by the *Westheer*; the defensibility of the bocage terrain; the frequency of enemy harassing fire, mortar attack, and sniper action;[46] the marked superiority of enemy armor; the lack of successful Allied advances; the frequency of local Allied reverses that compelled troops to incur further casualties by reattacking objectives they had gained previously but subsequently lost to enemy counterattack;[47] above all, the steady stream of casualties, that destroyed British small group cohesion; and particularly the severe casualties suffered among officers, that wrecked the effective function of units. All these served to exacerbate the inevitable, cumulative sapping of Allied physical and mental strength caused by lack of sleep, physical hardship, and the trauma of combat.[48] The combination of these factors took a serious toll on the morale fabric of Montgomery's command. Indeed, by mid-July, after six weeks of intense fighting, serious morale problems began to manifest themselves in several 21st Army Group divisions.[49]

Brigadier Hargest frankly recorded the morale problems that many British officers recognized but refused to admit openly, and observed that Allied troops lacked "the spirit essential to victory." Moreover, while Hargest conceded that Allied morale was higher than that of the enemy, he still confessed that the state of the former "frighten[ed] me." From this situation he concluded that senior British commanders would "do well to depend on air, artillery, and tanks."[50] Hargest's frankness highlights the methodological difficulties that dog historical analysis of morale problems; typically, the Allies did not openly admit such difficulties but discussed them behind closed doors in a euphemistic manner encapsulated in the term "stickiness."[51]

By mid-July, British morale problems in Normandy proved particularly bad within the very stretched forces of the I (British) Corps, under the command of John Crocker, which held the vulnerable yet vital eastern flank beyond the River Orne and Caen Canal. On 24 July 1944, the experienced Crocker informed Lieutenant-General Crerar, under whose First Canadian Army command Montgomery had just placed him, of these problems. Crocker stated that the 3rd British Division, which "had been fighting continuously since D-Day" and had suffered almost 6,000 casualties, "was tired out and had shown obvious signs of this exhaustion."[52] The existence of such a morale problem within his corps prompted Crocker to refuse to carry out Crerar's 22 July directive, the latter's first orders in the theater. This required the I (British) Corps to clear the Ouistreham area and Caen Canal from close enemy observation. Crocker, however, insisted that he "had no troops fit or available for any such operation."[53] By the time that Crerar had referred this dispute to Montgomery, the operational situation had changed and consequently, the I Corps never carried out the intended operations.[54]

By this time, morale problems also had emerged in both of the Canadian infantry divisions deployed in the theater—the 2nd and 3rd. The latter had spearheaded the D-Day assault, and both had spent long, continuous periods in the front, had suffered heavy casualties, and had had no chance to reorganize out of the line and properly absorb reinforcements. By the end of July 1944, these experiences had reduced the 3rd Canadian Infantry Division to a barely battleworthy state. Crocker reported that although the division had performed very well initially,[55] it soon "lapsed" into both "a very nervy state" and "a general attitude of despondency."[56] On 25–26 July 1944 the division participated in Operation "Spring," the first attack undertaken by the II Canadian Corps under the command of Lieutenant-General Simonds. "Spring" sought to secure the Verrières Ridge, but proved a failure, in part due to the unimpressive performance of the 3rd Canadian Division. Moreover, Crocker noted the failure of the divisional commander, Major-General Rod Keller, to exert a steadying grip on his deteriorating formation. Crocker concluded that Keller was "obviously not standing up to the strain"[57]—an indictment that Keller himself, in effect, soon admitted.[58] Crocker passed this information to Dempsey, who forwarded it to Montgomery, Crerar, and Simonds; all four concurred that a serious morale problem existed.[59]

As a result of the poor state of morale within these two Canadian divisions, Simonds felt compelled to use the green troops of the newly arrived Polish and 4th Canadian Armored Divisions for the crucial second phase of his 8 August 1944 "Totalize" attack. The inexperience of these troops contributed to the failure of this phase of the operation, which also resulted from dismal failure to use effectively the massive firepower available. Furthermore, morale problems immediately showed within the Polish Armored

Division, which performed very half-heartedly in this, its first operation, though it seems that Crerar placed on them more of the blame for the failure of "Totalize" than they deserved.[60] On hearing from Crerar of this stickiness, Montgomery angrily threatened that "if Poles not inclined for the battle we [will] take away their tanks to keep up [our] offensive strength and put [them] in def[ence]."[61] Part of the problem with the Polish division was that it had virtually no reinforcements. This manpower shortage compelled the formation both to join combat in Normandy on a reduced War Establishment, and to secure future reinforcements by combing Allied prisoner of war camps in Normandy for Polish troops whom the German army previously had conscripted.[62]

In Normandy, the veteran North African formations—the 7th Armored, the 50th (Northumberland), and the 51st (Highland) Divisions—all also experienced significant morale problems. The British army had brought back these three veteran divisions at Montgomery's request to provide backbone for the 21st Army Group's predominantly inexperienced forces.[63] Although using these veteran divisions seemed a sound military decision, in Normandy it soon became clear that this had been a serious mistake.

Signs of morale deterioration within the 50th Division became clear in early July 1944. Indeed, the high incidence within the division of what the authorities suspected were feigned cases of battle exhaustion led its chief medic to launch an investigation on 31 July. During that same month the division also experienced a high number of cases of soldiers either deserting or going absent without leave (AWOL). During August, the British army convicted no less than 150 soldiers from the 50th Division for these two offenses; this figure almost matched the number of soldiers convicted of these two charges during August for the rest of the entire Second (British) Army.[64]

Similar problems also surfaced in the veteran 51st Division. On 24 July 1944, Crocker informed Crerar that though the 51st Division "had not been nearly so heavily engaged" as the 3rd (British) Division, it "had done badly in the several operations it had been called upon to carry out." The 51st Division, Crocker concluded, "was not, at present, fit for battle." To make it battleworthy, he concluded, required "a new divisional commander, and a new point of view."[65] Dempsey and Montgomery received Crocker's doubts and concurred with them. Montgomery informed Brooke that the 51st Division currently was not "battleworthy" because it lacked "determination" in combat.[66] Divisional histories often remain more sanguine than critical, so it is significant that even the 51st Division's official history admits that "it was obvious all was not well with the division."[67] Montgomery replaced its commander, Major-General Bullen Smith; and the new commander, the highly respected Major-General Rennie, managed to impose a strong grip on the division and restore much of its morale in time for the autumn battles.[68]

Another veteran division, the 7th Armored, also made "a very poor show-ing in Normandy" according to Major-General Verney, who commanded the division from August 1944. Indeed he felt that both the 51st and 7th Armored Divisions "did badly from the moment they landed in Normandy" and hence "deserved the criticism they received.[69] The veteran 7th Armored demonstrated the "bifurcation" of initial "dashing recklessness" that soon gave way to "excessive caution" and a very sticky performance.[70] This caution resulted from the division's reaction to both German tank superiority and the effectiveness of enemy 88mm antitank guns.[71] Dempsey viewed the rever-sal suffered by the Desert Rats at Villers Bocage as a sign of this stickiness, and in late July 1944 he sacked several of the division's senior officers after a lethargic performance during Operation "Bluecoat."[72]

The main problem with the veteran divisions was the short time, after they had returned from Italy, spent in the United Kingdom prior to going to fight in Normandy. As Michael Carver's memoirs so poignantly illustrate, for some soldiers the prospect of leaving the wives, loved ones, relatives, and close friends with whom they had been so recently reunited after up to five years' absence, proved too much to bear; in some cases the influence of wives and sweethearts proved sufficiently strong to help turn heroes of the desert into reluctant soldiers.[73] After years of fighting, many veterans felt that they had done their bit in the war, and that now it was someone else's turn to risk their lives doing their duty for their country.[74] The picture they saw of the relatively safe existence of many troops based in the United King-dom no doubt fueled their resentment at this uneven division of the war's burden. While Churchill and his senior commanders sympathized, they rec-ognized the operational necessity of stiffening the majority of "green" troops with experienced soldiers.[75] Such troop resentment manifested itself in a serious AWOL situation among these veteran divisions in the period just before the invasion, especially in the 50th Division.[76] Consequently, some veteran soldiers who had performed superbly in the desert arrived in France determined to do just enough to do their duty but also return from the war alive; they had become, in army parlance, very "canny."[77] Prolonged expo-sure to combat, Major-General Verney observed, "does not make one more courageous. One becomes cunning, and from cunning to cowardice is but a short step." The "canny" infantryman "who does not want to 'have a go' can find opportunities to lie low at the critical moment," Verney commented, and "the tank man can easily find fault with his engine."[78]

In retrospect, it is easy to see that the British High Command could have done more during spring 1944 when these divisions were in the United Kingdom to limit these morale problems. More extensive retraining in close country tactics, stricter discipline, greater infusion of fresh recruits, and real-

location of veterans as cadres to "green" divisions may have resulted in a better battle performance in Normandy from the very forces intended to provide the backbone for the 21st Army Group.[79] The fact that by the end of
1944 the 50th Division largely had recovered from its earlier problems
under the inspired leadership of the "outstanding" Major-General D. A. H.
Graham demonstrated that these divisions were not beyond redemption.[80]

The fact that these veteran divisions had suffered relatively modest casualty rates in North Africa and Italy only served to exacerbate these morale
problems; consequently, these formations fielded large numbers of veterans
who had survived combat for several years and who appeared to have
exhausted their "stock" of combat effectiveness. This proved a critical factor
behind the surprising resilience of morale within German elite formations.
That the Allies, in prolonged hard fighting, had decimated several times
over the best Waffen-SS and German army panzer divisions may (paradoxically) explain why these formations consistently performed so highly.[81] Once
rebuilt and reequipped after periods in reserve, effectively they were new,
fresh divisions, but ones held together by tough veteran cadres, institutionalized professionalism, élan, and harsh realistic training. Hence, paradoxically,
high German casualty rates, despite the devastation these caused to primary
group—or small unit—cohesion, actually may have sustained German combat performance. Given that soldiers seem to have a finite stock of morale, of
combat performance, the high German casualty rate meant that few men in
a unit at a given time had been in combat long enough to have exhausted
this stock of courage.[82] Clearly, the influences on morale remain complex
and often contradictory, and the process observed may well have been coun-
terbalanced by the adverse effects of the destruction of primary groups.
Notwithstanding this, the existence of this process may be highly significant
in an examination of the morale of such a casualty-conscious formation as
the 21st Army Group. Indeed, many inexperienced Allied and German divisions, especially elite ones, displayed buoyant morale in their first actions
despite their inexperience, as the heroic resistance offered by the following
demonstrated: the previously untested youths of the 12-SS Panzer Division
Hitlerjugend; the recently formed, though superbly equipped, *Panzer Lehr*
Division; and the British 1st Airborne Division at Arnhem-Oosterbeek, which
had never before fought as a complete formation.[83]

Morale problems also emerged in other divisions within Montgomery's
command during the Normandy campaign. The overcaution displayed by
the 7th Armored also represented a charge laid at the feet of the Guards
Armored Division. The Secretary of State for War, James Grigg, had warned
de Guingand that the Guards Armored Division might use such claims about
the inferiority of British armor as a pretext for "canniness."[84] Curiously,

though, this was far from being the case in the division's sister formation, the 6th Guards Tank Brigade, which performed well throughout the campaign.[85] Furthermore, while the 43rd (Wessex) Division performed well throughout virtually all of the campaign, during Operation "Market-Garden" some of its exhausted troops displayed a certain "canniness," and the division experienced an increased incidence of feigned illness.[86] Indeed, toward the end of the Normandy campaign, significant morale problems had emerged in as many as seven of the 21st Army Group's total of sixteen divisions; in the worst scenario senior commanders assessed just nine divisions as completely reliable for offensive operations. In these circumstances, senior commanders could not allow divisions that were experiencing morale problems to deteriorate to the state of being completely unfit for battle.[87]

This degradation in Normandy of combat effectiveness at the divisional level was usually the cumulative effect of morale problems at the tactical level within units and subunits. In early July 1944, in one exceptional case, Montgomery had to withdraw the 6th Battalion, Duke of Wellington's Regiment (6 DWR), from its parent formation, the 49th Division, as it had become unfit for battle after suffering atypically high officer casualties.[88] Furthermore, unlike the resilient Germans, the morale of Anglo-Canadian units took a long time to recover from a single tactical drubbing, like that suffered by the 4th County of London Yeomanry at Villers Bocage.[89]

The frequent driving-out of Anglo-Canadian infantry units from their newly gained objectives by enemy mortar and artillery shelling forced their troops to incur further casualties reattacking these same objectives, and this further undermined Allied morale.[90] Just as the "Siegfriedesque" German commander Kurt Meyer had to rally the fleeing men of 89th Infantry Division during "Totalize" using only his cigar and considerable bravado, so too did the British commander of 6 DWR twice have "to stand at the end of a track and draw my revolver on retreating men."[91] Hargest similarly observed that although the 8th Durham Light Infantry easily captured St. Pierre on 10 June 1944, the next morning "while under heavy mortar fire, they panicked and some of them went right back to their previous day's start lines."[92]

Nurturing the morale, and thus the battleworthiness, of the formations and units fielded by the 21st Army Group proved a constant concern for Montgomery throughout the campaign. The morale problems experienced in Normandy, however, soon eased during the heady days of late August and early September 1944, when Anglo-Canadian forces surged through the interior of France and into Belgium. Montgomery commented that "there is no morale problem here at present; when soldiers win great victories they do not bother overmuch about the future."[93] Yet such spectacular success brought its own peculiar morale problems. An incredible wave of overoptimism, bordering on hysteria, swept through the Allied forces in Northwest Europe; the belief spread rapidly that the war was virtually won, and hence that it would be over in a matter of days or a few weeks.[94] Given the desperate nature of the Normandy struggle, and the desire that the slaughter be over, this curious phenomenon is intelligible. The result of this overoptimism was that, according to O'Connor, the commander of the VIII Corps, "everyone was looking over their shoulder,"' and hence that "nobody was quite prepared to take the same risks as they had earlier on in the campaign."[95] To Lieutenant-Colonel Turner Cain, commanding the 1st Herefords in the 11th Armored Division, it was obvious that in this period the soldiers "were a bit sticky about doing anything aggressive."[96] This caution contributed to the failures of both the Guards Armored and the 43rd Divisions to successfully meet up with the airborne forces dropped at Arnhem-Oosterbeek during the overambitious mid-September "Market-Garden" offensive.[97] The phenomenon of Allied overoptimism gradually died down during October as the German forces recovered their fighting power, but it reoccurred in the last weeks of the war; then few soldiers were prepared to take significant risks when victory was so close at hand.[98]

The determination of the senior commanders within the 21st Army Group to minimize potential morale problems frequently remained apparent during the dismal, waterlogged operations of the autumn and winter of 1944–45. Throughout the autumn, shortage of replacements hampered the effectiveness of the Polish Armored Division. After its poor first showing in "Totalize," the division had since "fought extremely well."[99] However, Simonds recognized that the desperate Polish reinforcement situation meant that "continued wastage at their present rates, will reduce them to impotence in a matter of weeks." Simonds, now acting commander of the First Canadian Army in place of the sick Crerar, implored Crocker to change his corps plans. Simonds urged his subordinate not to use the division offensively now, which he feared "would mean its finish," but instead to allow it time in reserve to reorganize so that it would become in the near future "a really effective fighting formation."[100] Equally, when Major-General Matthews assumed command of the 2nd Canadian Infantry Division in November 1944, he found the formation's morale in a poor state after the terrible experiences of its bitter fighting in the sodden polders of the Scheldt estuary—fighting not dissimilar in character from the waterlogged trenches of the Great War.[101] Consequently, the division required several weeks on a quiet sector of the front to revitalize its combat power.[102]

Although these examples indicate that serious morale problems existed within Montgomery's command, it should be remembered that the majority of units maintained reasonable morale. The crucial point for this study was that the morale fabric of the 21st Army Group remained essentially intact throughout the campaign. This formation both maintained its general offensive posture and continued to fight with reasonable effectiveness throughout the campaign. That the 21st Army Group managed to do so had much to do with the manner in which Montgomery fought the campaign; the very fact that the morale fabric of the 21st Army Group remained intact was the inescapable achievement of Montgomery's operational methods.

MAINTAINING MORALE AND MONTGOMERY'S CONDUCT OF THE CAMPAIGN

Montgomery's operational approach in Northwest Europe was designed to nurture this relatively fragile instrument toward an adequate, but sustained, combat performance. After all, as he and Brooke perceptively recognized, a reasonable combat performance, "assisted by competent generalship," sustained over the campaign, was all that was required to win this war of attrition in the long run, given the Allies' superiority in matériel. In particular, Montgomery had to avoid expending most of his army group's wasting resources in one initial burst, as Britain possessed only minimal reserves to replace her "Overlord" forces. Hence, it proved imperative for Montgomery to make "the most of the units he had" in order to deliver a sustained combat performance in the theater. The British commander recognized correctly that nurturing the morale of his meager total of sixteen divisions represented the key to the production of such a performance. And above all, the Field Marshal proved "uncommonly skilled" at maintaining the morale of his troops.[103]

Montgomery, while recognizing the relative morale fragility of the British army against the determined Germans, nevertheless understood that the British army of 1944 could defeat the cream of the *Wehrmacht* if—but only if—it was properly trained, fully rehearsed, truly motivated, carefully led, and backed by copious matériel. In late March 1944, Montgomery stated that if you had troops who were enthusiastic, tough, well trained, and properly equipped, then "*there is nothing you cannot achieve.*"[104] It is significant to note here that British morale fragility was not merely a factor in the genesis of a firepower-laden approach based on matériel, but unfortunately also was reinforced by the attritional approach Montgomery developed to manage these morale weaknesses. Though Montgomery's "Colossal Cracks" technique, termed *Matérielschlacht* by the Germans, helped to nurture morale by avoiding the imposition of extreme demands on British troops, the very existence of a "huge weight of firepower" influenced most soldiers to believe that "they possessed the means to dispense with anything resembling personal fanaticism on the battlefield."[105] Hence, not only was the "Colossal Cracks" approach a product of, and an appropriate response to, Montgomery's concerns over the maintenance of Allied troop morale, it (paradoxically) also perpetuated to some extent the very morale fragility behind its evolution. Montgomery's method, inevitably, remained a double-edged sword.

Montgomery made clear his position on the maintenance of morale immediately upon assuming command of the "Overlord" forces in early January 1944. He instructed, when laying down to his immediate subordinates his "battle doctrine" for the theater, that "particular attention must be paid to fighting spirit and morale."[106] He then began "his morale campaign" to raise the fighting spirit of the 21st Army Group while it remained in the United Kingdom so that it would cross the Channel in the highest spirits.[107] In the months before D-Day, once the Allies had finalized the basic "Overlord" plan, Montgomery gave morale-enhancing addresses to every formation within the 21st Army Group. Whatever his real thoughts on the prospects of success, he gave these addresses bristling with supreme confidence, striving to convince the troops not only that he knew that they would win, but also that they believed that they would win.[108] These morale-boosting efforts proved highly effective in raising the morale of the troops, so that by 6 June 1944 Montgomery had accomplished his aim of sending "them into this party seeing red."[109]

Surprisingly, Brooke's diary indicates that his usually trenchant mind failed to appreciate the significance of these measures; because Montgomery was "wandering around visiting troops and failing to get down to basic facts," the CIGS would have to "kick his back side again!!"[110] A "Brookie blasting" was the only censure Montgomery would accept because the CIGS was the one officer in the British army that the arrogant Montgomery truly respected.[111] Yet, Brooke's comments about his own positive image projection confirm the correctness of Montgomery's morale-boosting approach: "The hardest part of bearing such responsibility is pretending that you are absolutely confident of success when you are really torn to shreds with doubts and misgivings! But when once decisions are taken . . . what is required is to breathe the confidence of success into all of those around you."[112] Hence, even Brooke, Montgomery's staunch patron, misunderstood some aspects of the latter's morale-enhancing actions. Certainly, Montgomery had got carried away in talking to railwaymen and dockers, but this does not refute the validity of his work with the troops.[113] Brooke's view indicates that although his strategic genius made him irreplaceable as CIGS, he probably was not the best choice to command "Overlord" in the field.[114]

The methods Montgomery adopted throughout his Second World War battles reflected these morale-maintenance needs. Moreover, his methods in Northwest Europe particularly reflected these concerns, because the existence of a manpower shortage had greatly increased their significance. Montgomery appreciated that the key to high morale was success; in order to preserve morale, Montgomery ensured that any operation he launched would enjoy the best chances of success possible. He would, therefore, only launch attacks after careful preparation, and after concentration of a large numerical advantage in matériel. His approach ensured that he never lost a battle, even if in this process he let slip potential (but risky) opportunities to win major engagements, and hence ended up with an indecisive result. Montgomery encapsulated his "Colossal Cracks" approach, and illustrated the significance of the maintenance of morale in its genesis, when he observed that "to get" high morale he avoided "any failures" by limiting "the scope of any operation to that which can be done successfully." Moreover, he remained determined not to "launch the operation until I am ready," after which he "hit hard, and quickly."[115]

Some cynics have dismissed Montgomery's cautious approach as being largely designed to secure his own reputation, and his overweening egotism rendered him vulnerable to such criticism. In 1943 Crerar, for instance, jibed that "Monty's definition of an army with good morale is an army commanded by Monty."[116] In April 1943, Eisenhower encapsulated such suspicions of Montgomery's motives in a letter to General George Marshall, the American army Chief of Staff. His first impressions of Montgomery were that though he was "unquestionably able," he was "so proud of his successes to date that he will never willingly make a single move" until he had concentrated enough resources to make him "absolutely certain of success."[117]

Unlike Montgomery, such critics seem to have failed to appreciate that the morale of a commander's troops remained inextricably linked to his reputation, and that a commander's confidence formed a central part of this morale-boosting process. This duality allowed the Field Marshal, at one and the same moment, to both serve his personal vanity and be utterly professional by exaggerating this confidence for the benefit of his troops. Indeed, appreciation of this dichotomy facilitates a full comprehension of the Field Marshal's conduct of battle. Examination of the evidence refutes the suggestion that Montgomery's operational methods were designed primarily to satisfy his own personal ambitions; he was far too monkishly devoted to the professional art of war for this assertion to be true.[118]

Montgomery's concern to preserve troop morale explains the great caution and methodical nature of his operational technique. These concerns also lay behind his emphasis on preparation, extreme concentration of force, and reliance on massive firepower.[119] Some historians have argued, echoing Eisenhower's critique, that all Montgomery achieved in 1942–45 was to win battles that any competent general, given the superiority he enjoyed, should have won; that he in fact never started a "'losable' battle."[120] One has to concede that there is some truth in this, but such a verdict fails to consider the full picture.

The experience gained in Northwest Europe and on the Eastern Front during 1943–45 demonstrated that simple numerical superiority was not enough to ensure Allied victory on every occasion. The Germans, despite their marked numerical inferiority, remained capable of inflicting tactical and operational defeats on their enemies on both fronts, as at Targul Frumos, Romania, or Villers Bocage.[121] Equally, as this study demonstrates in chapter 4, Anglo-Canadian numerical advantage appeared greater on paper than it actually was in combat. Given the doctrinal techniques of "Colossal Cracks" and concerns over casualty conservation, Anglo-Canadian forces often only deployed at any given time a small proportion of their paper strength at the point of combat. Furthermore, Allied equipment often proved inferior to that of the enemy. Given these factors, that Montgomery ensured that all his 1942–45 battles achieved victorious outcomes—albeit marginally on occasion—represented a considerable achievement. Not once did he risk experiencing a major setback that put at risk the carefully nurtured morale of the British forces; the debacle of 1940 still remained very much in the minds of Britain's senior commanders. Equally, the dire impact on Allied morale exerted by the seven-week stalemate experienced in Normandy, prompts consideration of the impact that a major reverse would have exerted on the 21st Army Group. After all, the morale of certain American formations had faltered during the German Ardennes counteroffensive. Montgomery, therefore, did not blunt his army group in Normandy on several spectacular victories, but ensured it would achieve every task set it throughout the campaign. Indeed, despite the cumulative disintegrative effects of prolonged combat, waterlogged terrain, and the short-lived glimpse of victory in September 1944, the 21st Army Group maintained its morale integrity more or less intact; the success achieved during the desperately harsh and interminably long Operation "Veritable" during February 1945 supports this argument.

An analysis of operations in Northwest Europe indicates that Montgomery's generalship reflected his concern to sustain troop morale. The crucial point here concerns the relationship between the operational demands of the moment and the sometimes contradictory demands of preserving the morale fabric of the 21st Army Group—a necessity that was, in a sense, also an operational consideration. In Normandy, Montgomery proved unwilling to launch attacks that did not enjoy the most favorable circumstances for success, and postponed operations until conditions improved. A delay in build-up of artillery shells often proved sufficient to cause him to postpone an operation. During the storm of 19–20 June 1944, Montgomery complained to Simpson that "lying in ships off the beaches is everything I need to resume the offensive with a bang." Unless he got ashore a further division, and extra artillery ammunition, Montgomery warned, he would have "to postpone the attack."[122] Postponement also remained the likely consequence if bad weather occurred, as this prevented the Allies from using the awesome power of their tactical air forces. Montgomery signaled to de Guingand that not only had bad weather caused him to postpone the "Epsom" offensive until 25 June, but also that "each further day of bad weather will mean a further postponement of one day."[123]

Montgomery, however, weighed the demands of sustaining troop morale against the requirements of the current operational situation. His theater strategy for Normandy envisaged a series of holding attacks on the British sector designed to draw the bulk of the German forces to that front, thus permitting the Americans to advance in the west. His approach also strove to keep the initiative, thus forcing the Germans merely to react to Allied moves. All of this meant that the considerations of favorable operating conditions had to be weighed against these other concerns. Thus, while he was prepared to postpone the "Epsom" offensive until better weather was present, he understood perfectly that any postponement "would be of great nuisance as every day's delay helps the enemy."[124]

At times, however, the overall operational situation necessitated actions that ran contrary to Montgomery's cautious, morale-nurturing approach. In late July 1944 he ordered Operation "Bluecoat," the British drive from Caumont toward Vire-Vassy, to start as soon as possible in order to prevent the Germans from redeploying reinforcements against Operation "Cobra," the American breakthrough attempt. Montgomery ordered "Bluecoat" to commence almost immediately, leaving insufficient time for planning and stockpiling of matériel, and instructed that the divisions being redeployed for the attack be committed piecemeal as they arrived, in a fashion more reminiscent of the tactics that the Germans were often compelled to adopt.[125] Despite Montgomery's weighing of morale preservation against other operational requirements, American senior commanders believed that Montgomery, when weighing up these contradictory considerations, regularly erred too far on the side of caution. During the Normandy campaign, Bradley lamented in exasperation that "the old cautious, methodical Monty was back."[126]

Other aspects of Montgomery's approach reflected this principle of the maintenance of morale. The Field Marshal, like most commanders, sought to keep the morale fabric of his army group intact by not placing overwhelming burdens on his troops, or by sharing out this burden between forces and over time. Montgomery's concern over the dwindling combat power evident within his original D-Day forces led him to entrust the powerful late June "Epsom" offensive to a newly arrived, and hence fresh, force—the VIII Corps led by Richard O'Connor. Similarly, Montgomery made strenuous efforts to rotate divisions at the front for rests in reserve within the constraints of his theater strategy, the operational situation, the relative build-up position, and the manpower shortage. Unfortunately, these factors seriously limited Montgomery's scope of action in this regard. Soon after the D-Day assault, for instance, he could not release the 6th Airborne Division and the 1st Commando Brigade back to the United Kingdom as planned because of the level of enemy threat; consequently, these formations remained in the frontline under the command of the I (British) Corps until August 1944.

This principle of nurturing troop morale meant that the conscript soldiers of the 21st Army Group went into battle with all the material aids that Montgomery possibly could arrange. Generally, British and Canadian infantry only would attack with as copious fire-support as possible: This included not just artillery, tactical air, antitank and conventional armor assets, but also the specialized armored vehicles of Major-General Hobart's 79th Armored Division.[127] Consequently, throughout the campaign, the British undertook only a tiny proportion of their infantry attacks without artillery and armor support.[128] In contrast, unsupported attacks remained far more frequent among German forces.[129] Montgomery's intent to sustain troop morale exerted a strong influence on the genesis of such a firepower-reliant operational technique. Montgomery also desired that his soldiers have the best medical facilities possible, and that his subordinates undertook every effort to get hot meals forward to the fighting troops, including regular supplies of that essential item, a hot brew of tea.[130] Such zealous administration seemed less prevalent within the American army in Northwest Europe: The provision, for instance, of hot meals to forward troops proved marginally more efficient in the Anglo-Canadian forces than in the American.[131]

One fascinating manifestation of Montgomery's concern with troop morale in Normandy concerned his reaction to news of German tank superiority. When GSO1 (Liaison) reports began commenting on this superiority, while suggesting tactics to counter it, Montgomery felt compelled to suppress all such liaison reports, to avoid "the troops developing a Tiger and Panther complex."[132] Such censorship may have limited the development of such a complex, but did not prevent it. Hargest noted that on 12 June 1944 a solitary German Tiger tank "fired for one hour" and then "drove off unmolested" as "not one tank went out to engage it."[133] Montgomery's reaction to these reports is significant as it suggests that his concern to nurture troop morale inadvertently hindered his command's assimilation of the lessons of combat experience—a process Montgomery believed to be essential to success. Equally, morale concerns fostered a reluctance within the 21st Army Group to criticize commanders and troops for failures, and this reticence also hampered honest, searching self-appraisal.[134] Whether the morale advantages the 21st Army Group derived from such an attitude outweighed the resulting limitation in tactical development remains a moot point for historians to consider.

There is one aspect of Montgomery's desire to sustain morale that this study has not yet addressed. This was the necessity of avoiding unwarranted heavy casualties as a prerequisite for sustaining the morale of the troops. This study has left an examination of this issue to the end of this chapter because it establishes the connection between the maintenance of morale and casualty conservation, which this study examines in the next chapter. Montgomery, like many of his senior colleagues, recognized that avoidance of heavy casualties would help sustain the relatively fragile morale of his civilian troops. He explained to his army group staff on 28 March 1944 that "soldiers will follow you if they know you will not waste their lives."[135] Brigadier Edgar ("Bill") Williams, the army group's chief intelligence staff officer, observed that "we were always very aware of the doctrine, 'let metal do it rather than flesh.' The morale of our troops depended upon this. We always said: 'Waste all the ammunition you like, but not lives.'"[136] Equally, one of Montgomery's Brigade-Majors in Africa commented that "we knew he was dead against unnecessary casualties. One of the reasons we liked serving under [him] was that we had a better chance of surviving."[137] This approach contrasted with the rather less casualty-conscious approach of some American formation commanders. One such case was Patton's battering attacks against the German defenses at Metz during the autumn of 1944, which incurred heavy casualties but achieved only modest results.[138]

It is germane here merely to observe that heavy casualties exerted two major adverse effects on morale. First, the expectation, or fear, of severe casualties expedited degeneration into "stickiness." Secondly, actually sustaining casualties steadily unraveled the basic fabric of a unit. The devastating effect on morale that such severe casualties exerted on infantry battalions is attested by the atypical example of the 6 DWR. In fourteen days of combat in Normandy, an official report observed, the unit suffered severe wastage that amounted to 23 officer and 350 other rank casualties, or 66 and 43 percent of its war establishment, respectively. Deliberately targeted German sniper activity inflicted most of these heavy British officer casualties, and this prompted the surviving officers to remove their insignia of rank. The physical absence of "all the key" officers, now dead or hospitalized, plus the visual absence of the surviving officers, minus their insignia, wrecked utterly the effectiveness of a unit now so filled with fresh reinforcements that "half" the battalion did "not know" one another.[139] On receiving this damning report, Montgomery removed the battalion from the division and ordered it broken up for reinforcements.[140]

The avoidance of casualties, however, did not remain imperative for Montgomery solely on the grounds of sustaining morale. For the 21st Army Group also suffered from a chronic and insoluble manpower crisis in North-west Europe, which when coupled with the shadow of the slaughter of the Great War, led Montgomery to conduct the campaign in a way that did not incur severe casualties. It is to this second paramount influence on Mont-gomery's conduct of the 21st Army Group during 1944-45 that this study now turns.

CHAPTER 3

Casualty Conservation

The second foundation of Montgomery's "Colossal Cracks" operational technique was casualty conservation. Historians can only fully understand his methods, particularly his caution and reliance on firepower, in the light of his concern to avoid heavy casualties in the campaign. Prior to the 1980s the campaign's historical literature showed only limited awareness of the issue of casualty conservation. The British official histories only briefly mentioned this aspect, while the Canadian history merely produced a limited analysis.[1] In the mid-1980s, however, Carlo D'Este highlighted this issue and observed that "postwar British accounts of the Normandy campaign have not given sufficient emphasis to the seriousness of either the reinforcement problem or the effects it produced on Montgomery's strategy after D-Day."[2] D'Este emphasized the effects that the manpower shortage had on the campaign from the beginning of July 1944. D'Este argued that this problem was a new, temporary phenomenon that emerged after the opening of the second front.

This analysis goes farther than D'Este, arguing that the manpower problem was a long-term problem that the British had foreseen well before D-Day. The manpower crisis not only overshadowed the whole of the "Overlord" planning process but also shaped the campaign Montgomery intended to undertake on the continent. This fact, when coupled with Montgomery's long-harbored revulsion at the slaughter of the Great War, meant that casualty-conservation concerns influenced Montgomery's entire operational approach. Historians can fully appreciate the Field Marshal's predilection for the cautious, attritional, firepower-based set-piece battle only in the context of his desire to avoid heavy casualties. This work cannot overstate the complexity of the manpower issue; the vast array of manpower, casualty, and reinforcement statistics for the campaign are extremely confusing and often contradictory. Given this fact, together with limitations of space, this analysis cannot present a systematic examination of this manpower situation.[3] Instead, this study just demonstrates three assertions: first, that the 1944 British army manpower crisis was extremely serious; second, that the British High Command had anticipated this crisis long before the 21st Army Group landed on French soil; and third, that the crisis exerted a profound influence on Montgomery's conduct of the campaign.

THE MOTIVES BEHIND MONTY'S CASUALTY-CONSCIOUS METHODS

Four interconnected motivations lay behind Montgomery's desire to attain victory with tolerable casualties. First, as the previous chapter demonstrated, Montgomery realized that avoidance of unnecessarily high casualties would help to nurture sufficiently the relatively fragile morale of the 21st Army Group's civilian troops so that they could achieve final victory over the *Westheer*. Second, as he understood, Britain by 1943–44 was suffering a chronic manpower shortage in both the military and economic sectors of her war effort. During 1944 a chronic infantry reinforcement problem would hamper British army operations in general, and those of the 21st Army Group in particular. Third, the horrors of the First World War trenches—the shadow of the Somme and Passchendaele—had profoundly influenced Montgomery, as it had many of his peers. These commanders were determined in their conduct of this war to avoid a repetition of this slaughter of British troops. Finally, in impeccable Clausewitzian style, Montgomery fully appreciated the British politico-Imperial dimensions of the military campaign he was to conduct. Britain had gone to war, in addition to resisting Nazi aggression, to protect her influence in the Europe that would emerge after the war. Montgomery, like Britain's senior commanders and politicians, realized that being among the victors was insufficient to secure British war aims. If Britain emerged as one of the victorious Allies, but with her army destroyed, Britain's ability to influence the shape of postwar Europe would be diminished. This ability was already waning fast as the two nascent superpowers, the United States and the Soviet Union, steadily eclipsed Britain.[4] As Northwest Europe represented the major British (and Western Allied) effort of the Second World War in Europe, these political considerations dominated Montgomery's conduct of the campaign.

The combination of these four factors made Montgomery determined in Northwest Europe to avoid unnecessary casualties while seeking ultimate victory. After examining the last three of these four factors in more detail, this study then demonstrates that casualty conservation was the prime motivation behind Montgomery's attritional firepower-laden approach: Put simply, "shells saved lives."[5] Consequently, "at the end of a long and exhausting war all commanders" felt "that if the expenditure of thousands of tons of projectiles" saved "a few lives or made success more certain then it was fully justified."[6]

The Manpower Shortage

By 1943, the United Kingdom was suffering from an acute shortage of manpower. Given the enormous manpower requirements of both the armed forces and wartime industrial production, by 1942 Britain had mobilized all of its available manpower to these two sectors. Consequently, the British could only expand the manpower resources of one sector at the expense of the other. This situation strictly limited the amount of manpower available for the 1944 British army as reinforcements to replace casualties—or "wastage" as it was euphemistically termed. As early as 1942 the British army had become a wasting asset; manpower intakes did not match actual wastage, and hence the High Command had to disband field formations to provide reinforcements for combat divisions. The most acute reinforcement shortages existed in the rifle infantry, upon whom the majority of combat casualties fell.[7]

The British army had long anticipated that the 21st Army Group was likely to suffer some degree of manpower shortage in Northwest Europe. The War Office could not avoid the occurrence of some shortage during 1944, despite its strenuous efforts after autumn 1943 to minimize the problem. Though D'Este recognized the long-term precursors to the summer 1944 manpower problems experienced by the 21st Army Group, he nevertheless argued that this crisis emerged suddenly during July 1944 because the War Office miscalculated infantry wastage rates. D'Este also suggested that this miscalculation forced Montgomery to disband formations within the 21st Army Group.[8] Despite D'Este's arguments, the 21st Army Group simply could not avoid experiencing some degree of manpower shortage or the necessity to disband field formations to provide much needed reinforcements. In fact, the War Office's miscalculation of infantry wastage rates "merely served to exacerbate an existing and deep rooted problem."[9]

Long before D-Day the British army realized that a serious manpower crisis, especially with rifle infantry, would occur during the campaign. As early as 20 October 1943, the War Office recognized that it would have to dispatch large drafts from the six Lower Establishment Infantry Divisions to provide reinforcements for the 21st Army Group in Normandy. These six divisions, intended for home defense only, formed the bulk of the strength deployed by United Kingdom Home Forces, the formation tasked with defending the British Isles. As early as 28 December 1943, Home Forces expressed their anxiety that the required infantry drafts might "exceed the total available fit personnel" under their command.[10] Hence, just after Christmas 1943, it was clear to many British senior officers that the British army would need to bleed dry Home Forces, and thus to take risks with the security of Great Britain, in order to provide sufficient replacements to keep Montgomery's command operational in Nazi-occupied France.

Concerns over this manpower shortage overshadowed the whole of the "Overlord" planning process. On 19 March 1944, Montgomery informed Lieutenant-General R. M. Weeks, the Deputy CIGS (DCIGS), that "the situation" with regard to "reinforcements is not good." Montgomery, the military realist, added, "We must take things as they are and find the best answer," which was "to try and do this business with the smallest possible casualties." If the British played their "cards properly," Montgomery continued, "I believe we could do it fairly cheaply."[11] Weeks then made a verbal request to de Guingand connected with this exchange with Montgomery. This prompted de Guingand on 20 March to reply, "You asked me to ensure" that Montgomery "did not discuss the manpower situation with a certain individual. This will be all right."[12] It is unfortunate that the archives do not shed light on the identity of this individual. Certainly, Britain—for political reasons—often did not keep their American allies fully informed about the seriousness of the British manpower crisis.[13] Given this fact, one might speculate that de Guingand was referring to Eisenhower, but the identity of this person may never be firmly established. Many of the Anglo-American frictions evident during the campaign stemmed from British reluctance to admit the seriousness of their manpower problems. For this reticence made it much harder for American commanders to comprehend Montgomery's cautious operational methods.

As D-Day loomed closer, British concerns over manpower increased rather than abated. On 19 May 1944 Montgomery informed Brooke that "the implications of the manpower situation on the 21st Army Group are going to be very serious." For Montgomery's command was "already short of over 13,000 men of our W[ar] E[stablishment] plus authorised reinforcements even before we commence fighting," and this situation, Montgomery continued, "will deteriorate."[14] Similarly, on 30 May 1944 Major Peter Earle, Military Assistant to General Nye, the Vice-CIGS (VCIGS), noted in his diary that by June 1944 "we will be approximately 90,000 men short in 21 Army Group," and consequently "a reduction of some five divisions will have to be effected to provide reinforcements." In conclusion Earle observed that "we are about to enter on this vast project with only three weeks' reserves, which is unheard of in the annals of history."[15] This evidence demonstrates that these worries were not, as Horne observed, "a concern little voiced before" D-Day, but rather a long-recognized problem.[16] Given this "emergency" Montgomery urged Brooke to order "drastic pruning" of the training schools in the United Kingdom, so that the 21st Army Group could at least start the D-Day invasion at almost full strength.[17]

The War Office had long anticipated this looming manpower crisis, and as early as September 1943 had taken steps to minimize its consequences.[18] The Personal Minute that Grigg presented to the Prime Minister on 25

March 1944 referred to measures already taken to avert this shortage.[19] Grigg commented that an October 1943 Cabinet paper had observed that even if the army cannibalized the six Lower Establishment Divisions in the United Kingdom by June 1944 to provide reinforcements for Montgomery, expected infantry reinforcements would still not meet expected casualties in Normandy.[20] In February 1944 the War Office estimated infantry casualties for the first six months of the campaign as 61,255 all ranks; they based this figure on a "medium" definition of infantry that, in addition to rifle infantry, included commandos, Foot Guards and special service troops (see Table 3.1). The equivalent War Office casualty estimate based on a "wide" definition of infantry that also included machine-gun and motorized infantry was 67,132 men. These two estimates respectively amounted to 38 and 41.7 percent of the total 171,855 estimated British casualties for all ranks across all branches in the first six months of the campaign (see Table 3.1). These figures produced an average monthly infantry casualty rate of between 10,209 and 11,189 (on "medium" and "wide" definitions, respectively). This compared to an estimated total average monthly casualty rate of 28,642 soldiers of all ranks.[21]

TABLE 3.1

COMPARISON OF *PREDICTED* TOTAL BRITISH INFANTRY CASUALTIES WITH ACTUAL ONES (BOTH ALL RANKS, "MEDIUM" DEFINITION OF INFANTRY) WITHIN THE 21ST ARMY GROUP IN THE FIRST SIX MONTHS OF THE NORTHWEST EUROPE CAMPAIGN

	Predicted Infantry Casualties (All Ranks) [Source A]		Actual Infantry Casualties (All Ranks) [Source C]		
Month	Monthly Wastage	Cumulative Wastage	Period (1944)	Monthly Wastage	Cumulative Wastage
First	16,306	16,306	6 June–3 July	12,534	12,534
Second	9,067	25,373	4 July–9 Aug	21,775	34,309
Third	7,975	33,348	10 Aug–1 Sept	4,798	39,107
Fourth	9,067	42,415	N/A	N/A	N/A
Fifth	9,773	52,188	N/A	N/A	N/A
Sixth	9,067	61,255	N/A	N/A	N/A

Sources: Source A (Predicted), PRO, WO205/152; Source C (Actual), PRO, WO162/116, NWE British Battle Casualties. A "Medium" definition of Infantry includes Rifle Infantry, Foot Guards, Commandos, Special Service Forces, but excludes Machine Gun, Motor, Air Landing, Paratrooper and Glider Pilot personnel.

TABLE 3.2
COMPARISON OF *PREDICTED* TOTAL BRITISH CASUALTIES WITH ACTUAL ONES (BOTH ALL RANKS, "MEDIUM" DEFINITION OF INFANTRY) WITHIN THE 21ST ARMY GROUP IN THE FIRST SIX MONTHS OF THE NORTHWEST EUROPE CAMPAIGN

	Predicted Total Casualties (All Arms, All Ranks) [Source A]			Actual Total Casualties (All Arms, All Ranks) [Source B]	
Month	Monthly Wastage	Cumulative Wastage	Period	Monthly Wastage	Cumulative Wastage
First	39,446	39,446	6 June–6 July	24,464	24,464
Second	26,305	65,751	7 July–7 Aug	26,075	50,539
Third	25,282	91,033	8 Aug–7 Sept	14,597	65,136
Fourth	26,141	117,174	8 Sept–6 Oct	11,565	76,701
Fifth	28,540	145,714	7 Oct–13 Nov	26,776	103,477
Sixth	26,141	171,855	14 Nov–8 Dec 44	5,919	109,396

Sources: Source A (Predicted Casualties), PRO, WO205/152; Source B (Actual Casualties), PRO, WO162/116, Battle Casualties, NWE, handwritten notes at back of file.

Montgomery's Normandy campaign represented the British army's main effort during 1944. On 30 March 1944 the British army estimated that it required 102,250 infantry reinforcements to replace wastage across all war theaters during the nine-month period April to December 1944, at an average rate of 11,361 infantrymen per month. The army expected the 21st Army Group to incur 61,255 infantry casualties (as per the "medium" definition) during the first six months of the campaign, at an average rate of 10,209 infantrymen per month. Montgomery's army group required 90 percent of the British army's entire infantry reinforcement demands during the second half of 1944 just to prevent its infantry combat strength shrinking.[22]

The seriousness of the future manpower shortage was abundantly clear to the British High Command. Grigg's 25 March 1944 Minute concluded that if "Overlord" incurred casualties at the estimated rates, the British army would "be worse off by about 30,000 men than we had previously anticipated." Even with the Lower Establishment divisions broken up for drafting, "our total deficiency" in the field "will be in the order of 60,000, of which 40,000 will be infantry."[23] Similarly, at the 30 May 1944 Cabinet Meeting on manpower, Weeks concluded that, after replacement of estimated casualties, the British army as a whole "would be 100,000 men down by the end of the year" in comparison with December 1943.[24]

In response to these fears, Grigg urged that the army expand the process of combing out rear establishments that it had commenced in early 1944. He also calculated that the army would have to disband one operational division in both the Italian and Normandy theaters to provide reinforcements for other field divisions. From October 1944 onwards, Grigg concluded, "at best we can hope that the larger intakes which we are due to get into the army from March [1944] onwards, augmented by returning wounded and . . . [men] retraining from other arms as infantry might stabilize the situation and prevent a further weakening of effort." However, the reinforcements earmarked for 1945 were, he reported, inadequate.[25] In an attempt to minimize this manpower problem, on 30 March 1944 the Cabinet authorized the transfer of 35,000 men from the artillery and the R.A.F. Regiment for retraining as infantry.[26] Yet it would be many months before these men would complete their retraining and be ready for combat in France.

Implementation of these measures would leave, by August 1944, just one operational formation in the entire United Kingdom; this illustrates the extent to which this situation compelled the War Office to scrape the bottom of the manpower barrel. The sole operational formation located in the United Kingdom, the mountain-trained 52nd Infantry Division, had been held in the War Office Strategic Reserve since being earmarked at Chiefs of Staff level for Operation "Jupiter," the proposed invasion of Norway.[27] By August the British army entrusted the defense of the United Kingdom to just three reserve and one holding divisions, plus two cadre Lower Establishment divisions for retraining returning wounded; none of these formations was in any way fit for operational commitment abroad.

The extent to which the British army creamed off those Home Forces personnel considered fit for drafting overseas to boost the 21st Army Group's strength illustrates the scale of this manpower shortage. To be eligible for drafting to operational formations in combat overseas, an infantryman had to be in the Grade A1 medical category and be between 19 and 38 years old. As of 21 February 1944 there remained just 30,093 infantrymen within the active Lower Establishment infantry divisions in Home Forces, as the army already had transferred many such troops to Montgomery's command.[28] This figure, however, excludes those infantrymen serving in the reserve or holding divisions and other smaller miscellaneous units; yet the vast majority of these infantrymen remained unfit for drafting. By 1 April 1944 the 21st Army Group already had drafted 7,480 (or 25 percent) of these 30,093 apparently combat-fit infantrymen, to bring it up to full War Establishment plus authorized reinforcements. However, a significant number of the infantrymen within Home Forces were not fit for infantry duties in the field, on age and/or medical grounds. Home Forces calculated that some 20–25 percent of its infantrymen (that is, between 6,019 and 7,523 soldiers) remained unfit for drafting to the 21st Army Group.[29] Hence, some nine weeks before it even set foot in France, Montgomery's command had absorbed between 31 and 33 percent (7,480 out of between 22,570 and 24,074) of Home Forces' available draft-quality infantry strength. In addition, Home Forces dispatched 5,272 troops from branches other than the infantry to the 21st Army Group in the same period.[30] Thus, in the weeks prior to D-Day, the 21st Army Group also experienced manpower shortages in branches other than the infantry, especially within the Royal Armored Corps [RAC]; a shortage that was to persist throughout the Normandy battles.[31]

The War Office also planned in advance that Home Forces would give up 13,000 infantrymen during June and July 1944 as reinforcements to replace casualties incurred by the 21st Army Group in Normandy. In spring 1944, prolonged staff planning investigated the difficult question of how Home Forces could provide these drafts yet simultaneously fulfill its own burdensome tasks. Reduced by early June 1944 to a paltry 22,000 rifle infantry (of which only 14,200 were fit for drafting), the Lower Establishment divisions fielded by Home Forces still had to defend the United Kingdom, undertake marshaling duties for "Overlord," and most importantly both train new recruits and retrain wounded soldiers returned from combat. These commitments absorbed large amounts of manpower: The defense of the Orkneys and Shetlands alone accounted for 13,000 personnel, while "Overlord" marshaling duties required 17,961 personnel at its peak in early June 1944, before tapering off by August.[32] Clearly, by D-Day, Home Forces was stretched to the breaking point to fulfill its existing commitments, let alone to meet the demand for the dispatch of 13,000 infantrymen to the 21st Army Group during June and July 1944.

The dispatch of these 13,000 infantry soldiers to Montgomery during the first seven weeks of the Normandy campaign meant that by 7 August 1944, Home Forces' Lower Establishment divisions now fielded just 8,032 rifle infantrymen, of which staggeringly a mere 2,654 were draft-quality![33] Apart from the 8,000 operational infantry of the 52nd Division held in the War Office Strategic Reserve, the British army could immediately muster only a pool of under 2,700 available combat-ready infantry within the entire United Kingdom—while simultaneously in Normandy, Montgomery conducted the most important British army campaign of the entire war. The British High Command dispatched most of the remaining 2,700 draft-quality infantrymen deployed in the Lower Establishment Divisions to Montgomery during the rest of August 1944. Consequently, by the autumn, the 21st Army Group had absorbed virtually all the fit young infantrymen the United Kingdom could offer: By then Home Forces had been reduced to a force consisting of young lads, old men, and the unfit.

Given that Montgomery's command had bled Home Forces dry of draftable riflemen by September 1944, from this time on those new British army infantry recruits who each month had completed their standard training represented the only future source of infantry reinforcements for the 21st Army Group—unless the High Command took the drastic step of withdrawing field forces from other theaters for disbandment. Short of this desperate measure, the War Office also could supplement this paltry monthly infantry manpower output both with recovered wounded who had completed refresher training, and with troops from other branches who had completed their retraining as infantry.

This evidence casts the gravest doubts on D'Este's conclusions at the end of his analysis of manpower. Here, he produces new evidence, contradicting his earlier argument, that he believes "casts serious doubt on the legitimacy of the infantry reinforcement shortage."[34] Citing War Office documentation, D'Este observes that on 30 June 1944 there were no fewer than 6,373 infantry officers and 109,251 infantry other ranks deployed within the United Kingdom in addition to those forces allocated to the 21st Army Group.[35] D'Este, despite admitting that some of these troops were needed to defend the British isles, and that others were either involved in the training process or earmarked as future reinforcements for France, nevertheless concluded that the "availability of vast numbers of uncommitted infantry [sic] poses several disturbing questions." D'Este then pondered "why were none of these troops used in Normandy" and "why were United Kingdom-based infantry units not disbanded instead of line infantry units of the Second [(British)] Army?" In answer to this question, D'Este mused "were they deliberately withheld" by Churchill because he either "so mistrust[ed] the eventual success of Overlord" that he remained "simply unwilling to commit them to Montgomery," or because he wished to "place limitations on the numbers of men he was willing to sacrifice at this stage of the Second World War?"[36]

Unfortunately, nothing could be farther from the truth; there simply were not "vast numbers of uncommitted infantry" still in the United Kingdom on 30 June 1944. On paper there remained over 100,000 infantry within the United Kingdom outside those in the 21st Army Group. The simple truth is that only a tiny fraction of these forces were fit for active combat duties in France; Home Forces, as his study already has demonstrated, had been virtually bled dry of draftable infantry by August 1944. Of these 100,000 infantry, there were, as D'Este rightly concedes, no less than 52,916 other ranks in training, depot, and miscellaneous units. Training units typically consisted of a small cadre of trainers, and a bulk of new recruits undergoing training. Though most of the trainers possessed combat experience, many were not fully fit or had previously shown signs of battle fatigue, and hence the High Command deemed them unfit for infantry combat overseas. Equally, the training of infantry recruits was a long and thorough affair. Just like the German army until 1944, the manpower crisis within the British army did not prompt more than minor curtailing of the thoroughness of infantry training. To send men half-trained into combat was a guarantee that many would swiftly die for their inexperience, and quite correctly this was something that Britain was not prepared to do.[37] Therefore, as of 30 June 1944 the vast majority of these 53,000 troops were not available immediately as reinforcements for the 21st Army Group. Over the next six months, however, approximately some 50–75 percent of these infantry troops would arrive in France as replacements for Montgomery's forces.

The other 57,612 infantrymen in D'Este's 30 June 1944 inventory belonged to 93 regimental infantry battalions and 15 independent companies.[38] At first glance, it seems possible that these troops may have been available as replacements for the casualties incurred by the 21st Army Group. The fact that the War Office undertook a series of extensive reorganizations of Home Forces throughout 1944, however, prevents anything more than an approximate analysis of the composition of these 108 units. Despite this, such an analysis of these 57,612 infantrymen clearly demonstrates that the vast majority of these troops were not draft-quality—and therefore remained unavailable as reinforcements for Montgomery's command. This analysis is depicted Table 3.3.

Some 8,000 of these 57,612 infantrymen remained unavailable to Montgomery as the War Office held them as its Strategic Reserve. The vast majority of the 22,000 personnel in the training formations remained only partially trained, and thus not yet fit for combat overseas. Neither could Montgomery draft the instructor cadres in these units without seriously disrupting the training of new recruits, which now constituted Britain's main source of infantry reinforcements; furthermore, as this study has already observed, many of these instructors were medically or psychologically unfit for drafting. By 30 June 1944, the only sources of drafts for Montgomery's command were the roughly 13,000 combat-fit infantry in the Lower Establishment divisions. However, the War Office had always intended to use this source to meet the manpower demands (for 13,000 infantry) of Montgomery's forces during the first two months of the campaign. However, not only did the entire defense of the United Kingdom rest on their shoulders, but they were already on average at 50 percent of their War Establishment; further drafting could only bring into question their remaining integrity as units. Therefore, by August 1944 after the War Office had dispatched these 13,000 troops to France, there remained very few draftable troops available in the United Kingdom, even after strict combing. If the 21st Army Group suffered especially heavy

TABLE 3.3: BRITISH RIFLE INFANTRY PERSONNEL (ALL RANKS) IN U.K. UNDER HOME FORCES/ WAR OFFICE CONTROL, 30 JUNE 1944[40]

Function	Formations or Units	Total Rifle Infantry	No. Inf Bns	Estimated Draftable Infantry	Estimated Draftable 21 Army GP
War Office Strategic Reserve	52 Inf Div	8,140	9	8,140	0 {a}
War Office Control	9 Dorsets	347	1	347	0
UK Home Forces	7 Inf Bde	875	3	875	875
Total UK Operational Field Forces	**N/A**	**9,362**	**13**	**9,362**	**875**
UK Home Defense	38, 45, 47, 55, 61 Lower Est Inf Divs	17,845	42	c. 13,000 {b}	c 13,000
Training	48, 76, 80 Reserve Divs 77 Holdng Div 8 Sherwood F	22,355	30	c. 1,100	c. 1,100
Young Boys Bns	5 × bns	3,524	5	0	0
Local Def Coys	15 × Coys	2,892	15 coys	0	0
Other	Lovat Scouts{c} 1/5 Leics 4 R Berks	1,612	3	844+	0
Total Rifle Infantry, UK Home Defense	**N/A**	**48,228**	**80**	**c. 14,944+**	**c. 14,100+**
Grand Total UK Rifle Infantry	**N/A**	**57,590**	**93 +15 coys**	**c. 24,306+**	**c. 14,975+**

infantry casualties during the Normandy campaign, it would only be able to replace this wastage by breaking up some of its own field formations to provide the necessary reinforcements.[39]

The infantry reinforcement crisis of 1944, therefore, represented a long-term problem that the War Office undoubtedly exacerbated by its underestimation of infantry casualty wastage rates for the Normandy campaign. In fact, the War Office estimation of total casualties for all branches in the campaign's first six months remained higher than the total losses actually suffered; 109,396 total casualties suffered up to 12 December 1944 against a predicted figure of 171,855 casualties up to 5 December.[41] However, predicted infantry casualties proved significantly lower than actual infantry wastage. The 21st Army Group incurred 39,107 infantry casualties by 1 September 1944, compared with 33,348 predicted casualties (on a "medium" definition) by 5 September.[42] Actual infantry casualties exceeded estimated ones by some 17 percent.

The War Office miscalculated the proportion that infantry casualties represented out of the total casualties incurred over all branches by Montgomery's forces in Normandy. The February 1944 War Office casualty projection estimated that infantry casualties would constitute between 38 percent and 45 percent of total casualties, depending on which definition of infantry was used.[43] This estimate proved to be far too low for the fighting experienced in Normandy. Within the Canadian forces employed in Normandy, the actual infantry casualties (based on a "wide" definition) incurred between D-Day and 17 August 1944 amounted to no less than 76 percent of their total casualties.[44] The corresponding British figure was 63.7 percent for (medium definition) rifle infantry other ranks, and 47 percent for officers. Use of the broadest definition of infantry produced a figure for other ranks of 71.3 percent.[45] The Allied infantry bore hardest the intense, constricted, fighting experienced in Normandy. After the successful Allied breakout of mid-August 1944, the proportion of total casualties represented by infantry wastage declined markedly. By 16 September 1944, total British rifle infantry casualties amounted to 55.7 percent for other ranks and 43.1 percent for officers. The corresponding figures using a broad definition of infantry were 65.7 percent and 51.2 percent, respectively. In Normandy, therefore, higher-than-expected infantry wastage exacerbated Montgomery's pre-existing problems of infantry reinforcement shortages.

The fear that the reinforcement pool would run dry remained a constant concern for Montgomery. It was more the fear that this pool would be exhausted, rather than it being physically exhausted, that strongly influenced Montgomery's handling of the campaign. The problems the 21st Army Group experienced getting forward available reinforcements to replace casualties in frontline troops also compounded these manpower concerns. The British reinforcement pool never ran dry, largely because Montgomery cannibalized two British divisions for reinforcements before this pool became exhausted.

However, the Canadian pool became exhausted by August 1944. Canadian formations suffered heavily throughout Normandy, and their reinforcement problem peaked in August and early September as a result of the heavy casualties incurred during Operations "Totalize" and "Tractable." In August 1944 the authorized War Establishment of the First Canadian Army in terms of infantry other ranks amounted to 20,599 troops. On 2 September 1944 the deficit in infantry other ranks within Crerar's command peaked at a staggering 19.2 percent—some 3,917 soldiers. Such a deficit in infantry strength threatened seriously the long-term combat viability of Canadian formations. As this study discusses in chapter 7, during September 1944 General Crerar conducted cautiously the Canadian operations designed to open up the channel ports along the Pas de Calais and the Belgium coast. His caution is explicable in the context of the severe manpower crisis that enveloped the First Canadian Army after late August 1944. The Canadians found it hard to remedy these infantry shortages, and even with the caution displayed by Crerar during September, the infantry other ranks deficit in the First Canadian Army still amounted to a dangerous 10.69 percent as late as 7 October 1944.[46]

These manpower concerns persisted throughout the campaign, and hence continued to influence the manner in which senior British and Canadian commanders conducted their operations. By early 1945, however, three factors had ameliorated the British infantry other ranks reinforcement shortage within the 21st Army Group: First, Montgomery had disbanded the two British infantry divisions previously mentioned; second, from late 1944, the higher monthly number of troops that had completed their basic training boosted the flow of reinforcements to Montgomery's command; and third, from December 1944, soldiers who had completed their retraining from other arms to infantrymen began to arrive on the continent.[47] Nevertheless, during early 1945 there remained a serious shortage of infantry officer reinforcements. On 22 January 1945 Montgomery complained to Grigg that he was 350 officers short and that he expected this to rise to 1,100 by March 1945 despite the reinforcements already promised him. Montgomery implored that "the most ruthless measures must be adopted, both on my side and by your side, to comb out every source and try and get a thousand officers for the infantry by the end of March."[48] Irrespective of whether the infantry reinforcement shortage fell on other ranks, as in 1944, or on officers as in 1945, this problem haunted Montgomery's handling of the 21st Army Group throughout the campaign.

The Shadow of the Somme
The third influence on Montgomery's desire to avoid casualties was the legacy of the Great War. Many of the senior officers in the 21st Army Group had witnessed the slaughter of "the poor bloody infantry" on the Western Front

in the 1914–18 War. Many of these, as well as senior British politicians, remained determined in the Second World War to avoid the "chateau generalship" that had contributed to the decimation of a generation which had so damaged Britain in the interwar period. Montgomery commented that the Canadians at Passchendaele in 1917 had forgotten "that the whole art of war is to gain your objective with as little loss as possible."[49] This concern contributed to a British grand strategic approach during the 1939–45 War that sought to weaken the Germans on the peripheries rather than engage the main body of enemy forces.[50] Historians need to discuss with care the humanitarian feelings of generals, because in wartime it is an unavoidable part of their job to send troops to their deaths. Nevertheless, during 1939–45, many of these senior British officers remained determined to avoid a repetition of the terrible slaughter of the infantry of the Great War. Their approach sought to achieve operational objectives while avoiding unnecessarily large casualties as much as possible. To Montgomery and his senior subordinates the infantry of the 21st Army Group did not constitute mere cannon fodder, even though, like most campaigns, the majority of casualties inevitably fell on the infantry. Consequently, in Northwest Europe Montgomery refused to waste the lives of his men by continuing with offensive operations that stood little chance of success.

According to Richard O'Brien, one of Montgomery's personal liaison officers at army group tactical headquarters, the Field Marshal had been "horrified by the loss of life" incurred during the Great War and remained "determined not to repeat the mistakes made by the First War generals." O'Brien felt that Montgomery's desire "to lose as few men as possible" constituted the "main explanation of the caution he showed in preparation for his battles."[51] Similarly, Grigg thought it "absurd" to describe Montgomery "as timid" simply because "he was determined not to subject his troops to anything like the carnage of the Somme or Passchendaele."[52]

The Political Dimension

Britain's political objectives during the Second World War constitute the fourth motivation behind Montgomery's desire to avoid heavy casualties in Northwest Europe. By 1943 senior British military commanders, Montgomery included, were acutely aware that if the British army suffered devastating damage during the process of defeating successfully the Germans, this would diminish British Imperial influence on the postwar world and especially postwar Europe. For it simply was not enough for the British Empire to have won the war—it had to win the peace as well.[53]

Brooke's enthusiasm that Montgomery should command the 21st Army Group, and all Allied forces in the theater, reflected his recognition both of Montgomery's operational abilities, and of the fact that the Field Marshal shared his viewpoint on Britain's role in the world.[54] Brooke realized that the forceful Montgomery represented the best commander to pursue British aims in Northwest Europe. Many of Montgomery's actions in the campaign, especially his protracted argument with Eisenhower over theater strategy and the command setup, reflected his determination "to maintain the course of the campaign" on "lines most suitable to Britain."[55] Montgomery displayed a marked Clausewitzian influence when he stated in his *Memoirs* that "war is a political instrument" and that "it was of no avail to win the war strategically if we lost it politically."[56]

While Montgomery's own personal pride also remained very much at stake on the command issue, so too did his ability to protect the interests of the British army within the campaign. Montgomery's overweening vanity has led historians to underestimate the influence of British aims on his behavior. While Montgomery stressed the need for full operational cooperation between the Allies in order to defeat the enemy, he also sought (somewhat contradictorily) to protect British interests within the wider Allied effort in the theater.

Montgomery's pursuit of British interests in Northwest Europe begs consideration of whether he received any formal instructions from the British government concerning his conduct of the campaign. There is no evidence to support the existence of such instructions. However, given that these instructions would have been highly controversial in the context of inter-Allied cooperation, it seems certain that Churchill or Grigg would have issued them privately and verbally. Moreover, in all probability, no such instructions were necessary because Churchill, Brooke, and Montgomery shared a common British viewpoint. It is inconceivable that somebody in as senior a position within the British army as Montgomery, and someone so close to Brooke, would not have been fully aware of the wider politico-strategic agenda of the British government.[57] Moreover, Montgomery's behavior in the 1939–45 War prior to Normandy displayed that he shared fully the arrogant Imperial outlook of the British élite. To name but one example of many, Montgomery persistently treated the Canadian General "Harry" Crerar in a supercilious manner.

Despite being a self-professed apolitical general, Montgomery's behavior suggests that he correctly remained concerned by the wider politico-Imperial dimension of the campaign. In May 1944 Field Marshal Jan Smuts, the South African president, influenced Montgomery in urging him to "speak out" when "the war was nearly over."[58] Montgomery's notes of their conversation demonstrate that both men remained acutely aware of Britain's perspective on the grand strategic or international political dimensions of the war. "Smuts is worried that we may lose the peace," Montgomery recorded. The South African argued that even though "Britain, with American aid, won the

Great War," after 1918, the "tired" British nation "stood back" and allowed "France to take first place in Europe," and this precipitated "the present war." In Smuts' view, once the Allies had defeated Nazi Germany, Britain had to "remain strong" so as to "stand firm as the corner stone of the new structure of Europe."[59] Hence, Smuts argued, Britain's victory in 1918 remained chimerical, because in the process of securing military victory, she had failed to preserve the influential political role in Europe that had been part of the reasons for going to war in the first place. In 1944, with two superpowers emerging rapidly, history seemed to be repeating itself. This was the political context that sat consistently at the back of Montgomery's mind during the 1944–45 campaign.

In Northwest Europe, the vital theater for the Western Allies during the Second World War in Europe, the link between the 21st Army Group and Britain's international standing remained clear. Churchill was extremely conscious of the connection between the dwindling forces fielded by the 21st Army Group and the decreasing international influence exerted by Britain. The rising influence exerted by America, an ally of Britain that was by "no means friendly to the British Empire," only served to increase Churchill's sense of unease.[60] As early as November 1943 the Prime Minister had stated that he "should like to be able to tell" the Americans, that "we will match you man for man and gun for gun" in Normandy, because this would "maintain our right to be effectively consulted in operations which are of such capital consequence."[61] Churchill, moreover, informed Montgomery on 12 December 1944 that he "greatly fear[ed] the dwindling of the British Army as a factor in France as it will affect our rights to express our opinion upon strategic and other matters."[62] By the time of Germany's defeat, American forces in the theater outnumbered the Commonwealth's best effort for a significant military force by well over three to one. Churchill, obsessed with "bayonet" strength, remained determined to avoid reduction in the 21st Army Group's peak 1944 strength of sixteen divisions. Yet the manpower crisis compelled Montgomery to break up several divisions to provide reinforcements for other formations in his army group. On 3 December 1944 Churchill angrily ordered Montgomery to halt the disbanding of the 50th Division as soon as Brooke had informed him of the decision.[63] Churchill only reluctantly reversed his halt decision after the Chiefs of Staff had backed a firm message from Montgomery that informed Churchill that he had already begun the disbandment, that he could not easily reverse these actions, and that any attempt to do so would cause severe damage to British prospects in the theater.[64]

Brooke shared Churchill's concerns over Britain's international political eclipse. The CIGS revealingly responded to a proposal by Major-General Harding, Alexander's Chief of Staff in Italy, that this theater should become an all-British front, with forces withdrawn from Europe. Brooke inquired whether Harding "thought it advisable that the offensive on the main front [Northwest Europe], responsible for the final defeat of the Germans, we should leave the task entirely to the Americans and take an insignificant part?"[65] Brooke believed that the maintenance of Britain's international influence necessitated that British forces assume a prominent role in the prosecution of the vital Northwest Europe campaign. The 21st Army Group, however, scarcely possessed sufficient forces to achieve such a military prominence. Montgomery's decision-making throughout the campaign remained impaled on the horns of this politico-military dilemma.

The desire of senior British commanders to preserve Britain's international position made them highly concerned to avoid heavy casualties that might decimate the British army—the very institution that embodied this position. Churchill intervened directly in the conduct of the campaign at least once by raising the matter of casualty conservation in a telephone call to Eisenhower. Major-General Kenneth Strong, chief intelligence officer at SHAEF, noted that Churchill asked Eisenhower if he could "avoid too many British casualties" because "British losses had been severe, and Britain was being assaulted by the V weapons." According to Strong, Eisenhower told Churchill that "if Britain wished to be in the van of the battle, as Montgomery had suggested, British casualties could not be avoided."[66]

One of the keys to Montgomery's conduct of the campaign lies in understanding these contradictions—for the Field Marshal remained caught in an intractable dilemma throughout the campaign. He recognized that his army group command could secure for Britain a significant role in deciding the political fate of postwar Europe by its assumption of a prominent role in the military defeat of Germany. To a large degree, Britain's postwar political prestige rested on the glory that her soldiers won on the battlefields of Europe. However, if Montgomery maintained such a high profile by using the 21st Army Group to spearhead the Allied onslaught against the *Westheer*, his formation would incur severe casualties, particularly in infantrymen. Given the British infantry reinforcement crisis, such high losses would force Montgomery to disband additional divisions. Consequently, the order of battle of the 21st Army Group would decline further from its meager peak strength in Normandy of sixteen divisions. The fewer the number of combat-experienced divisions that the British army emerged with at the end of the war, the smaller her influence on Europe was likely to be in the face of the growing military might of the two nascent superpowers. This paradox remained as clear to Montgomery as it was insoluble. For if the British commander-in-chief strove to secure a significant British political influence in postwar Europe through the maintenance of a high military profile in the Northwest Europe campaign, he risked destroying the very force—the 21st

Army Group—that would secure this political agenda. Montgomery's gener-alship in Northwest Europe constituted an attempt to solve this paradox: He sought the achievement of a high British military profile in the theater while avoiding the inevitable casualties that went with such a profile.

Montgomery, unfortunately, faced another thorny dilemma in North-west Europe. The longer the war lasted, the smaller would be the British effort in comparison with that of the Americans, as the latter gradually deployed their full numerical might. In consequence, the British politically remained more interested in achieving victory quickly than the Americans, because "the British economy and man-power situation demanded victory in 1944: no later."[67] The 21st Army Group, however, possessed insufficient resources to achieve early victory by itself, unless the Germans collapsed unexpectedly. Equally, Montgomery could not afford to sustain the heavy casualties that would be incurred in a British-dominated attempt to secure quick victory over the *Westheer*. Should such a full-blown British offensive effort fail, Montgomery's emasculated army group might be reduced to a secondary role in the theater, condemned merely to watch from the side-lines as the Americans achieved the glory of ultimately defeating the *Wehr-macht*. Britain might be on the war's winning side yet still lose the peace. The motivations behind Montgomery's atypically bold "Market-Garden" offensive are more intelligible in this context. The operation constituted his exploita-tion of a unique battlefield opportunity for him to gamble his forces realisti-cally in an attempt to secure for Britain a prominent profile in an Allied victory over the *Westheer* achieved during 1944.

Montgomery remained both an ardent military professional and a staunch champion of British political interests: an uneasy bifurcation, at best. He faced a double dilemma: how to strive to win both the war and the peace by seeking a high military profile in the wider Allied campaign and/or by seeking an early, British-dominated victory—yet in both cases to do so with-out destroying his army group and wrecking the force that stood the best chance of achieving these political aims. Montgomery's simple solution to this double dilemma was to attempt to remain as theater Land Forces Com-mander after the end of the Normandy battles. With Montgomery com-manding all forces in the theater, any success, irrespective of the nationality of the forces achieving it, would reflect on him, and hence on Britain. No doubt, retention of this command appointment also assuaged his rampant personal glory-seeking.

By remaining as Land Force Commander, Montgomery also could ensure that Allied operations conformed to a clear theater strategy. Not only was this operationally sound, but it served British interests. For a clear the-ater strategy could select, and justify operationally, the northern line of advance toward the Ruhr, and such a strategy would ensure a key profile for the 21st Army Group within the theater. Lastly as Land Forces Commander, Montgomery could allocate logistical priority to the 21st Army Group to ensure that his forces had the resources necessary to enable them to achieve significant advances. Given that Montgomery's retention of overall control of all land forces was so vital to both British politico-strategic interest and his own personal ambition, it is not surprising that he waged such a long and insubordinate campaign against Eisenhower to get himself reinstated in the position.

Montgomery, however, utterly failed to comprehend the huge impact that public opinion, especially that in America, would exert on the Allied conduct of the campaign. His rigid military mind could not grasp the fact that American numerical superiority in the theater after August 1944 meant that there would have to be an American Land Forces Commander. Montgomery seemed to have learned little from his own previous personal experiences of inter-Allied tensions in Africa, Sicily, and Italy. His decision-making, with its narrow focus on British interests and strictly operational matters, could not grasp the subtle realities of inter-Allied cooperation, unlike Alexander in Italy. Montgomery "appeared to have been temperamentally incapable of recognizing that operational requirements (no matter how correct on their own terms) would have to be subordinated to the paramount need of holding the Grand Alliance together."[68] In Northwest Europe, this weakness in Montgomery's generalship came very close to undermining the professional inter-Allied operational cooperation he deemed so vital to the achievement of victory over the *Westheer*. In reality, Montgomery struggled to maintain the delicate balancing act required to effectively marry his strict operational professionalism with his ardent British patriotism in order to produce effective British participation in a wider, successful Allied campaign.

When Montgomery failed to get himself reinstated as Land Force Commander during autumn 1944, he strove for a "half-way house" position by cajoling Eisenhower to accord him the power of operational coordination over Bradley's army group. Montgomery's other compromise position was to persuade Eisenhower to place American formations under the direct command of the 21st Army Group. In this way Montgomery, and hence Britain, would enjoy a greater military profile than his own dwindling forces could obtain in the field. These measures also reflected Montgomery's casualty-conscious approach. For Britain would receive most of the glory achieved by the forces within these command arrangements, but this success would be secured, at least partially, by both American efforts and casualties.

Given the nature of this agenda, it is not surprising that many senior American commanders in the theater hated Montgomery, a view subsequently entrenched by the American historical literature about the campaign. Montgomery's caution in front of Caen, for example, prompted "unpleasant comments" by senior American officers at SHAEF that Montgomery was attempting "to save British lives at the expense of those of his Allies."[69] Senior American officers often interpreted Montgomery's actions as examples of personal aggrandizement. The fact that British reticence prevented American appreciation of the true extent of Britain's manpower crisis only served to foster such suspicions. Equally, few American commanders appreciated the extent to which Montgomery's pursuit of British national interest in the theater at the expense of Allied interests served to reinforce his personal ambitions.[70]

Historians also have not awarded the crucial, yet shadowy, role maintained by Brooke in Montgomery's defense of British interests in the campaign the attention it deserves. Brooke was ready to blame Montgomery's behavior on the latter's vanity, yet he approved of the Field Marshal's defense of British interests. Brooke supported Montgomery's military logic, and staunchly defended his protégé in the latter's campaign against the Americans over the command issue. Yet when Montgomery went too far and threatened the stability of the Alliance, Brooke castigated his subordinate. Within parameters, Brooke backed Montgomery as the best individual to defend British interests in the campaign.[71]

CASUALTY CONSERVATION AND MONTGOMERY'S CONDUCT OF THE CAMPAIGN

When combined, the four aspects discussed here produced a powerful motivation for Montgomery to conduct the campaign in a casualty-conscious manner. Having examined the factors that led to Montgomery's casualty conservation, this analysis now examines how these worries manifested themselves in Montgomery's conduct of the campaign. The senior German commanders that faced the 21st Army Group during the campaign deduced the existence of casualty-conscious motivations behind Montgomery's utilization of an attritional approach based on massive firepower. On 10 July 1944 General Gehr von Schweppenburg, commanding the *Panzer Gruppe West*, astutely observed that although the Anglo-Canadian troops "were magnificent," the "slow and rather pedestrian" Allied high command "was not making the best use of them" by merely seeking "to wear down their enemy with their enormous material superiority."[72] Schweppenburg considered it possible that "Montgomery had received private instruction from his Government to avoid for the British troops another bloodbath such as they had suffered in the First World War."[73] Another German report of November 1944 concluded that "the Allies believe in material superiority; instead of attacking energetically they attempt to smash the enemy by means of their heavy weapons and to occupy ground without having to light for it, thereby avoiding heavy casualties."[74] The Germans grasped correctly that the essence of "Colossal Cracks" was the "application of overwhelming firepower" to "avoid, to the maximum possible extent, the need for close combat."[75]

During 1944, several senior British commanders noted the existence of casualty-conscious approaches in certain Commonwealth ground operations. On 31 March, Brooke noted that in Italy "Freyberg has been fighting with a casualty-conscious mind." Freyberg, Brooke continued, "has been sparing" his New Zealand infantry and "hoping to accomplish results by use of heavy bombers and artillery, without risking too much infantry."[76] The predictable result, Brooke concluded, was that Freyberg's operation had failed. Brooke's postwar comment on this diary entry demonstrates that casualty conservation was not the product of the operational limitations of commanders, but of circumstances beyond their control. Brooke agreed with the widely held view that Freyberg was one of the most able Allied commanders, but understood that by 1944 Freyberg had received instructions from his national government "not to risk losing too many soldiers as casualties were already very high" that made him "loath to risk heavy losses."[77]

Moreover, in an apparently whimsical culinary metaphor, Brooke made a penetrating observation that pinpointed the operational side-effects of conducting battle in a casualty-conscious manner. "Unfortunately it is hard in war to make omelettes without breaking eggs," Brooke remarked, "and it is often in trying to do so that we break most eggs!"[78] Brooke clearly recognized that the operational repercussions of fighting in a casualty-conscious manner sometimes meant that Allied forces squandered fleeting tactical opportunities. Not only were such consequences inherent to casualty-conscious operational techniques, but they also may have actually prolonged the war and hence led to more casualties. Today it "seems hardly surprising" that such techniques "had the reverse effect to the one desired."[79] This was, and remains, the fundamental paradox that dogs casualty-conscious operational methods.

Given both the importance that Montgomery placed on casualty conservation and his belief in unity between theater strategy and individual operations, it is not surprising that the Field Marshal's strategy for Normandy reflected his concern to avoid casualties. That Montgomery allocated the Americans a larger role in establishing the outer limits of the Allied lodgment area reflected both their greater resources and British casualty concerns. Montgomery's strategy did not necessarily mean that the Anglo-Canadian forces would incur fewer casualties. On the contrary, Montgomery recognized during the "Overlord" planning that the Anglo-Canadian attacks would face a larger concentration of enemy forces, especially armor; for the enemy remained highly sensitive to any advances from the Allied eastern flank toward Paris. However, the fact that Montgomery could conduct Anglo-Canadian attacks as a series of limited offensives designed to pin down German armor on that flank enabled him to halt attacks that incurred high casualties without undue detriment to his overall planned development of the campaign.

For obvious reasons of inter-Allied cooperation, the British could not admit explicitly to the Americans the extent of their concern over casualties nor the impact this had on Montgomery's theater strategy for Normandy. Senior American commanders displayed some understanding that the Commonwealth effort in Northwest Europe inevitably was limited, as suggested by their temporary allocation of an American army to the 21st Army Group at several points in the campaign.[80] In times of crisis, however, opinion at SHAEF and among the American forces in Normandy sometimes suspected that the British were not pulling their weight.[81]

The principle of casualty conservation also exerted a significant impact on Montgomery's day-to-day conduct of the campaign. The first few days of the invasion saw the 21st Army Group fail to make full use of the operational surprise gained by the D-Day landings to capture Caen easily before the German defensive crust could harden. After this Montgomery initially remained prepared to push Second (British) Army hard to capture the vital strategic town of Caen, and consequently incur heavy losses. This determination was evident during Operation "Epsom," the 26 June bid to encircle Caen from the west through the Odon Valley, in which infantry casualty rates reached Great War dimensions at over 50 percent.[82] It was also apparent during "Charnwood," the 8 July British attack that captured the northern half of Caen. However, after the capture of Caen, Montgomery did not continually smash the Second (British) Army against the strong German defenses to the south of the town, located along the Bourguébus Ridge. It was the scale of casualties incurred that prompted Montgomery to halt Operation "Spring" in late July. Moreover, the operational reality once the Allies had captured Caen was that Montgomery remained reluctant to suffer massive casualties; his correspondence, however, still suggested disingenuously that he was relentlessly smashing the Second (British) Army against the formidable German defenses.

It was reinforcement shortages, together with the effectiveness of enemy resistance, that forced Montgomery to modify his operational activities from the broad blueprint he had conceived before D-Day. In the "Overlord" planning phase, Montgomery stated his determination to reach Falaise as soon as possible. However, after the bitter five-week battle for Caen, Montgomery was less concerned to advance rapidly further south, unless this could be achieved without heavy casualties.[83] Montgomery certainly wanted to increase the depth of the Second Army bridgehead, for reasons of security, adminis-tration, and maneuver, as well as for the airfields located south of Caen. He was not, however, prepared to massacre the Second Army in the process. Montgomery made this attitude clear to Dempsey in his 10 July orders, which stated that "the south side of the [River] Orne opposite Caen will be secured and a bridgehead thus gained, if this is can be done without undue losses." Montgomery, however, was "not prepared to have heavy casualties to obtain this bridgehead" on the grounds that his forces were likely to suffer "plenty" of casualties "elsewhere."[84]

Montgomery, therefore, remained flexible in the manner in which he fulfilled operationally his broad strategic plan, a flexibility noted by Brigadier Edgar Williams.[85] Montgomery was well aware long before D-Day that merely the threat of the Second (British) Army launching a major advance toward Paris from the eastern flank would attract German armor to that flank. Hence, Dempsey's army could achieve its role in the theater—to attract Ger-man armor to its front—without necessarily undertaking massive break-in operations that would inevitably incur heavy casualties. The motive of casu-alty conservation explains why Montgomery terminated operations like "Goodwood" soon after he realized that relatively easy success was unlikely.

In retrospect, this approach has led some historians to accuse Mont-gomery of excessive caution. Examination of the casualty and reinforcement contexts, as well as his need to nurture troop morale, however, reveals that Montgomery had sound reasons for this caution. Given the politico-Imperial dimension of the campaign, there was little point in Dempsey's army captur-ing Caen in the first week after a bloody, all-out battle in which it had incurred such massive casualties that its long-term effectiveness was under-mined. Britain did not possess the resources in 1944 to rebuild badly cut-up divisions; it proved impossible, for instance, to rebuild speedily the 1st Air-borne Division after its decimation in Operation "Market-Garden." It was imperative for Montgomery to protect the long-term viability of his inevitably shrinking army group so that it would play an important part in the final defeat of the enemy.

Casualty conservation influenced Montgomery's methods most conspic-uously in the 18 July "Goodwood" offensive. Just prior to this, the Adjutant-General, Ronald Adam, had warned Montgomery that he could no longer guarantee the dispatch of sufficient infantry drafts to France.[86] This infantry manpower shortage led Dempsey to persuade a reluctant Montgomery to launch an attack by an all-armor corps. In mid-July, Montgomery's forces needed to resume offensive action to keep German armor tied down in the eastern half of the bridgehead prior to the American "Cobra" offensive in the west. An all-armor attack also was logical because Dempsey could not afford to loose infantrymen, but could afford to lose armors.[87] "Goodwood" contravened Montgomery's stated policy never to employ a corps comprising entirely of armor.[88] This policy reflected both the often poor performance of Allied armor during break-in operations in North Africa and the realities of modern warfare, which now required intimate infantry-tank cooperation. Ironically, the shortage of adequate infantry support for the armor constituted the biggest factor in the failure of "Goodwood." The extent of Montgomery's concern over casualty conservation during this operation is demonstrated by the explanation of Montgomery's intentions for "Goodwood" made by his military assistant, Kit Dawnay, to the War Office, that "Montgomery has to be very careful of what he does on his eastern flank because on that flank is the only British army there is left in this part of the world."[89]

Casualty conservation manifested itself throughout the 21st Army Group down through the hierarchy of command. Even though such concerns constituted an established facet of the British army's approach to war long before D-Day, the critical manpower situation in 1944 powerfully reinforced these concerns. To what extent knowledge of this situation filtered through the army group remains unclear. It seems that all formation commanders down to divisional level, if not to brigade level, knew something about the severity of the British manpower crisis and of the need to avoid heavy casualties. The Americans also possessed limited knowledge of the problem. On 24 July, Harry Butcher, Eisenhower's naval aide, recorded the American opinion that Montgomery and Dempsey were "so conscious of Britain's ebbing manpower that they hesitate to commit an attack where a division may be lost" because "to replace the division is practically impossible."[90]

In Northwest Europe such concerns led British senior commanders to halt attacks that met strong resistance and thus incurred high casualties, especially if a breakthrough seemed unlikely. At the lower formation (brigade) level, and below that at unit level, British and Canadian commanders soon called off attacks that met strong resistance, and then arranged a new, larger, fire-plan so that their forces could repeat the attack the next day. The main impulse of this cautious attitude was Montgomery, as demonstrated by his explanation to Simpson of his 21 July 1944 orders on proposed future operations. The third phase of immediate future operations, Montgomery envisaged, would entail an operation by VIII Corps east of the River Orne passing through II Canadian Corps and advancing down the Falaise road toward St. Sylvain and Conteville. Montgomery believed that "if the form is not too good, we can always withdraw into our own lines of the Canadian Corps firm base and repeat the operation a few days later."[91]

This intended operation formed part of Montgomery's post-"Goodwood" alternate-thrusts approach, which he adopted to maintain future casualties at acceptable levels. Alternate thrusts involved a series of attacks at various parts of the front as the preliminaries for a decisive attack. The 21st Army Group had already suffered heavy casualties at "Epsom" and "Spring." Yet with the American breakthrough offensive imminent, Montgomery realized that his forces had to keep the pressure on the Germans to prevent them redeploying armor to the American sector. An alternate-thrusts policy achieved this objective without incurring heavy casualties. Through attacks at different sectors of the front, the British forces created uncertainty within the enemy and kept the latter's powerful armored forces on the move from one attack to the next, and thereby limited the casualties these forces could inflict on attacking Allied forces.

The principle of casualty conservation explains in part the unimpressive combat performance of Anglo-Canadian forces troops in Northwest Europe. It sheds light on why numerically superior forces fielded by the 21st Army Group failed to achieve decisive penetrations. As a result of both casualty conservation concerns and of the practice of extreme concentration (particularly the echeloning of assault formations in depth on a narrow front), only a fraction of Anglo-Canadian forces actually engaged the enemy at any one time. Campaign analyses have placed great emphasis on citing crude comparative figures of numerical advantages, but such figures can be misleading.[92] As Dupuy demonstrated, there exist marked diminishing returns to scale for a side with numerical advantage, largely due to the impact of Clausewitzian friction.[93] These diminishing returns also result from a concept that Dupuy terms "challenge"—the "response of a force of inferior strength to the challenge posed by such inferiority," in that within certain parameters "the psychological pressure of coping against odds unquestionably stimulates the weaker force to intensified efforts."[94] From this concept, one can extrapolate the idea of "negative challenge," that the existence of numerical advantage in itself encourages a less-than-satisfactory combat performance through the lack of the motivating force of dire necessity. "Negative challenge" sheds further light on the modest combat performance of the 21st Army Group in Northwest Europe.

In this campaign, moreover, Anglo-Canadian numerical advantage in personnel proved of limited significance because the existence of a serious manpower reinforcement problem prevented Montgomery from undertaking prolonged and costly battles. Montgomery's need to avoid heavy casualties negated the benefits that ought to have accrued from his numerical superiority in men and machines. If Montgomery possessed abundant manpower resources, it seems likely that the Second (British) Army would have

advanced much quicker than it did. Additionally, if British senior commanders had developed a greater disregard for casualties, similar to that displayed
by the Germans and Soviets, the Second (British) Army might have advanced
much quicker. Or rather, it might have advanced faster initially, but then
ground to a halt. For it seems likely that if Montgomery had utilized his
troops without care to avoid casualties, this would have exerted a serious
impact on the morale of civilian, conscript troops who lacked strong ideolog-
ical motivation. If Montgomery had handled the 21st Army Group with a disregard for the lives of its soldiers reminiscent of certain Soviet commanders,
the consequent damage to troop morale quickly would have undermined the
combat effectiveness of his forces. John English cites Kurt Meyer's conception of how the Soviets would have successfully enacted Simonds' "Totalize"
offensive; the Soviets would have advanced "not by tactical maneuvering, but
with guns blazing to either Falaise or a 'glory finish.'"[95] Even though this
approach may have achieved a much better short-term success than Simonds'
corps plan, the crucial point is that such methods remained inappropriate
for the civilian soldiers fielded by the 21st Army Group. Though such methods held out the prospect of swifter initial successes, they did little to nurture
in the long-term either the morale of Montgomery's soldiers or the number
of divisions he was able to deploy. Such tactics were scarcely conducive to the
achievement of the particular set of politico-military objectives that Montgomery pursued in Northwest Europe.

Montgomery, however, also weighed the principle of casualty conservation against other operational necessities. He was prepared to accept heavy
casualties when he felt it operationally vital to do so. Montgomery was more
prepared to incur heavy casualties both before the capture of the strategically vital town of Caen, and in mid-August when attempting to close the
Falaise pocket. Similarly, the slow progress of Allied operations to clear the
Scheldt estuary to enable use of the vital port of Antwerp prompted Montgomery on 16 October to order that these attacks now be pursued with the
utmost vigor irrespective of casualties.[96] On 8 February 1945, he also
launched the great "Veritable"' offensive knowing that the planned southern American pincer to the assault, "Grenade," had been delayed by the
enemy's deliberate flooding of the Roer valley. He was aware that consequently his army group would take the full butcher's bill of the stubborn
German defense.[97]

The evidence presented clearly demonstrates that Montgomery "more
than most manifested an abiding concern with avoiding unnecessary casualties."[98] The caution he displayed in his operational technique, as well as his
reliance on firepower, resulted from his determination to minimize casualties. D'Este perceptively observed that "what has never been understood" by

CHAPTER 4

"Colossal Cracks" I:
The Set-Piece Battle

This chapter examines the key characteristics of Montgomery's operational technique in conducting this campaign, and demonstrates the overwhelming contribution that Montgomery made to the operational methods utilized by the 21st Army Group. Before commencing this investigation, a brief discussion of doctrinal development in the British army in the years 1939–44 is necessary. The 1939–45 British army—following a long tradition—relied heavily on extemporaneous pragmatism rather than on a formally expressed doctrine of war.[1] There existed two influences on the development of British army methods during the Second World War: First, the War Office in London formulated official doctrine and disseminated this through *Army Training Instructions* and *Memoranda*, plus *Military Training Pamphlets*; second, the personal experiences and policies of British higher formation commanders in the field produced doctrine in practice.[2] Despite the existence of official policy, in practice the methods of British higher formations in the field reflected the individual policies of their commanders. The latter were free to issue their own doctrinal memoranda as long as these policies did not substantially contradict the official War Office position.[3] In this process of doctrinal development the dissemination of operational and tactical ideas flowed both ways between field commanders and the War Office, and through this process a broad consensus on "a particular Commonwealth style of fighting" emerged "between Dunkirk and 1944."[4]

As a result of this lack of explicit doctrine, however, the development of the British army's operational methods relied heavily on the experiences and policies of individual field commanders; the War Office typically reflected these developments rather than initiated them. Wartime doctrinal development up to D-Day naturally derived much of its substance from the 1940–43 combat experiences in North Africa. This decentralization of doctrinal development permitted substantial variance to emerge between the field policies of senior commanders and official doctrine. Throughout 1943 General Montgomery, commanding the Eighth Army in North Africa and Italy, argued persistently with the War Office over the correct organization of the armored division, as well as the related distinctions between the infantry/

cruiser tank and the armored/tank brigade.[5] The policy of the 21st Army Group in Northwest Europe denied any such distinction, in contradiction to the War Office position.[6] Though historians justifiably might reproach Montgomery for the vitriolic and vain manner in which he debated these issues, they ought also to display some sympathy with the resentment of didactic field commanders to the doctrinal instructions issued by War Office "arms" directors, some of whom possessed less recent combat experience than those in the field.[7]

Despite these disagreements, a broadly similar school of operational thought had emerged by 1944, originating after Dunkirk via the experiences of El Alamein and the desert. An important source in the development of this common doctrinal approach was the didactic Montgomery. Montgomery's military policies, though progressive in their professionalism, remained grounded in the conservative bedrock of British military thought of the 1916–39 period.[8] The foundations of Montgomery's orthodox approach, based on traditional gunner methods, had been formed as early as his Western Front experiences of 1917–18.[9] As commander of Southeastern District in 1942, he imparted his operational policies to the Canadian Corps, and he further developed his methods in North Africa.[10] His high profile in doctrinal development resulted not just from the unrivaled success of his recent combat experience but also from the support of General Brooke, the CIGS. Back in England during spring 1944, Montgomery outlined his technique to his new army group command, while in Italy his former subordinate Oliver Leese continued to utilize the Montgomery method in its author's absence.[11]

It was not surprising that the operational technique utilized by the 21st Army Group in Northwest Europe mirrored Montgomery's methods, given the following: Montgomery's professionalism, dogmatic opinions, didacticism, and his successful field experience; his good relations with the CIGS; his desire to impose his will on the 21st Army Group; and last, his appointment of trusted former Eighth Army subordinates to many of the army group's senior staff positions. Consequently, Montgomery made the most important individual contribution to the manner in which the 21st Army Group conducted this campaign.

Montgomery's contribution, however, reflected just one of several influences on the way in which the 21st Army Group conducted the campaign. Consequently, historians must assess his participation in the context of the institutional framework of the army group; his influence interacted with the contributions of other institutions, including his army group staff and his two subordinate armies. Nevertheless, Montgomery was not a typical army group commander and his influence on the 21st Army Group was more significant than other such commanders, like Alexander in North Africa. His determination to disseminate his undoubted experience to those serving under him in the 21st Army Group sometimes led him to "overcontrol" subordinates—particularly, to give tactical instructions direct to officers beyond his immediate subordinates in the chain of command. Consequently, though historians must analyze the contribution that Montgomery made to the conduct of this campaign within the wider context of this formation's senior command framework, his own policies nevertheless pervaded the 21st Army Group.

METHODOLOGY FOR ANALYZING MONTGOMERY'S OPERATIONAL APPROACH

This study now analyzes Montgomery's operational methods by using two approaches. The first examines what Montgomery wrote or said about operational technique by utilizing three types of evidence—his contemporary verbal discussions, the instructional pamphlets he wrote during and immediately after the war, and his postwar published works.[12] This analysis considers whether Montgomery was consistent in what he said or wrote on operational method. The second approach analyzes the operational actions that the Field Marshal ordered to be undertaken in Northwest Europe. This material includes his directives to his subordinate army commanders, his discussions with senior officers, his memoranda, messages, and telegrams. This analysis investigates whether Montgomery's operational conduct of the campaign remained consistent with his thoughts on operational technique: Did the circumstances of the campaign allow Montgomery to utilize his usual approaches, or was he forced to modify these policies?

An analysis comparing what Montgomery said or wrote about operational technique with what he did in the field is dogged by methodological problems. Much of what Montgomery said was misleading and needs careful interpretation. Many of the Field Marshal's buoyant speeches and optimistic reports were rhetorical public relations exercises designed to keep up the morale of his troops and also maintain his reputation;[13] these two were complementary because, as Montgomery recognized, his troops needed complete faith in their commander-in-chief if they were to possess high morale.[14] Interwoven with this feature was Montgomery's exaggeration of his own achievements in order to avoid sharing "the slightest sliver of glory" with his colleagues.[15] Shabby examples of Montgomery's sordid glory-grabbing include his grasping of the media limelight both for the 1943 Allied victory in Tunisia, and the American repulse of the German December 1944 Ardennes counteroffensive.[16] This rhetoric and exaggeration create methodological problems for historians attempting to analyze Montgomery's statements.

Another problem with interpreting the Field Marshal's stated intentions was that he sometimes misled his colleagues—Eisenhower especially—about these aims. In order to receive greater air support from SHAEF for Operation "Goodwood," VIII Corps' armored thrust that sought to outflank Caen from the east, Montgomery deliberately exaggerated to Eisenhower his expectation that the operation would achieve a decisive breakthrough. Dempsey admitted to Liddell Hart the "confidential" fact that "misunderstanding" over Montgomery's true intentions during the "Goodwood" offensive was "increased because of Monty's reticence to Ike." Nor was this deception uncommon, for according to Dempsey, Montgomery regularly told him, "There's no need to tell Ike."[17] This deception has caused historians to debate the real aims of "Goodwood" ever since. Indeed, perhaps the only officers who knew Montgomery's real intentions were Major-General de Guingand and Brigadier Belchem, respectively the 21st Army Group's Chief of Staff and Brigadier, General Staff (Operations).

Interpretation of Montgomery's aims is also complicated because his stated intentions often remained vague. His orders for "Goodwood," for instance, did not explicitly state that a breakthrough was intended, though the comments on possible exploitation were sufficiently explicit to permit him to take the credit if VIII Corps achieved a significant advance.[18] This hedging-your-bets approach to the intended results of operations was apparent at other times in the campaign, and was characterized by his use in orders of informal, nonmilitary terms, such as to "crack about" and to "find the form."[19] Montgomery remained too aware of the vagaries of the battlefield to nail his flag to any one predicted outcome of an operation. This attitude also reflected both his operational flexibility and his belief that defeating the enemy was more important than capturing ground; for example, Montgomery stated that Operation "Bluecoat," the late July drive on Vire, would "have no geographical objective" but would instead continue the Second (British) Army "policy" of engaging "the main enemy force" while First US Army advanced.[20]

Montgomery, despite his assertions to the contrary, was often flexible in his conduct of the campaign. After D-Day, Montgomery did not feel bound by the indications he had made to the Air Chiefs in the pre-invasion planning that his forces would capture swiftly the enemy airfields south of Caen.[21] When Kit Dawnay, his military assistant, arrived in Normandy, he soon realized that Montgomery "did not care a damn about those airfields, as long as he could draw all the German armor onto that [eastern] side and give a chance for the [American] right swing to break out."[22] Montgomery later admitted that "it became impossible to meet" this earlier promise without altering "the whole strategy of the battle," which he "was not prepared to do."[23] Montgomery's flexibility compounded the misunderstanding of his intentions already fostered among senior Allied commanders by his imprecision and rhetoric.

Interpretation of Montgomery's intentions is further complicated by the increasingly distorted view with which Montgomery looked back on the war. Montgomery's recollections increasingly exaggerated his successful generalship and the subordination of events to his grand design.[24] Montgomery strove in his postwar accounts to demonstrate the patently false suggestion that virtually everything that happened in the campaign went precisely according to plan.[25] Montgomery's chief intelligence officer, Brigadier Bill Williams, commented that Montgomery's "idea of fairness and truth" would "sometimes chill me inside."[26] Unfortunately, this characteristic not only made Montgomery enemies and obscured the real issues of the campaign, but it also obfuscated appreciation of his actual achievements in Northwest Europe.

Gradually over the subsequent years, many of the campaign's senior participants also increasingly viewed the events of 1944–45 in a distorted manner. This innocent distortion—which was often connected with perceived injustices suffered at the time—explains the prevalence of postwar controversies between these senior officers.[27] In de Guingand's mind, for instance, germinated the story that he had saved Montgomery from the sack in October 1944, and Belchem's determination to defend Montgomery's Normandy master plan led to gradual alterations in his version of events.[28]

These methodological problems reinforce the confusions in the subsequent historical debates that resulted from inter-Allied frictions. Consequently, it is unlikely that historians will reach a definitive solution to the campaign's more contentious issues, such as Montgomery's theater strategy in Normandy, the real objective of "Goodwood," the single thrust/broad front controversy, and the relationship between Montgomery and Dempsey. These methodological considerations must be borne in mind during an examination of Montgomery's operational approach, but they can be surmounted if the available evidence is used carefully and related to what is known about the campaign as a whole.

CATEGORIZATION OF MONTGOMERY'S OPERATIONAL APPROACH

Categorization of the aspects that comprised Montgomery's operational technique is problematic due to the connections that exist between these characteristics. The principle of concentration, for example, was inextricably associated with that of economy of force and security, while Montgomery's conception of grip was as much a part of his concept of leadership as of his operational approach.[29] Similarly, his emphasis on balance not only also related to the principles of concentration, economy of force, security, and grip, but also reflected his emphases on caution, the minimization of casualties, and the nurture of morale. While historians should bear in mind the complexities of these interconnections, the purposes of analysis require that this study break down Montgomery's overall operational technique into its constituent elements.

In 1945, Montgomery defined eight principles of modern war that constituted the "essentials of success." These included four aspects that only had become important in this war—air power, administration, the initiative, and morale—together with four "old stagers"—surprise, concentration, cooperation, and simplicity.[30] Although the classification presented in this study is based in part on Montgomery's writings, it does not just slavishly follow these views. Rather, it reflects an interpretation of the significance of these characteristics as illustrated not just by Montgomery's writings but also by his conduct of the campaign. Consequently, in this study, the operational approach used by Montgomery in Northwest Europe is analyzed in terms of the following eleven fundamental, interconnected characteristics: the maintenance of morale and casualty conservation; the master plan, concentration, firepower-based attrition, and caution—these four being the key components of the set-piece battle; the complementary technique of alternate thrusts; plus the initiative, balance, administration, and air power. Associated with these eleven fundamental characteristics were seven other, ancillary, facets: grip, surprise, flank protection, flexibility, cooperation, simplicity, and the assimilation of combat lessons. This chapter examine the first five of these—the master plan, concentration, firepower-based attrition, caution, and alternate thrusts, which together formed the crux of Montgomery's set-piece battle approach. Chapter 5 then examines the remaining four fundamental tenets of Montgomery's operational technique, together with the seven ancillary characteristics.

THE FUNDAMENTALS OF MONTY'S OPERATIONAL TECHNIQUE
The Master Plan
Montgomery's concept of the master plan represented a crucial part of his operational technique. This notion, a classic military principle, referred first to the development and maintenance of a clear plan for how an operation or campaign would develop, and then the utilization of forces to enact this plan.[31] Montgomery's conception existed in three forms that might be termed the operational level, suboperational, and single operation senses of the master plan; these related, respectively, to the overall development of a campaign, to the development and sequence of several operations in fulfillment of the operational master plan, and to the development of a particular

operation. In reality, however, Montgomery's practical soldier's mind used the term master plan indiscriminately to refer to any of these three senses. This imprecision exacerbated the misunderstandings that emerged between senior officers during the war and in the postwar literature—in part based on their misconstruction of which of these senses was intended by a commander's use of the terms master plan or plan. To avoid such confusions, it is important to establish which of these senses Montgomery meant when he discussed his master plan concept.

In his postwar writings, Montgomery often lumped together the operational level and suboperational senses of his master plan concept. He believed that "on the operational side a C[ommander]-in-C[hief] must draw up a master plan for the campaign he envisages."[32] This sentence illuminates the haziness of the distinction between the operational and suboperational senses of Montgomery's master plan concept. As it appears that he is referring to an entire campaign, it seems that he is discussing the operational level sense of his master plan, but in fact he is referring to both this and the suboperational senses. For he is arguing not just that an overall conception of the development of the entire campaign is necessary, but also that a more detailed operation-by-operation plan for achieving this theater strategic conception is required.

Montgomery's written thought also emphasized this master plan concept in its individual operation context, concerning the development of a single operation. He believed that an operation "must develop within a predetermined pattern of action" and that a commander must decide both how he will "fight the battle before it begins" and then "use the military effort at his disposal to force the battle to swing the way he wishes it to go."[33] As it is the corps that typically plans and fights individual major operations, Montgomery's statements represent an admonition to his senior subordinate commanders to conduct their respective battles in this manner.

Montgomery also believed that once the master plan of an operation had been devised at the corps level, it had to be adhered to and protected from distortions "created by subordinate action" that did "not suit the master plan." Though Montgomery conceded that "the master plan must never be so rigid" that the commander could not "vary it to suit the changing tactical situation," he insisted that "nobody else may be allowed to change it . . . especially, not the enemy."[34] Clearly this concept was based on Montgomery's desire to seize the initiative and thus impose his will on the battlefield.

Montgomery's emphasis on preplanned control of individual operations sheds light on his attitudes both to the conduct of battle and to the British army. This approach suggests that Montgomery possessed both supreme belief in his own abilities, and a certain distrust of his subordinates, as well as concern that subordinate action might distort the intent of superiors. In

Montgomery's opinion, adherence to a master plan minimized the risk of error during an operation. Through the individual operational master plan and the meticulous planning and preparation it entailed, every soldier taking part in an operation would know both his particular role and contribution to the overall battle. This prior planning and preparation enabled formations and units to undertake specific training and full-scale rehearsals of the types of action they would undertake in the next operation. This preplanned approach suggests that Montgomery both sought to achieve the maximum potential out of a force whose limitations he fully recognized, and possessed a neat mind that sought to create order out of the chaos inherent in active operations. This command style is far removed from the mission-analysis approach of the modern, professional British army, which stresses the exercise of initiative by subordinates within the superior's overall intent, to enact successful maneuver warfare.

Montgomery's emphasis on the master plan also formed an integral part of his style of leadership. The latter reflected some distrust of the staff because Montgomery was determined to remain the central impulse on operations, especially with planning, where the staff's influence was potentially strongest. Throughout his career after reaching battalion-command level in September 1918, Montgomery felt that once a commander produced an outline plan his main task was to ensure that "the basic foundations" were "not broken down" by the detail worked out by the staff.[35] His concern over the role of the staff manifested itself during the planning of Operation "Husky," the invasion of Sicily, where he inherited a finalized staff plan that he considered unacceptable. He savaged the notion that an operation could be planned with just a planning staff but without a commander. The correct procedure, he insisted, was for the commander who was to implement the operation to make "the original outline plan" and only then should the staff plan the details.[36] When Montgomery assumed command of the 21st Army Group for "Overlord," he faced the same situation, inheriting the prepared COSSAC D-Day plan, with which he was far from satisfied.[37]

Having examined how Montgomery's master plan was depicted in his writings, this study now examines how this concept manifested itself in his conduct of this campaign. Montgomery placed much emphasis on his operational-level master plan in his writings, and in practice he did conceive, with the cooperation of his senior colleagues, an overall master plan for the Normandy campaign.[38] Historians have debated ever since what precisely this strategy was and whether Montgomery stuck to it.[39] Despite this considerable debate, this author is convinced that the contemporary evidence demonstrates that Montgomery always intended that the Second (British) Army would engage substantial German forces on the eastern flank to facilitate an American advance in the west.[40] The Second (British) Army operational plan of 21 February 1944 stated that its task was to "protect the flank of the US Armies while the latter captured Cherbourg, Angers, Nantes and the Brittany ports" and indicated that "there is no intention of carrying out a major advance" until "the Brittany ports have been captured."[41] Similarly, Montgomery signaled de Guingand on 11 June 1944 that "my general object is to pull the Germans on to Second Army so that First [US] Army can extend and expand."[42] Montgomery largely stuck to this broad plan and resisted pressures from the Americans, and from Dempsey in "Goodwood," to radically alter this conception. However, this is far removed from Montgomery's totally specious claim that the Normandy campaign went "exactly as planned."[43] At best the campaign developed similarly to a broadly based operational-level vision. That it did so reflected Montgomery's determination to develop his sequence of operations along lines appropriate to fulfill his operational-level master plan.

During the early part of the Normandy campaign, however, Montgomery displayed considerable flexibility in the development and sequence of operations he ordered in pursuit of his operational-level master plan; he utilized a flexible suboperational master plan to fulfill his more rigid operational-level master plan. Montgomery remained flexible when deciding the location, sequence, and development of the series of corps offensives undertaken in Normandy. Rather than adhering rigidly to a fixed program of planned operations decided before D-Day, Montgomery rightly permitted himself considerable leeway in the manner in which his individual operations achieved the ultimate objectives of the operational-level master plan. That the 21st Army Group planned many more corps operations to fulfill this master plan than it carried out is evidence of this flexibility.[44] This formation, for example, never undertook its early June plan for a double envelopment of Caen from east and west, nor its planned mid-June "Dreadnought" attack to outflank Caen from the east. This flexibility resulted from operational circumstances that forced Montgomery to modify his intentions. Despite what he said, it is not surprising that a commander as experienced as Montgomery could be flexible in his methods, just as he had been at Alamein and at the Battle of Mareth in March 1943. Moreover, whereas Montgomery was determined to adhere to his operational-level master plan, he remained more flexible as to how his suboperational or individual operation master plans fulfilled this strategy.

After the collapse of the German defense of Normandy, Montgomery's conduct of the remainder of the campaign reflected greater adherence to a more rigid suboperational master plan. Having been replaced by Eisenhower as Land Forces Commander on 1 September 1944, Montgomery no longer directly decided theater strategy. Yet, after Normandy, Montgomery's conduct of his army group's operations reflected greater continuity in planning in that he managed to plan the next operation while the current one was still being conducted.[45] Such a practice was feasible only if the current operation unfolded as planned, because the next operation could only commence as planned if the present one achieved its final objectives, which represented the starting points for the next operation. In Normandy, the battlefield situation meant that operations typically did not go as planned and, hence, future operational planning had to be flexible. After September 1944, however, Anglo-Canadian operations achieved their objectives more frequently than in the earlier period. In late February and March 1945 the Second (British) Army planned Operation "Plunder," the assault crossing of the River Rhine, while the First Canadian Army conducted "Veritable," the precursor to "Plunder" that sought to reach the Rhine's west bank; "Plunder" could commence as planned only if "Veritable" was a success.[46] This process reflected a growing confidence within the 21st Army Group that it could dictate events on the battlefield.

These planning principles also were evident when on 22 September 1944 Montgomery ordered planning to commence on the successor operation to "Market-Garden," code-named "Gatwick." This attack aimed to advance from the eastern flank of the "Market-Garden" penetration up to the Rhine.[47] However, given the precarious state of the "Market-Garden" salient and the failure to clear the flank-threatening enemy salient at Venlo, Dempsey postponed and then shelved "Gatwick."[48] By ordering the "Gatwick" planning to commence on 22 September, Montgomery already had abandoned his intention of pursuing the "Market-Garden" advance north beyond Arnhem some five days before the beleaguered 1st Airborne Division withdrew from the Oosterbeek perimeter.

Montgomery's conduct of individual operations—rather than a series of offensives—also reflected his master plan concept. Montgomery was determined to see that his diligently preplanned and well-prepared operations were carried out according to the original master plan. He continued Operation "Veritable," for example, inexorably day after day in accordance with the phases outlined in the original plan.[49] This determination was also evident in the twinned Operations "Nutcracker/Mallard," in which convergent thrusts by the XII and VIII Corps eliminated the German salient west of the River Maas at Maeseyck.[50]

Montgomery's influence on the conduct of individual operations, however, did not always remain devoid of flexibility in response to changing tactical situations. Even though most of these flexible initiatives came from subordinate corps commanders, both the army commander and Montgomery had to approve these modifications before they were enacted. In Operation "Switchback," II Canadian Corps' 6 October assault on the Breskens pocket south of the Scheldt estuary, the main assault at Eede made little progress. Consequently, General Simonds transformed the diversionary assault across the Savojaards Plaat inlet into the main effort.[51] Similarly, when "Market-Garden" ran into difficulties, a new plan was formulated that swung 43rd (Wessex) Division west, outflanking the German defenses, to reach the endangered 1st Airborne Division at Oosterbeek; but this could not be implemented before German pressure forced the 1st Airborne to withdraw.[52] Yet despite this flexibility within individual operations, in general Montgomery conducted his operations in Northwest Europe in terms of pre-conceived operational-level, suboperational, and individual operation master plans.

Concentration

The second key characteristic of Montgomery's operational approach in Northwest Europe was concentration of force. This classic military principle concerned the deployment of massive force at the decisive point of battle; as such it was inextricably associated with the principles of economy of force and security. To Brooke, Montgomery described this approach as smashing "through towards the selected objective" by both concentrating "great strength" and having ready "fresh divisions to exploit the success gained."[53] Montgomery would only commence offensive operations after thorough preparation that included copious stockpiling of logistical supplies, especially artillery ammunition. In Northwest Europe the Field Marshal concentrated maximum offensive strength on a narrow frontage, with two division attacks like "Tractable" and "Totalize" being launched on a front ranging from two to four miles, respectively. Moreover, Montgomery echeloned his offensive forces in great depth behind this narrow frontage. His January 1944 theater policy instructed that divisions should attack on a narrow front with only one brigade up and the remainder echeloned in the rear."[54] Allied air superiority in the theater made concentration of such high troop densities possible by removing the threat of heavy casualties incurred by enemy air attack.[55]

Concentration of force on a narrow frontage with units echeloned in depth ensured maximum offensive power at the point of break-in. Once the assaulting units had achieved their initial objectives, commanders redeployed the echeloned follow-up units through the forward troops in order to attack the next set of objectives. This passing through of echeloned forces in pursuit of modest objectives both helped sustain combat power and maintain attack momentum by keeping assault forces relatively fresh. Though this method sustained offensive momentum, the tempo of unfolding operations remained

slow as this frequent passing through of units consumed much time and created tactical pauses. During Operation "Veritable," the First Canadian Army's
February 1945 drive to the Rhine, commanders passed fresh assault units
through forward troops between one and four times each day.[56] Furthermore, echeloning in depth enabled corps commanders to insert reserve formations into the break-in battle to widen and deepen the penetration.
During "Veritable," Horrocks erred by inserting his reserve divisions too soon
along restricted communications routes, causing massive congestion.[57] In
Montgomery's brand of concentration, armored forces were held in reserve
ready to exploit success. Once his forces had completed the break-in battle,
Montgomery released the armor. More than armor firepower, however, concentration relied on the firepower of massed artillery. In this campaign, concentration meant, above all, massing all available artillery to provide fire
support for the attack, augmented when possible by "flying artillery"—
bomber aircraft. Operation "Veritable," during which the 21st Army Group
deployed nearly two-thirds of its entire resources in one location, epitomized
Montgomery's emphasis on concentration.[58] On 8 February 1945, five
infantry divisions attacked on an eight-mile frontage, backed by 1,056 guns,
with a three-divisional central thrust on a two-mile front.[59] This approach was
also evidenced by Montgomery's refusal in late December 1944 to attack the
northern shoulder of the Ardennes salient until he had gathered ample
forces for his assault.[60]

Another aspect of Montgomery's emphasis on concentration was "tidiness," which reflected other facets of his technique such as balance, flank
protection, and the master plan. Tidiness reflected Montgomery's concern
both to control an orderly battle and to achieve and maintain concentration
before and during an operation. To Montgomery tidiness meant ensuring
that an attack was "teed off" properly—that he had deployed correctly his
forces and had allocated appropriately to them available supporting
resources. Montgomery did not "tee-up" Operation "Goodwood" effectively,
because the narrowness of the starting line in the Orne bridgehead forced
him to deploy his three armored divisions one behind the other. This dilu-
tion of shock combat power, plus the consequent restriction on tactical
maneuver, contributed significantly to the failure of the operation.[61]

Montgomery sought to ensure tidiness during offensives (and thus both
orderly control and concentration) by conducting operations where possible within well-defined battle areas delimited by topographical features like
rivers. His plan for Operation "Veritable" selected the River Maas to delimit
the western and southern ends of the battle area and the River Rhine the
northern and eastern ends.[62] Similarly, he selected the River Maas to delimit
three sides of the combat area for Operation "Nutcracker/Mallard." Such

delimitation was prominent in Montgomery's winter 1944–45 operations because the topography of Belgium and Holland, with numerous watercourses, proved conducive to such delimitation; in Normandy there were fewer such opportunities.

This geographical restriction of the battlefield maintained concentration by avoiding dispersion of forces over an expanding battleground—a feature of some American operations that Montgomery deplored. Furthermore, this restriction ensured continued concentration of the spearhead, economy of force, and security, because only modest forces had to be diverted from the main thrust to protect flanks hinged on easily defensible topographical obstacles. Last, such delimitation helped keep the advance orderly and facilitated Montgomery's tight control of a relatively rigid combat situation.

Montgomery sought in his operations to avoid untidiness—situations where the front had become ragged and extended, with troops dispersed rather than concentrated. Such untidy situations hampered tight command and control, represented uneconomical disposition of force, and presented opportunities for German counterattacks to pinch off Allied salients. If untidiness occurred, Montgomery often halted an operation in order to let his forces regroup. Despite his instruction that "Veritable" be continued "night and day" until the Rhine was reached, when by 20 February 1945 the II Canadian Corps had become untidy, Montgomery ordered it to cease offensive action for forty-eight hours "to sort itself out" before recommencing their attack.[63]

Though the British and American armies utilized similar operational techniques in the theater, American doctrine did not display the same emphasis on extreme concentration. Although both armies relied heavily on concentration in the sense of massed aerial and artillery firepower, the Americans conducted offensive operations on a broader front—a technique caricatured by Brooke as "engaging the enemy along the whole front."[64] In the American approach, commanders conducted offensive action on a more regular basis rather than the "start-stop-rebuild-start-stop" nature of the British approach. In comparison with Anglo-Canadian offensive operations in the theater, American ones typically saw larger proportions of available combat power deployed forward over a wider front with less extensive echeloning in depth. Unlike Montgomery, the Americans often launched their attacks after only quite modest logistical build up and continued them "in spite of bad weather" that prevented the use of their awesome tactical air power.[65] Bradley contrasted Montgomery's crude approach based on "dragg[ing] up everything he had for an all out" attack with the American technique that both "constantly nibbled away" at key enemy positions and "constantly kept him knocked off balance."[66]

Montgomery also emphasized keeping the enemy off-balance, but by using feints and raids rather than by frequent major attacks. Anglo-American differences in offensive technique, however, did not revolve around simply the issue of degree of concentration but also the semantics of what this principle meant. To American commanders, concentration meant "the simultaneous effort of all possible forces,"[67] whereas to British ones it meant deploying massive force echeloned in depth on a narrow front. Given that the Americans deployed a higher proportion of their forces in the front line than did the British, they consequently possessed fewer reserves. This often resulted in American troops, especially infantry, remaining in contact with the enemy for longer than that typical of Anglo-Canadian operations. To Montgomery, such "continuous fighting without relief" reflected poor "man-management" and undermined troop morale.[68] Given the more modest build-up program, often American artillery not only could fire fewer rounds per day than that typical of an Anglo-Canadian operation, but did so across a wider offensive frontage. Whereas an allocation of 200 rounds per gun per day was common in Anglo-Canadian operations, American batteries often received an allotment of just 100 rounds.[69] Montgomery tactlessly derided these American methods as a "futile doctrine" and condemned the American's conduct of their November 1944 offensive toward Cologne because it lacked sufficient concentration, attacked on too wide an assault frontage, deployed inadequate artillery support, and held back too few reserves.[70]

Any comparison of the relevant merits or disadvantages of these national operational styles has to tread carefully to avoid becoming embroiled in the prejudices of inter-Allied rivalries. Both approaches had advantages and drawbacks, and the evidence from Northwest Europe does not demonstrate that one was more effective than the other. Neither approach proved impressive given the natural tactical advantage enjoyed by the defense in 1944, as well as the skill and determination of the *Westheer*. Neither technique achieved a major penetration of the German defensive zone in Normandy in the seven weeks prior to "Cobra," and neither avoided becoming bogged down in the mud of autumn 1944. Furthermore, in "Cobra," the most successful American attack in Normandy, "the despair of the Bocage deadlock" drove Bradley to adopt a plan "uncharacteristic of the American army" in its "concentration of power on a narrow front."[71] That this successful American attack utilized the same extreme concentration so typical of Montgomery's "Colossal Cracks," only complicates any balanced comparison of the relative merits of these two approaches.

Several inherent drawbacks, however, existed in Montgomery's technique of concentration along a narrow front. First, the narrowness of the penetration restricted the scope for maneuver, which both denied the potential fruits of Allied mobility and restricted actions to obvious frontal assaults. Both commanders of the armored divisions involved in Operation "Totalize," for example, believed that their frontages were too narrow and requested in vain for more room to maneuver.[72] Equally, the limitation of the spearhead advance of "Market-Garden" to just one road enabled the enemy to discern the position of the decisive localities and redeploy their meager defensive forces accordingly.

The narrowness of Anglo-Canadian attack frontages, and hence penetrations, also restricted the availability of axes of advance, which often hampered the forward movement of artillery and logistic supplies, and resulted in congestion like that experienced in "Goodwood" and "Veritable." A narrow penetration also placed substantial responsibility on flanking formations to maintain their defensive positions against enemy pressure. The failure to secure the high ground of the Rauray spur on the right (western) flank of the "Epsom" offensive seriously hampered the successful development of this operation. Furthermore, Anglo-Canadian forces often found offensive momentum difficult to sustain as unsuppressed enemy fire from the flanks could halt forward movement in the center.[73]

Another flaw with concentrated Anglo-Canadian effort on a narrow frontage was that it enabled the Germans to counterconcentrate available reinforcements against the Allied penetration. Consequently, Montgomery's operations were sometimes a race to exploit initial break-in success before enemy reinforcements restabilized the front. In "Veritable," once the 21st Army Group had staved in the German front with a massive fire-plan, its forces had to race to secure exits from the restrictive terrain of the Reichswald Forest onto the open Goch-Calcar Plain before the Germans brought up reinforcements.[74] Those commentators who have extolled Montgomery's narrow-thrust strategy over Eisenhower's broad-front one have rarely given due regard to the issue that extreme offensive concentration facilitated enemy defensive concentration against it.[75]

The advantage of the American approach was that it ensured better opportunities for maneuver and war often accompanied by more boldness and at times a quicker tempo of operations, as typified by "Grenade." However, American operations often lacked sufficient strength at any given point for penetration, further dispensed force to the battle unfolded, and experienced declining combat power due to the troop fatigue that resulted from inadequate retention of reserves. Irrespective of the merits and disadvantages of these two national operational approaches, neither succeeded in easily overcoming the effectiveness of the German defense. Both the Anglo-Canadian and American approaches, however, concurred that the key to unlocking this resilient German defense lay in lavish use of massed firepower.

Firepower-based Attrition

Montgomery's reliance on firepower-based attrition combined with his emphasis on concentration formed the foundation of his operational technique. The key to his conduct of battle was utilization of overwhelming concentration of massed artillery firepower, supplemented by aerial bombardment where possible, in a set-piece style of war based on attrition, which the Germans termed *Matérielschlacht*. Attrition based upon massed artillery fire, together with the antitank action of the six-pounder gun, had brought success at Alamein, and this "impressed itself indelibly upon" Montgomery's mind, "almost to the exclusion of everything else."[76] The principal lesson of the North African campaign was that only Allied attacks with strong artillery support could overcome German defensive power.[77]

With this firepower-laden approach, Montgomery never suffered a serious operational defeat after his initial success at Alamein.[78] His methods sought to blast the infantry onto their objectives with an overwhelming weight of shell. This was not dissimilar to the artillery bombardments of 1914–18, as his detractors observed with some justification. Unfortunately for Montgomery, this comparison conjured up the associated connotations of Great War Chateau generalship. This comparison was ironic because Montgomery's operational approach could trace its origins to his revulsion at this very type of generalship with its callous disregard for the lives of the troops. However, the crucial point was that Montgomery adopted methods similar to those used in 1918 specifically to save lives, not throw them away needlessly.

Between 1939 and 1944, the British army enhanced enormously the effectiveness of its use of artillery. This improvement resulted largely from technical developments such as improved communications that enhanced command and control (C^2), and thus tactical handling.[79] In Northwest Europe, the 21st Army Group could bring down simultaneously the accurate fire of hundreds of Allied guns on an enemy target. The combination of this effectiveness with copious availability of pieces enabled Montgomery to centralize artillery concentrations wherever possible at the corps level or that of the Army Group, Royal Artillery (AGRA).[80]

Montgomery's emphasis on firepower resulted both from the prevalence of traditional gunner doctrine within the British army and his appreciation that the 21st Army Group could utilize effectively the large number of guns available. Undoubtedly the most effective arm within the 21st Army Group, the artillery made a contribution to ultimate Allied victory only equaled by that of air power. In contrast, the effectiveness of German artillery in Normandy proved poor, although by winter of 1944–45, the *Westheer* managed more effectively to concentrate defensive artillery fire.[81]

In the constricted Normandy bridgehead, the 21st Army Group managed to provide a massive scale of artillery fire support—typically 500–750 guns—for its major operations.[82] A German combat report noted the "incredibly heavy" Allied artillery fire and concluded that the Allies were "waging war regardless of expense."[83] After August 1944, however, the army group typically could provide fire support of between 300 and 450 guns for major operations, the reduction caused by the extension of the army group's frontage.[84] Not until the 1,056-gun Anglo-Canadian "Veritable" fire-plan of 8 February 1945—the largest and most sophisticated of the entire campaign—did the fire support the army group provided surpass the Normandy peak. [85] Montgomery's command adhered rigidly to the principle that it would support any operation with the largest amount of guns possible, and hence censured any artillery officer who "left even a single gun idle that was in range or could be moved in range."[86]

The fundamental problem with this firepower-laden approach—particularly if Montgomery employed strategic bombers in a direct support role—was that it devastated the area over which the troops were to advance. The resulting cratered terrain hampered enormously the movement of motorized transport along communication routes or across country. While this weight of fire facilitated the success of the initial break-in battle, the ensuing devastation restricted severely the tempo and momentum of the unfolding Allied attack and allowed the Germans time to move up reserves to halt any further Allied penetration of their tactical zone of defenses.[87]

This devastation proved a particular problem for Allied forces because all their divisions, including infantry, were motorized. In contrast, most German infantry divisions remained predominantly horse-drawn throughout the Second World War.[88] Given this motorization of Anglo-Canadian divisions, all offensive operations witnessed the movement of thousands of vehicles. Such heavy Allied use of available communication routes often churned those already damaged by Allied fire support into impassable bogs—such as the morass created in the first days of "Veritable."[89] Hence, even when these massive Allied fire-plans broke initial enemy resistance, subsequently assault troops often could not advance rapidly enough to take full advantage of this success and effect a significant penetration; by the time the attacking Allied juggernaut had rolled forward, German reserves had often improvised another defensive line in the rear.

The other main consequence of Allied reliance on massive firepower was that it hampered attempts at maneuver warfare. Many assaults undertaken by the 21st Army Group remained obvious frontal blows, and the limited tactical maneuver it attempted remained ponderous. That some of the most impressive, or potentially promising, Anglo-Canadian actions in the campaign involved rare examples of tactical maneuver indicates the significance of the loss of the potential fruits of this approach. In one such case, Dempsey switched the 7th Armored Division's axis further west to exploit a gap in the German front, which enabled it to advance on Villers Bocage on 12 June 1944. Conversely, according to Kurt Meyer, commanding the 12th SS Panzer Division *Hitlerjugend*, the sluggish Canadian exploitation of the success achieved by its initial nighttime assault in "Totalize" during 7/8 August 1944 let slip one of the best opportunities of the entire Normandy campaign.[90]

This utilization of massed firepower also reduced built-up areas, like Caen, to rubble, and this inadvertently created excellent defensive positions where even a few determined German soldiers could resist effectively, as when a mere sixty *Hitlerjugend* soldiers held out in the ruins of Falaise for three days.[91] The Germans soon adapted their defensive tactics and held urban areas just with weak forces, and strongly reinforced these positions only after Allied saturation bombing, which indicated an imminent attack. Horrocks later bitterly rued his decision to let Allied bombers—even with bombs with a reduced cratering effect—devastate Cleve during "Veritable," as the devastation aided more than disrupted the motley German defenders and simply delayed forward movement of Allied forces. Montgomery appreciated the destructive effects of this "Colossal Cracks" technique, and commented in June 1944 that "Montebourg and Valognes have been 'liberated' in the best 21 Army Group style, i.e. they are both completely destroyed!!"[92] Clearly, Montgomery believed that the advantages of this firepower-laden, attritional approach outweighed its inherent disadvantages.

Another drawback with this approach centered around the complexities concerning the utilization of strategic bombers in a direct support role, particularly the operational requirements of the aircraft and the difficulties of arranging such strikes with Allied air commands.[93] During the early Normandy offensives, these problems led the Allies to undertake such strategic air strikes several hours before the ground forces attacked, as during the 8 July "Charnwood" assault around Caen; but unfortunately this alerted the enemy to the imminence of an attack. Above all, the complexity of such arrangements meant that Allied commanders had to make key decisions early in the planning process, and once made, these were not easily reversible. In "Totalize," it proved psychologically impossible for the Allies to cancel the bombing at the last minute, due both to the enormous effort made by the First Canadian Army staff to arrange the strike and to the twenty-four hours' notice required by the air commands to cancel the bombing runs; consequently, Simonds could not adjust his "Totalize" plan to take account of last minute intelligence that the Germans had begun to redeploy troops from the forward defense zone to their secondary one.[94]

Kurt Meyer savaged this whole Anglo-Canadian approach, as exemplified by "Totalize," as an egregious example of both "inflexible, time wasting method" and "too much planning" that "transferred the initiative" from "leading combat elements" to "timetable acrobats" at corps headquarters.[95] Many German reports criticized the rigid prior staff planning inherent in the Anglo-Canadian approach but failed to show any appreciation of the ways in which this operational method represented an appropriate utilization of Allied resources.[96]

Montgomery was not overly concerned over the retarding effect this fire-power-reliant method had on the tempo of operations, as his own approach was slow and methodical. To some extent this emphasis on increasing fire support proved self-defeating, because even if the fire-plan crushed enemy resistance, the devastation that it caused prevented the Allies from the exploitation of any success.[97] However, other powerful considerations—ones that Meyer failed to appreciate—justified Montgomery's methods. Though this method was crude, however, it enabled Allied troops to get onto their objectives with tolerable casualties. Montgomery not only never lost a single major battle with this operational method from El Alamein onwards, but also secured—admittedly modest—victories with tolerable casualties.

Assessing the effectiveness of artillery support proved complicated, as the scientists attached to the 21st Army Group discovered in 1944.[98] Even with the most massive artillery bombardments, the physical damage inflicted on the enemy—the "lethal effect"—was not large in terms of equipment, and even more limited with personnel.[99] Troops in well dug-in positions could sometimes withstand the most incredible scenes of devastation without suffering vast casualties, even if the fire proved accurate. The lethal effect of artillery always remained out of all proportion to the copious resources expended.

In contrast, the "moral effect" of artillery—its ability to stun, incapacitate, or smash the morale of enemy troops—proved highly significant. An accurate, concentrated bombardment would temporarily stupefy enemy troops or substantially reduce their morale, and even if the victims were seasoned elite troops, the effect remained significant. British artillery, for example, hit so hard the troops of the II SS Panzer Corps as they prepared to counterattack the British "Epsom" penetration, that even these fanatical troops could not manage an attack for the rest of that day.[100] It was through this temporary stunning of the enemy—"neutralization"—that artillery fire support enabled the infantry to gain objectives with reasonable casualties.[101] An accurate bombardment was sufficient to neutralize even the best troops for a short while, so that if the follow-up troops remained close behind the rolling barrage, the initial German defensive crust could be penetrated with relatively light casualties. Neutralization was short-lived; and the better the troops, the shorter it lasted, so it was vital that assault troops "leaned-into" the rolling barrage.[102]

The bombardment of Bauchem during Operation "Clipper" on 20 December 1944 proved the most effective Anglo-Canadian artillery fire-plan of the campaign. Uniquely, this bombardment alone secured the almost total collapse of German resistance in this hamlet, and the assaulting infantry met virtually no opposition. The bombardment was not only incredibly intense but sustained at this enormous intensity for no less than four hours. The small scale of the target permitted a vast expenditure of ammunition to be concentrated on one small area. Despite the startling success of this bombardment, this formula was not repeated because it was impracticable for the 21st Army Group to use with any frequency such vast ammunition expenditures on extremely small targets.[103] Even though most typical concentrations never achieved anything like this impact, the use of massive firepower proved effective. The initial fire-plans for "Goodwood," "Cobra," and "Veritable," for example, proved successful in suppressing German defensive fire and getting the infantry onto their initial objectives with tolerable casualties.[104] Scientific research in 1945 showed that there existed a strong correlation between the scale of firepower employed and casualties sustained in achieving a tactical objective.[105] The major problem experienced by Allied commanders remained the translation of initial success during break-in operations into a significant penetration of the enemy's defensive zone.

Allied commanders, however, failed to effectively adjust the target discrimination of these massive fire-plans to deal with the depth of the German defensive zone. These commanders only recognized slowly that the Germans merely held lightly their forward defense zones, and hence these massive Anglo-Canadian fire-plans continued to concentrate their efforts on the devastation of what was merely a lightly defended enemy outpost line. Consequently, the rolling barrage sometimes only carried the advancing Allied infantry through these devastated first localities right onto the scarcely damaged main German position that was defended by now alerted troops who fielded intact their powerful screen of antitank weapons.[106] Anglo-Canadian gunner officers also experienced major difficulties in redeploying forward hundreds of guns across cratered terrain in the early phases of an assault so that the advancing spearheads remained within range of available fire support. These failings explain why the 21st Army Group achieved only a modest combat performance in this campaign.

Brigadier Matthews—the Corps Commander, RA (CCRA) at Simonds' II Canadian Corps—organized the most innovative Anglo-Canadian fire-plan of the Normandy campaign for the 8 August "Totalize" attack. This was the only fire-plan to get to grips fully with the depth of the German defense, through incorporation of a second aerial-artillery strike against the second German defensive line. It proved ironic, therefore, that this creditable attempt by Simonds and Matthews to address this flaw in Anglo-Canadian offensive technique inadvertently led the II Canadian Corps to let slip one of the best opportunities of the entire Normandy campaign. Tragically, the operational pause Simonds built into his "Totalize" plan to permit this second aerial strike bought the Germans sufficient time to shore up their front that—unbeknown to Simonds—the initial Canadian night attack already had torn apart.[107] Only slowly during the campaign did artillery commanders produce fire-plans of increasing sophistication and target discrimination to deal effectively with the German defense zone throughout its depth—a process that culminated in the highly effective "Veritable" fire-plan.[108]

Montgomery's firepower-based attritional style also proved effective in other ways. Even if British attacks did not successfully penetrate the German defenses, the enemy was forced to expend many lives and much matériel preventing Allied thrusts—resources the enemy could ill-afford to lose. Partly unsuccessful Allied operations, like "Goodwood," that nevertheless produced a rough parity in relative casualty rates or even a slight disadvantage to the Allies, still constituted long-term strategic successes despite being immediate tactical failures. For the Allies could afford reasonable combat losses sustained over time—especially equipment ones—better than the Germans could; this was the inexorable logic of an attritional war of matériel. This approach, furthermore, also reflected the realities of combat in the period after 1943. With both the Allied and German armed forces not completely mismatched in terms of combat power—broadly speaking, resources multiplied by effectiveness—and with the Germans in prepared defensive positions, battles had become attritional slogging matches. The dashing days of Blitzkrieg had waned, because the opportunities for such mobile warfare could only be obtained after a period of hard attritional fighting that significantly wore down enemy cohesion and fighting power.

Attrition based on concentrated firepower, however, represented a two-edged sword. In general terms it represented a most appropriate way for the British army to achieve victory over the Germans with tolerable casualties. However, the drawbacks inherent in "Colossal Cracks" prevented the 21st Army Group from the achievement of more than an adequate operational performance in Northwest Europe. One major weakness in Anglo-Canadian operational technique was that its reliance on firepower tended to be self-reinforcing—it became an increasing tactical crutch upon which other combat arms could lean. The branch of the Major-General, RA (MGRA) at army group headquarters increasingly became concerned at the growing demands for fire support requested by junior commanders for even minor raids. A June 1944 report recorded that one corps had fired no less than twenty Victor targets, involving all the guns in a corps firing simultaneously, in just one day.[109] At times during "Totalize" an entire AGRA supported each of the two assault divisions, in addition to the latter's organic artillery.[110] In another extreme example, no less than two field artillery regiments supported Operation "Flo," a single-platoon raid. Another MGRA report denounced the overuse of artillery in fire-plans that often were "nothing more than a fool's answer to a target which he has failed to hit with one gun."[111]

The availability of such an effective resource meant that as the campaign progressed, the artillery became an increasing tactical crutch on which the other arms within the 21st Army Group could lean.[112] Anglo-Canadian armor, for example, sometimes hung back giving supporting fire to the infantry from hull-down positions in the rear in the knowledge that the gunners could be relied on to smash enemy resistance.[113] Furthermore, the infantry also often halted and called down artillery fire at the first sign of enemy resistance, rather than attempting to fight their way forward using their own small-arms firepower.[114] Above all, Allied troops relied excessively on the success of artillery to defeat German resistance by itself. Consequently, a significant imbalance arose in the cooperation of all arms necessary for superior combat performance. The domination of the tactically effective artillery arm within the operational technique utilized by the 21st Army Group exerted inadvertent side effects that undermined the combat performance of the forces employing these techniques.

Caution

Montgomery's operational technique was also characterized by its caution and methodical nature. He stressed the need for patience in the conduct of operations and appreciated that it might take his forces time to fulfill his strategic plan for Normandy. Montgomery's cautious approach led him to launch an offensive only after his command had planned carefully and fully established the administrative foundations, and concentrated such numerical superiority, so as to maximize the prospects of success. This caution had been the hallmark of the Montgomery method even before El Alamein, and it led to the "concentrate-start-stop-rebuild-start" rhythm so characteristic of the way in which the 21st Army Group conducted this campaign; but this caution also infuriated both senior American commanders and British air force commanders like Coningham and Tedder.[115] In Normandy, this caution led Montgomery to postpone operations on many occasions because he believed that there was insufficient artillery fire support deployed or because bad weather prevented his forces utilizing the awesome power of Allied tactical air forces. Typically, any small disadvantage to his troops proved sufficient for Montgomery to postpone an operation. The Field Marshal, for example, canceled "Epsom" several times due to the combination of bad weather and the delays in build-up caused by the storm of mid-June 1944.

Montgomery's caution over the commencement of offensive action, however, did not always overwhelm other operational considerations. At times, if Montgomery thought the operational situation demanded it, he was prepared to order operations to commence at short notice at the expense of his typical standards of preparation and build-up. In Operation "Bluecoat," Montgomery demanded a start time that permitted just forty-eight hours for planning, and even though only two divisions had managed to deploy in time, he ordered the attack to commence with the admonition that the other divisions be "thrown into the battle as they arrive."[116] This haste reflected his desire to prevent German redeployment away from the British sector to block the progress of the American "Cobra" offensive. Similarly, Montgomery launched the uncharacteristically bold "Market-Garden" offensive at a time when logistical build-up was only marginally sufficient to support such an operation. Though the motivations behind this operation are complex, one factor was Montgomery's appreciation that this was the last opportunity, with the *Westheer* in rout, for the British army to win the war in 1944 with one last mighty blow.

A second characteristic of Montgomery's caution was that he was not prepared to take risks in seeking a decisive breakthrough, in pushing a penetration deep, or in exploiting success.[117] This caution had allowed Rommel's Afrika Korps to escape destruction during its retreat after El Alamein. In Normandy, Montgomery sent Kit Dawnay to the War Office before "Goodwood" to clarify his intentions during this operation: "Having broken out in country southeast of Caen," Montgomery had "no intention of rushing madly eastwards," which would extend and hence weaken the security of Second Army's flank.[118] Montgomery's request to O'Connor during "Goodwood" that he maintain both "thrustfulness" from the armor and the security of this eastern flank left the corps commander caught between two stools; the shortage of infantry that resulted from not taking risks with the security of this flank contributed to the failure of the attack. Even on 11 August 1944, with the German front close to collapse, Montgomery remained as concerned to hold a "secure" eastern flank as to exploit the imminent German disintegration.[119]

Montgomery was correct to be concerned over this flank because, as he appreciated, a successful German attack in that area could seize the high ground that dominated the eastern beaches. During June and July 1944, senior Anglo-Canadian commanders in Normandy "always" experienced "real anxiety" because the consequences of mistakes "could be catastrophic."[120]

Montgomery's concern, however, was not justified given the battlefield situation of mid-August. His ingrained caution often rendered him unwilling to take risks almost to the exclusion of other tactical considerations, such as the opportunities his caution was letting slip away.

Even after the decimation of the *Westheer* in the Falaise pocket, Montgomery's concern with the security of the eastern flank slowed his pursuit of the beleaguered enemy back to the Seine, so that once again he failed to capitalize on an excellent opportunity to destroy disorganized, retreating enemy forces. One has to concur with Thompson that Montgomery remained loathe to let fluid operations develop as such a situation would not allow him to conduct operations in his accustomed manner, with both careful preparation and firm control; his orderly command style could not rise to meet the needs of the fluid, impromptu battle, and this failing excludes him from the ranks of the "great captains" of history.[121]

In many ways, though, Montgomery's cautious approach was operationally appropriate. His caution ensured that the 21st Army Group did not present the enemy with "any opportunity" to deal it an unsettling blow.[122] Moreover, this caution reflected Montgomery's determination to nurture the morale of his troops. He believed that it was only through continued Allied success, and the avoidance of even minor setbacks and local enemy successes, that his formation could sustain reasonable morale within its civilian soldiers. Much of historians' criticism of Montgomery has focused on the caution he displayed in Normandy, and this has some validity because at times he was overcautious.[123] Yet often these critics have overstated this criticism, largely because they have assessed this aspect in isolation to the other aspects of his operational technique; historians can only fully comprehend Montgomery's caution in the context of his complete operational approach. Although his caution represented in part a long-established, integral part of his natural approach to battle, in Northwest Europe it also reflected his appreciation of the following three issues: the realities of the set-piece battle; German tactical effectiveness; and the need to both nurture troop morale and conserve manpower. In this respect, Montgomery's approach remained broadly in line with how British army operational doctrine had developed between 1939 and 1944.

First, the nature of the set-piece battle reinforced the natural caution and methodical style that Montgomery always possessed. The frequent passing-through of units, and the reliance on both elaborate artillery fire-plans and the movement forward of the guns during an advance, engendered a ponderous operational style that made difficult the exploitation of fleeting opportunities. Second, Allied recognition of German tactical abilities, learned at such heavy cost during 1939–44, also encouraged a cautious approach. The worst Allied tactical setbacks in Normandy, such as the Villers

Bocage débâcle and the destruction of Worthington force in "Totalize," occurred when infantry or armor advanced boldly without adequate support from other combat arms, especially artillery.[124] These examples dull the gloss historians have attached to the concept of audacious mobile warfare after the onslaught of the Blitzkrieg in 1939–42. Bold maneuver warfare was very risky, if conducted against an enemy as tactically skilled as the German army, even if the latter was markedly inferior in matériel. The Allied air commander-in-chief, Leigh-Mallory, perceptively observed on 27 June 1944 that Rommel was "building up" his reserve armor, and "waiting for Montgomery to stick his neck out" so that he could counterattack any exposed Allied flank.[125] Not surprisingly, therefore, many commanders of all levels within the 21st Army Group conducted their operations in a cautious fashion.

Third, Montgomery's concern to nurture troop morale and conserve manpower also reinforced his naturally cautious operational technique. This approach compared unfavorably with Patton's bold, high-tempo exploitation of the initial success of Operation "Cobra" that demonstrated the great operational benefits of audacity. Yet Patton's success has obscured the considerable risks involved. His success was as much the product of the impact of both the Allies' previous two months of attrition and the timely collapse of German logistics, as it was with Patton's bold generalship.[126] But even in these circumstances, some risk existed during "Cobra" that several American divisions might be smashed, just as the Desert Rats were at Villers Bocage; any attempt at such operational audacity earlier in the campaign courted disaster. Most significantly, though the Americans could cope with the loss of two divisions, the 21st Army Group most definitely could not afford any such loss.

It is clear, therefore, that Montgomery's caution in Northwest Europe can only be understood in the light of his concerns over casualty conservation and the maintenance of morale. Montgomery realized that the way he fought his battles coincided with the best way, all things considered, to fulfill Britain's war aims—attaining victory within a larger Allied effort without a massive butcher's bill. Although the Montgomery method constituted a crude, cumbersome, and cautious example of the art of war, it nevertheless represented an appropriate way for him to achieve a reasonable, sustained performance from his troops.

These characteristics—the master plan, concentration, firepower-based attrition, and caution—formed the main components of the set-piece battle approach that epitomized Montgomery's operational style in this campaign. The utilization of this approach by the 21st Army Group produced two interconnected operational consequences that impacted its conduct of the campaign: a dearth of activity at the operational level, particularly through a lack of simultaneity; and second, a failure to commit more than a modest proportion of available combat power.

First, the nature of the set-piece battle did little to encourage activity at the operational level of war. The 21st Army Group conducted these largely attritional operations in pursuit of limited, geographic objectives, and the direct contribution that success in many of these operations made to overall decisive victory remained at best hazy. Montgomery's utilization of the set-piece approach also hampered the use of simultaneity in his operations; this in turn restricted his capability to effectively coordinate tactical action to produce fully integrated, synchronized activity at the operational level. For the use of such an approach by the 21st Army Group virtually precluded both of its subordinate armies undertaking full-scale operations at the same time. There were insufficient artillery guns within the army group to support simultaneous major attacks by both armies on the lavish scale to which Anglo-Canadian forces had become accustomed; the "Colossal Cracks" approach inadvertently institutionalized the psychological belief that attacks always required the maximum possible fire support if they were to succeed. While the First Canadian Army undertook "Veritable," for example, the Second (British) Army assumed a defensive posture. Similarly, Montgomery had to halt prematurely the Second (British) Army's Operation "Constellation," its October 1944 attack on the German salient west of the River Maas, in order to reinforce the First Canadian Army's faltering operations to clear the Scheldt estuary and open up the vital port of Antwerp.[127]

Once information reached both armies that major new operations were imminent, they both commenced a bargaining process in which they requested that the army group allocate them extra resources, particularly artillery pieces and ammunition quotas. But even the copious artillery resources available within the army group often proved insufficient to meet the full demands of each army, because both generally requested a generous provision of guns for their next task. Not surprisingly, when the 21st Army Group allocated only moderate resources to a subordinate army, the latter found it difficult to achieve its objectives, just as the First Canadian Army did in the Scheldt. The evidence suggests that, in part, this was a problem of mind-set; the availability of only modest fire support both restricted what commanders considered to be operationally possible, and eroded their usually marked determination to achieve their objectives despite the considerable costs involved.[128]

The 21st Army Group also proved unable to sustain simultaneous major operations by both its armies due to the existence of a similar bargaining process over specialized vehicles such as flail tanks or Kangaroo armored personnel carriers (APCs). After their "invention" by Simonds during "Totalize," the army group raised two regiments of APCs, one Canadian and one British.[129] At times, both army's planning for major operations requested two APC regiments, resulting in demand that outstripped supply.[130] The 21st

Army Group recognized that at any given moment it only could support one full-scale army operation to the scale that corps commanders expected and to which they had grown accustomed. In September 1944, Montgomery allocated the Second (British) Army the copious resources it had requested to achieve his "Market-Garden" plan, but merely awarded the First Canadian Army for its Scheldt operations limited resources out of proportion to the ambitious objectives he had ordered it to accomplish; consequently, the Canadian forces only managed to advance slowly.

The inability of the 21st Army Group to undertake two simultaneous army attacks created similar consequences to those already observed in the comparison between British and American offensive methods. Concentration, through operation on a single army front, ensured a powerful attack, yet allowed enemy counterconcentration against such a thrust. Critically, such concentration also may have allowed the Germans to maintain the integrity of their precarious front during September and October 1944. If the army group had undertaken simultaneous army operations, each necessarily with reduced fire support, this might have pushed the *Westheer* into total collapse. For if Montgomery had utilized this method, he may have undermined German ability to maintain their beleaguered front through redeployment of their panzer "mobile fire-brigades" from crisis to crisis, and hence caused total enemy collapse. For most of the campaign, the German defenders sought desperately to avert looming collapse, and their ability to do so demonstrated both their resilient morale and tactical abilities, as well as to the consequences of Montgomery's operational approach.[131] Though the set-piece approach would get the 21st Army Group to victory eventually, genuine opportunities would be missed on the way. The Field Marshal, however, had to weigh the benefits of simultaneous army operations against significant drawbacks, not least the adverse impact this method would have on Allied troop morale and casualty rates; in this respect, Montgomery—perhaps predictably—erred on the side of caution.

Montgomery's utilization of this set-piece approach also restricted simultaneity because it encouraged his command to conduct a series of single-corps attacks. At first glance many of his operations seem to be army-scale offensives, but often—as at "Goodwood"—only one corps undertook the main assault while both neighboring corps launched limited flank-protection attacks, and fired much of their artillery in support of the central attack delivered by the spearhead corps. The tendency of the 21st Army Group to undertake a series of predominantly single-corps battles did little to foster effective coordination or generalship at the operational level.[132]

When Montgomery's tendency to undertake offensives with just a single corps, and often by only one army at a time, combined with his casualty avoidance motives and his brand of extreme concentration (in which he retained large forces echeloned in reserve), the tactical result was that his offensives engaged just a fraction of potential Allied combat power at any given moment. The constant exception to this was artillery, which the army group utilized to the full. Many of Montgomery's contemporaries misconstrued his failure to bring to bear on the enemy more of his numerical superiority as evidence of willful lack of determination; a reaction encapsulated by Tedder's dismissal of Dempsey's attacks on Caen as "company exercises."[133] What these critics failed to appreciate, however, was that much of Montgomery's failure to deploy more than a fraction of his potential strength was the result of the nature of his set-piece approach, and in particular—in an illusory paradox—his brand of extreme concentration.

Alternate Thrusts

The 21st Army Group utilized this set-piece battle approach on virtually all its operations, irrespective of their scale; hence, multicorps offensives like Operation "Veritable," single-corps battles like "Spring" and "Constellation," and even divisional ones like the 4 July Canadian Operation "Windsor" assault—all these Montgomery conducted as set-piece "Colossal Crack" battles. Some historians, however, have viewed another operational method utilized by Montgomery—"alternate thrusts"—as an alternative to the set-piece battle approach; but in fact this method usually represented an integral, complementary component to his set-piece approach. For many of Montgomery's set-piece battles fought on a varying scale from multicorps to divisional thrusts also reflected his alternate-thrusts technique. This approach manifested itself many times during Montgomery's Second World War campaigns. His alternate-thrusts technique took two main forms, one suboperational, which related to his development of a sequence of operations, and the other tactical, which related to the development of a single battle. This technique, in its suboperational sense, typically consisted of Montgomery first making a medium sized thrust in one area. When enemy forces had been attracted to this assault and held there, he would undertake another modest, but unexpected, blow in another part of the front. Once enemy reserve formations had been drawn to this attack and the enemy was hence unbalanced, he would unleash a "Colossal Crack" at yet another part of the front.[134] Montgomery had switched his thrust lines within an individual battle first at El Alamein. Later, during the March 1943 Battle of Mareth, after the failure of his initial, narrow, frontal "Colossal Crack," Montgomery swung his southern flank round in a successful outflanking attack.[135] The only significant difference between these two forms of alternate thrusts was that they were enacted at different scales in terms of duration and size.

Montgomery's utilization of this alternate-thrusts method to unbalance the enemy was also prominent in Northwest Europe. He used this technique in the series of right and left hook envelopments of Caen that he ordered in June 1944. He also utilized this approach in the series of right-left-right hook attacks made by the Second (British) Army south and southwest of Caen in late July and early August. Montgomery launched Operation "Bluecoat," for instance, on the extreme right (western) flank of the Anglo-Canadian sector, then followed this with a couple of feints and then a few days later still by the large "Totalize" offensive striking towards Falaise on the eastern flank. Montgomery's use of this technique was evident in his description to Simpson of the operations he intended to carry out now that the "bottleneck of Caen" had been passed: "I have ordered Second Army to do a series of left-right-left blows east-west-east of the [River] Orne, so as to keep [the enemy] guessing. And then a really heavy blow towards Falaise."[136] Montgomery's elaboration of these intended operations illuminated what precisely his alternate-thrusts policy meant in operational terms. His envisaged sequence of operations included the following: first, a Canadian attack "east of the Orne to capture Fontenoy" on 25 July; second, "an attack by 12 Corps west of the Orne to capture the area Evrecy-Amaye" on 28 July; third, "an operation by 8 Corps east of the Orne" to help the Canadian Corps capture the woods around Garcelles on 30 July; and finally, after these "preliminary" actions, "a very large scale operation toward Falaise," ultimately code-named "Totalize."[137]

Though Montgomery utilized this approach most frequently in Normandy, he still employed it later in the campaign. One example of this was the twin Operation "Nutcracker/Mallard" launched on 14 November 1944, which was followed four days later by Operation "Clipper;" Montgomery only launched the latter after these twin attacks had commenced and thus had attracted most of the German reserves. In "Clipper" the XXX Corps made a thrust through Geilenkirchen toward Linnich on the River Roer to protect the northern flank of the U.S. Ninth Army in its drive on Cologne.[138] In this post-Normandy period Montgomery also used this alternate-thrust approach in a modified form—a pair of converging attacks, one preceding the other. One example of this was Operation "Constellation," O'Connor's October 1944 thrust to clear the Venlo salient. Operation "Veritable" also followed this characteristic, if only by force of circumstances rather than by design. Originally, Montgomery conceived the operation as the northern half of a great pincer movement aimed at Wesel on the Rhine, with the American Operation "Grenade" forming the southern half of this pincer with an advance northeast from the Roermond-Jülich area. However, the enemy's deliberate flooding of the River Roer delayed the American thrust. Nevertheless Montgomery decided to push ahead alone, even though he realized that in doing so he would incur additional casualties as his forces would attract all the German reserves; at the same time this would facilitate the subsequent advance of "Grenade."

General, and from September 1, 1944, Field Marshal, Bernard Law "Monty" Montgomery commanded 21st Army Group in Northwest Europe from D-Day through the end of the war. His two army commanders were Lieutenant-General Miles Dempsey, Second (British) Army, and Lieutenant-General Henry "Harry" Crerar, First Canadian Army.

A Canadian corporal with a sten gun guards German prisoners taken on D-Day on Juno Beach. As the Allies moved inland, the German defense became even more fierce.

A Sherman tank rolls ashore in Normandy as part of the massive build up in men and supplies for Montgomery's "Colossal Cracks."

A Bren gun team from the 8th Canadian Infantry Brigade in a dug-in position near Carpiquet Airport, July 4, 1944. The Bren gun provided the infantry with supporting fire as they advanced on German positions.

Members of a patrol of the East Yorks come under artillery fire. Normandy proved ideal terrain for the German defense, but the Allies were determined to push through.

Canadian medics tend to a wounded soldier. The casualty rate among infantry was disproportionately high compared to other branches of the military during the Normandy campaign.

Invented by Canadian Corps Commander Major-General Guy Simonds, the un-frocked Priest, or Kangaroo as it came to be known, was the first fully tracked armored personnel carrier that allowed soldiers a significant degree of protection from bullets and shrapnel. Here, soldiers from the British 51st Highland Division roll forward on August 7, 1944.

GIs examine a burning German 251 halftrack. For the duration of the Normandy campaign all ground forces, including American, were under Montgomery's control as Land Forces Commander.

The German defeat in Normandy was comparable to their defeat at Stalingrad, and had some thinking the war would be over by Christmas 1944.

A vehicle park in Normandy filled with captured German equipment.

Montgomery conferring with Air Marshals Coningham and Leigh-Mallory and First Canadian Army Commander Lt. General Crerar. Air support was seen as vital in helping to overcome German resistance, especially the much feared Tiger tank.

German POWs being sent back from the front lines to spend the rest of the war in captivity. The Germans greatly feared being captured by the Russians. As the war drew to a close, German units made desperate attempts to head west in the hopes of being taken prisoner by British, Canadian, or American soldiers.

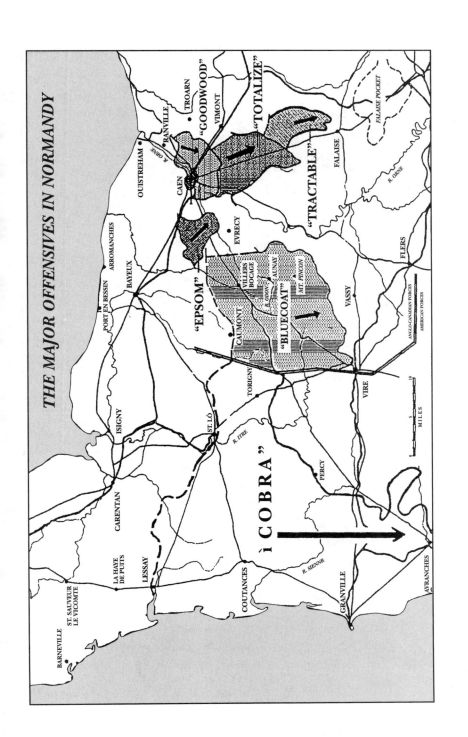

THE MAJOR OFFENSIVES IN NORMANDY

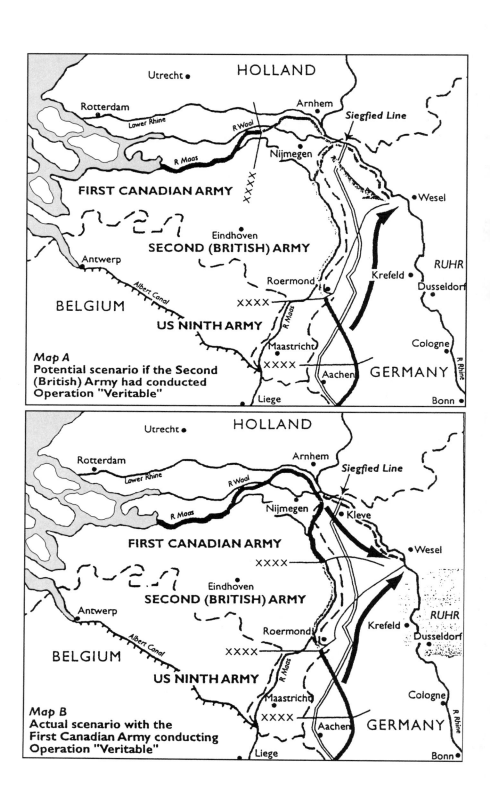

Utrecht •

HOLLAND

Rotterdam •

Lower Rhine

Arnhem •

Siegfied Line

R Waal

R Maas

Nijmegen

FIRST CANADIAN ARMY

xxxx

• Wesel

Eindhoven

SECOND (BRITISH) ARMY

RUHR

Antwerp •

Albert Canal

Roermond

Krefeld •

Dusseldorf

BELGIUM

xxxx

R Maas

US NINTH ARMY

Cologne •

Maastricht •

xxxx

Aachen

GERMANY

R Rhine

Map A
Potential scenario if the Second (British) Army had conducted Operation "Veritable"

Liege •

Bonn •

HOLLAND

Utrecht •

Rotterdam •

Lower Rhine

Arnhem •

Siegfied Line

R Waal

R Maas

Nijmegen

• Kleve

FIRST CANADIAN ARMY

xxxx

• Wesel

Eindhoven

SECOND (BRITISH) ARMY

RUHR

Antwerp •

Albert Canal

Roermond

Krefeld •

Dusseldorf

BELGIUM

xxxx

R Maas

US NINTH ARMY

Cologne •

Maastricht •

xxxx

Aachen

GERMANY

R Rhine

Map B
Actual scenario with the First Canadian Army conducting Operation "Veritable"

Liege •

Bonn •

CHAPTER 5

"Colossal Cracks" II: The Other Elements

Having examined those key tenets of Montgomery's "Colossal Cracks" technique that comprised the crux of his physical conduct of set-piece operations, this chapter analyzes the other four fundamental components of his operational technique: maintenance of the initiative, balance, administration, and air power. This study then examines the following seven ancillary characteristics that comprised the remaining components of Montgomery's operational technique: grip, flank protection, surprise, flexibility, cooperation, simplicity, and the assimilation of the lessons of combat experience.

THE OTHER FUNDAMENTALS OF "COLOSSAL CRACKS"
Maintenance of the Initiative

A key concept in Montgomery's operational approach was the classic military principle of the initiative—imposing one's will on the enemy. The Field Marshal believed that the events of the 1939–45 war demonstrated that the achievement and maintenance of the initiative over the enemy in combat had become essential to victory. By the initiative Montgomery meant that a commander had to "make the battle swing [his] way" and "make the enemy dance to his tune from the beginning, and never vice versa."[1] To maintain the initiative a commander had to "continue relentlessly with his own plan." To be able to do this, his dispositions had to be "so balanced" that he "need not react to the enemy's move." Put simply, it was crucial for a commander to appropriately position his readied reserves to swiftly block previously anticipated enemy countermoves before they achieved any degree of tactical success.[2] Hence to Montgomery the initiative meant that a commander had to ensure that operations developed according to a predetermined plan. Such actions would force the enemy merely to react, rather than be able to instigate his own measures. A force that successfully undertook offensive action and maintained a grip on the initiative accrued distinct moral advantages, and Montgomery hoped that such an operational approach would facilitate his concerns to nurture the morale of his civilian forces.

The Field Marshal believed that the need to maintain the initiative applied equally to commanders at the strategic, operational, and tactical levels.

Montgomery's directives, written thoughts, and actions in Northwest Europe all indicate that maintenance of the initiative represented a key concern in his conduct of the campaign. Variants of the slogan "We must keep the initiative and not let the enemy 'dig in'" appeared frequently in his instructions.[3] Indeed, by 1944 the Field Marshal felt that the maintenance of the initiative was so important that a commander could not "win without it."[4]

Maintenance of the initiative dominated Montgomery's Normandy plans at the theater-strategic or operational level. He sought to ensure that his Anglo-Canadian forces kept hold of the initiative to prevent the Germans redeploying their armor from the eastern flank to the western, American sector.[5] Operationally, Montgomery also strove to make the German commander-in-chief of *Heeres Gruppe B*, Field Marshal Erwin Rommel, merely react to Allied moves during the Normandy campaign. Allied commanders correctly feared that the *Westheer* might manage to concentrate an armored reserve with which to launch a counterattack against the precarious "Overlord" bridgehead. Montgomery sought to control the initiative through being on the offensive, with the aim of preventing the Germans from using infantry to relieve the panzer forces deployed in the front line, permitting the latter to pass into reserve.[6] In Normandy, Montgomery was delighted to discover that Rommel had been forced to commit his panzer reserves to plug the holes that Allied offensives had torn in the German line, instead of concentrating them as a counterattack force.[7] In mid-June, Rommel had been compelled to commit his newly arrived reserve, the 2nd Panzer Division, to seal off the Villers Bocage penetration. Similarly, Allied intelligence concerning the recent arrival at the front of the II SS Panzer Corps provided a powerful incentive for the British to launch their "Epsom" offensive. This operation ensured that Montgomery kept the initiative because it forced Rommel to commit the powerful II SS Panzer Corps to halt "Epsom" rather than to use it for his own planned counterattack.[8]

The 21st Army Group strove to ensure that it maintained the initiative by assuming an offensive posture as often as possible in the circumstances, as this orientation continually would force an enemy reaction. However, obvious frictions existed between this requirement and other elements of Montgomery's operational technique. The retention of the initiative through offensive action conflicted with three other considerations: Montgomery's determination to attack only after he had concentrated copious resources so as to prevent the occurrence of any "set-back or reverse"; his resolution to remain balanced, for offensive operations often left dispositions ragged and unbalanced; and his abiding concern with casualty conservation and the maintenance of morale.[9]

Some historians have criticized Montgomery—with some justification—for his frequent postponement of impending Anglo-Canadian attacks in Normandy on the grounds of insufficient matériel. These delays in part resulted from the Field Marshal's desire to avoid battering his forces against the powerful enemy defenses in the Caen area. But despite this, throughout the campaign as a whole, the 21st Army Group maintained a reasonable record for time spent on the offensive; even though their American allies spent a marginally larger proportion of the campaign on an offensive posture. Montgomery's commencement of Operation "Plunder," the assault crossing of the River Rhine just thirteen days after the completion of the massive "Veritable" offensive, showed this commitment to continued offensive action, even though there is some justification that "Plunder" should have been launched even sooner given the weakness of the German defenses. Overall, Montgomery sought to assume an offensive attitude whenever possible within the powerful constraints of his cautious, casualty-conserving, and morale-nurturing methods. Furthermore, on one occasion, Operation "Market-Garden," the Field Marshal launched an offensive when his administrative system could barely support such a thrust. His motivation for undertaking this operation was an appreciation both of the fleeting operational possibilities of the moment and the prospects of achieving the Montgomery/British agenda in the Anglo-American debates over command and strategy.

Significant tensions existed between the need to maintain the initiative and other elements of "Colossal Cracks," particularly Montgomery's desire to nurture troop morale and avoid heavy casualties. To surmount these frictions, Montgomery had to utilize techniques other than full-scale offensive action. When the Field Marshal believed that the 21st Army Group was unable to assume an offensive stance, he sought to maintain the initiative by ordering limited Anglo-Canadian attacks, raids, and feints.[10] In Normandy, these actions sought to provoke a German response and prevent them from transferring their armor to the American sector. In late July 1944, for example, Montgomery ordered that Crerar's static First Canadian Army undertake several small-scale raids with the purpose of pinning down German armor in the Bourguébus Ridge area, to prevent Rommel from redeploying it against either the unfolding American "Cobra" offensive or the imminent British "Bluecoat" attack.[11]

The 21st Army Group proved highly successful in maintaining control of the operational initiative during the majority of the campaign. The Allies only once lost control of this initiative to the enemy during the latter's mid-December 1944 Ardennes counteroffensive. This lapse resulted largely from

faulty Allied dispositions—poor balance—that arose from intelligence failures that were compounded by a tinge of complacency. The Allies also maintained a much weaker grip on the operational initiative during their
crawling advances in autumn 1944. But even during this period the Germans only twice seriously challenged the hold exerted by the 21st Army
Group on the operational initiative—during their resistance to "Market-Garden" and their counterattack at Meijel in late October; both these instances,
however, represented nothing more to the Allies than local setbacks.[12]

The ability of the 21st Army Group to maintain the initiative in Northwest
Europe proved a crucial factor in its victory over the *Westheer*. It prevented the
Germans from successful concentration of any significant counterattack force,
with the one exception of their Ardennes counteroffensive. Once the Allies
had secured the "Overlord" lodgment area, the Germans stood little chance
of preventing the eventual Allied liberation of Nazi-occupied Europe unless
they managed to undertake successfully an operational-level counteroffensive
that denuded substantially Allied morale. Through their stranglehold on the
initiative for most of the campaign, the Allies imposed on the *Westheer* a reac-
tive defensive posture based upon a series of negative, delaying, and unimagi-
native fighting withdrawals.[13] Frequently, Allied attacks compelled the *Westheer*
to desperately throw into the front line whatever reinforcements had just
arrived, to shore up a front line in imminent danger of collapse. An examination of the deployments of the *Westheer* during the Anglo-Canadian "Veritable"
offensive reveals the desperate nature of the repeated German attempts to
prevent a major Allied penetration.[14]

Balance

Montgomery's orders to his commanders and his messages to Brooke also
reveal that he placed great emphasis on balance in Northwest Europe.[15] Balance was a facet of concentration and its sibling classic military principles,
economy of force and security: The *Field Service Regulations* defined the concept as the correct combination of these three characteristics.[16] Montgomery's sense of balance was interconnected with his emphases on the master
plan, caution, maintenance of the initiative, and flank protection. Balance
referred to a commander's ability to deploy his forces so effectively with
regard to terrain, communications, and likely enemy reaction, that these
forces could easily accommodate, rather than react to, any countermove by
the enemy. Hence, balance reflected Montgomery's intent both to enact a
master plan and maintain his grip on the initiative, because balance permitted a commander "to proceed" relentlessly with his plan.[17] Moreover, Montgomery's emphasis on balance in Northwest Europe also facilitated his

objective to sustain troop morale, because balance enabled Anglo-Canadian forces to speedily halt enemy penetrations before they could achieve tactical success that might damage Allied morale. Balance also reflected the fixation the cautious Montgomery maintained over tidiness—his concern to avoid dangerously exposed salients and an untidy, ragged front line that might offer the Germans opportunities for successful local counterattacks.

During 1944–45 the Field Marshal's concern with balance was most noticeable in his fears over the vulnerability of the eastern flank of the Normandy lodgment area. Given the potential risk of Allied forces in the east of the Normandy bridgehead being swept back into the sea by enemy counterattack, the cautious Montgomery remained determined to keep his dispositions balanced even if this meant postponing impending operations: This was the motivation behind his suspension of offensive operations for forty-eight hours on 14 June 1944. Hence, even though balance in some ways facilitated Montgomery's intent to maintain the initiative in Northwest Europe, real tensions pervaded the relationship between these two elements of his overall operational technique. In reality, the Field Marshall's concerns with balance, the nurture of troop morale, and the avoidance of excessive casualties reinforced his innate caution and encouraged him to adopt a defensive or limited offensive orientation. Yet neither of these two postures facilitated Montgomery's attempts—through the combination of repeated, successful, offensive action and continued grasp of the initiative—to maintain troop morale and achieve victory in the theater on his desired terms. To Montgomery, victory meant the achievement of Britain's particular politico-military campaign objectives through the securing of a high national profile within a larger Allied effort that successfully brought the German army to decisive defeat. Like most higher field commanders, Montgomery's generalship revolved around the art of balancing all these contradictory objectives and concerns within the context of a rapidly changing battlefield situation.

Administration

Another fundamental aspect of Montgomery's operational approach was the administrative dimension. Administration concerns the organization of logistical supply—the transportation from depots in the rear up to the front line of the ammunition, petrol, oil, rations, and all other supplies necessary to sustain a fighting force in the field. Montgomery based his operational technique on the principle that "administrative arrangements must be equal to the strain imposed in carrying out the strategical or tactical plan."[18] What Montgomery believed to be logistically possible determined his consideration of what was operationally feasible; operational possibilities remained principally a function of logistical ones. Consequently, administration proved integral to Montgomery's theater strategic master plan for Normandy. The "Overlord" plan sought to establish, by about D+90, a lodgment area that stretched from the River Seine in the northeast, to the River Loire in the south, and to the Brittany Peninsula in the west. The Allied High Command intended to rapidly open the ports within this lodgment area to facilitate the importation of the many thousands of tons of logistical supplies required each day by the Allied Expeditionary Forces. Montgomery planned to launch a decisive campaign only after D+90, when the 21st Army Group—plus the newly formed American Army Group—had successfully established this administrative network.[19] In reality, the campaign developed contrary to Allied expectations because the enemy decided to stand and fight a decisive battle west of the Seine in Normandy. Consequently the Allies fought their crucial operations before they reached the Seine, rather than afterward as they had planned.[20]

The overriding concern within the Allied "Overlord" planning process was to establish a sufficiently rapid rate of build-up of men and matériel within the lodgment area established in Normandy. This was a difficult task because the Germans could reinforce their troops more quickly by land than the Allies could across the waters of the Channel. The Allied staffs devoted vast amounts of labor to the production and frequent updating of these hugely complex daily build-up tables.[21] The 21st Army Group staff recognized only too well that "the outcome of this battle will depend primarily on whether our rate of build-up can match the enemy rate of reinforcement."[22] The maintenance of adequate rates of build-up relative to those of the enemy constituted a crucial factor in the Allied success in Normandy. In this achievement, the Allies owed much to the huge success of their aerial interdiction campaign prior to "Overlord."[23]

The administrative dimension so dominated Montgomery's operational methods during the 1944–45 campaign that one critic described him as a "general-manager"—rather than a general—who was "enslaved by logistics" in a campaign dominated by matériel.[24] With one exception, Montgomery never undertook an operation when the administrative situation was not completely satisfactory. The central issue in Montgomery's operational planning was the scale of ammunition supply. He would not commence an operation until his forces had completed stockpiling a more than adequately large supply of ammunition. Though some historians have criticized this cautious, firepower-laden, administratively dominated approach, this method constituted a crucial factor in the eventual Allied attainment of victory.

In contrast, during the Second World War the German army consistently neglected logistics in preference to their concentration on tactical excellence. It is a chilling thought that the spectacular German triumphs of 1939–41 would have been even more successful if the German army only had devoted the same professionalism and efficiency to the logistical dimension as they did to the tactical sphere. In Normandy the Germans once again focused on their skills at the tactical level to the detriment of the strategic or operational levels, and woefully neglected the logistical dimension. Indeed it is only recently that historical research has convincingly demonstrated that the failings of the German logistic system in Normandy made a far greater contribution to Allied victory than previously had been believed.[25] In stark contrast, during the Northwest Europe campaign, Montgomery oversaw, through generalship based on both competence and a justified logistical orientation, the utilization of crude tactics to produce an appropriate, if unimpressive, Anglo-Canadian operational effort. Moreover, the fact that the development of modern warfare since 1945 has affirmed the ever-increasing dominance of logistics on military activities vindicates Montgomery's great concern with the administrative dimension.[26]

Several historians have suggested that Montgomery's operational method remained too concerned with ensuring an excellent administrative situation before launching operations. The Field Marshal certainly let slip excellent operational and tactical opportunities because he was not prepared to take chances on logistical matters, as say Patton did. Montgomery's innate caution and lack of awareness of exploitation were evident in his early military career, because he omitted the latter subject in a tactical guide he drew up in 1924.[27] During the 1939–45 war, a pattern, initiated at Alamein, emerged in Montgomery's conduct of operations: He consistently failed to fully exploit successes he had achieved.[28]

Montgomery, however, fully recognized the fact sometimes overlooked by historians that logistics constituted the foundation blocks for victory. Moreover, in defense of Montgomery, the evidence indicates that whereas he was highly concerned with the logistical dimension, his army group staff and subordinate staffs were even more concerned with such matters. The operational planning process of the First Canadian Army in its autumn 1944 operations to clear the Scheldt estuary, for example, remained dominated by considerations of simple weight of artillery shells.[29]

Very occasionally, when Montgomery felt that the operational situation absolutely required it, he was prepared to take risks and launch operations when the administrative situation was barely adequate, as in Operation "Market-Garden." As an official report put it, this offensive "had to commence for operational reasons at a time when the administrative resources were barely able to support it."[30] Similarly, in Operation "Bluecoat," Montgomery also sacrificed his usual regard for administrative safety to the operational requirements of the moment. Despite these exceptions, however, administrative issues dominated Montgomery's handling of the 21st Army Group and reinforced his predilection for a series of cautious, firmly controlled, fire-power-laden, set-piece offensives.

Air Power

Another key component of Montgomery's firepower-reliant operational technique was his emphasis on the use of air power. Once the Allies had achieved air superiority over a theater, the army could call upon air assets in pursuit of the following five missions: tactical reconnaissance; ground and naval fire direction; tactical air support, where fighter-bomber aircraft directly supported land operations; the use of strategic air assets—medium and heavy bombers—in a direct role to support ground operations; and the use of both tactical and strategic air assets for battlefield air interdiction. By 1944 Montgomery had concluded that "experience in this war has shown that all modern military operations are in fact combined army/air operations," and that air power was "a battle winning factor of the first importance."[31] Montgomery believed that at the strategic level "it is necessary to win the air battle before embarking on the ground battle."[32] The experience of maneuver warfare over the subsequent fifty years has vindicated entirely this belief.[33] It was Montgomery's Eighth Army in North Africa that first emulated the techniques of the German Blitzkrieg through their development of intimate tactical cooperation between the army and the Royal Air Force. When Montgomery returned to Britain in January 1944, the lack of effective cooperation that existed between the 21st Army Group and the tactical air forces allocated to support it horrified him. His guiding impulse and the experience of cooperation in the early stages of the Normandy campaign quickly honed Allied air power into an awesome instrument with which to support ground operations.

During the Northwest Europe campaign as a whole, the Allied tactical air forces inflicted extremely heavy damage on German armor and motor transport and severely disrupted German logistical resupply activities. The dreaded Allied fighter-bombers proved so effective that they compelled the enemy to move its vehicles only at night and forced them to rely on bicycles as the principal source of daytime mobility.[34] By Operation "Goodwood" the Allies had all but perfected the cab-rank system whereby Allied fighter-bomber flights circled continually overhead until directed onto enemy targets by forward air controllers on the ground.[35] The Allies demonstrated the effectiveness of these tactical air support methods by the particularly terrible slaughter they inflicted on the German forces desperately attempting to escape entrapment in the Falaise pocket.[36] The frequency with which Montgomery called off ground offensives when poor weather limited the extent of available aerial support illustrates the importance that he attached to air power. On 20 June 1944, after Montgomery had postponed "Epsom," the attack by the VIII Corps toward the Odon, he signaled de Guingand that "each further day of bad weather will mean a further postponement of a day."[37] Tactical air power made an enormous contribution to eventual Allied success, and some authors have even argued that the campaign "was decided by Allied superiority in the air."[38]

The Allies based their organization of land-air cooperation in Northwest Europe primarily at the level of army, the highest echelon link between ground formations and the tactical air forces. During 1944–45, British and Canadian forces further honed the organizational techniques first developed in North Africa. In Northwest Europe, both of the British and Canadian army headquarters in reality constituted joint army and tactical air force headquarters, with adjacent layouts and common representation in the Joint Battle Room.[39] Moreover, the 21st Army Group ensured that it integrated direct air support with the proposed development of the land battle to produce a single combined—in modern parlance, joint—bi-service plan. Such integration not only constituted a fundamental element within the operational technique utilized by the 21st Army Group but also contributed crucially to ultimate Allied success. A tactical group, RAF or RCAF each supported the two Anglo-Canadian armies fielded by the 21st Army Group. Every day in the campaign, weather permitting, both armies allocated fighter-bomber targets to their respective supporting tactical air forces for them to attack to assist land operations. Essentially, therefore, Anglo-Canadian utilization of tactical air power simply represented another method for applying effectively massive firepower onto enemy positions. The awesome power of such fire support, when combined with effective, massed artillery fires, constituted a devastatingly potent weapon with which to weaken the combat power of the *Westheer*.

ANCILLARY ELEMENTS OF MONTGOMERY'S APPROACH

Seven other ancillary tenets together formed the remaining characteristics that completed the overall operational technique implemented by the 21st Army Group in the 1944–45 Northwest Europe campaign. One such aspect was Montgomery's concept of "grip." This notion had two senses, one concerning leadership and the other operations. Grip formed part of Montgomery's conception of command, whereby he tightly controlled the activities of his immediate subordinates—his two army commanders. Undoubtedly, Montgomery's firm emphasis on grip sometimes led him to "overcontrol" these subordinate commanders. Clearly, the issue of grip dominated Montgomery's relationships with his two subordinate army commanders, albeit in

subtly different ways; the nature of these relationships forms the substance of
the analysis that this study presents in the following two chapters.

Grip

Grip in its operational sense was a means by which Montgomery sought both
to retain the balance of his dispositions and to ensure that operations developed according to his master plan. Grip meant that the Field Marshal mon-
itored closely the development of an operation. Montgomery believed that
"the modern battle can go very quickly off the rails," and that "to succeed,"
an army group commander had to firmly grip "his military machine." For
such grip was the only way a commander could ensure that his force maintained "balance and cohesion" and thus developed "its full fighting potential."[40] He felt that it was not enough for commanders, "once their plan was
made and orders issued," to take "no further part in the proceedings, except
to influence the battle by means of reserves." To Montgomery a firm grip
was essential to keep an operation unfolding according to his predetermined master plan. In particular, such grip helped him ensure that his master plan was not distorted by other influences. Without grip, Montgomery
feared, an operation might become merely "a compromise" between the
master plan and circumstances: namely, that the plan might be distorted by
either subordinate intent, the tactical outcome of subordinate action, or the
results of the enemy's seizure of the initiative.[41]

Montgomery recognized, at least in principle, that "this firm grip does
not mean interference, or the cramping of the initiative of subordinates,"
and indeed acknowledged that "it is by the initiative of subordinates that the
battle is finally won."[42] In late July 1944, for instance, the Field Marshal
warned Crerar for cramping Crocker's conduct of his corps. Despite this,
Montgomery overstepped that fine and subjective dividing line between an
army group commander's proper handling of his formation and his impinge-
ment on the appropriate authority of subordinate army and corps commanders to fight their respective battles. Montgomery did not just give his
subordinates the minimum detail necessary for them to complete their
detailed plan to fulfill his directive. Montgomery's personality, his experience
of not being gripped by Alexander when commander of the Eighth Army in
North Africa, and his packing of army group headquarters with trusted former subordinates, all reinforced his strong influence on the army and corps
level within the 21st Army Group. One historian, for instance, concluded that
in Northwest Europe, Montgomery acted more like an army commander
than the head of an army group.[43]

One reason behind the Field Marshal's emphasis on grip was his unshak-
able belief in his own abilities and his limited confidence in the abilities of

his subordinates. This attitude appeared widespread within the senior command echelons of the 21st Army Group. Although Montgomery clearly was guilty of overcontrol, this also remained true of his senior subordinates. Dempsey gripped his subordinate corps commanders, and Simonds' lack of confidence in his divisional commanders, Keller and Foulkes, after Operation "Spring," led him to control them more tightly in their next operation, "Totalize."[44] This predilection to overcontrol subordinates is a recurring theme in the remainder of this analysis. In addition to Montgomery's tendency to overcontrol his army subordinates, the techniques inherent in "Colossal Cracks" also served to limit the contributions made by these two army commanders. The nature of this operational approach meant that most attacks remained single-corps affairs, and this reduced the relative role of army and increased that of corps. This fact may explain in part why the campaign's historical literature often portrays these army commanders as mere ciphers.

Flank Protection

Maintaining the security of the flanks exposed by offensive action formed another ancillary facet of Montgomery's operational technique. This aspect reflected Montgomery's emphases on caution, sustaining morale, balance, security, and tidiness. His great concern over the security of flanks reflected his healthy regard for German tactical capabilities. His determination to keep the flanks of his advancing forces secure denied the Germans opportunities to take advantage of Allied audacity to inflict local defeats. In Normandy, Montgomery's concern over flank protection was evident in his emphasis on maintaining the security of the vulnerable eastern flank. The Allies remained greatly concerned throughout June and July 1944, as they established a lodgment area, that a German armored counterattack would roll up the bridgehead from this flank, or at least interrupt the Allied logistic build-up over the beaches.[45] It was no coincidence that Montgomery entrusted Crocker, one of his most experienced and capable armored corps commanders, to defend this vital flank. For most of the Normandy campaign, Montgomery deployed Crocker's corps in defensive positions, and consequently the position of the front on that flank scarcely changed as the campaign unfolded elsewhere. Indeed, as late as mid-August, when the German front was in the process of collapse, Montgomery continued to issue orders that stressed the need to keep this eastern flank, now extended as far south as Falaise, firm and solid.

The manner in which Montgomery and his senior subordinates developed offensive operations also reflected his concern with flank protection. Sometimes the existence of natural obstacles that advancing Anglo-Canadian could use to protect their flanks influenced Montgomery's selection of the areas over which he would launch major operations. Use of such obstacles facilitated both concentration and tidiness, as well as minimized the threat posed by possible German counterattacks on the flanks. In a classic example of this concern, Simonds' "Totalize" offensive utilized the Laize River to screen its right (western) flank from German countermoves.[46]

Montgomery remained concerned about substantial German counterattacks on the flanks of Anglo-Canadian penetrations throughout the 1944–45 campaign. This fear prompted him in late June 1944 to halt the "Epsom" attack. Similarly, he canceled the October 1944 "Gatwick" offensive because the American 7th Armored Division had been unable to clear the enemy-held Venlo salient on the southern flank of the offensive. If this salient remained in enemy hands, the attacking forces would have to advance with two exposed flanks to the north and south. The most notorious occasion, however, when Montgomery abandoned his concern with flank protection was during the "Market-Garden" offensive, which represented the antithesis of a typical Montgomery operation. This unique operation demonstrated that in certain circumstances Montgomery was prepared to abandon flank protection in favor of potentially significant operational gains. The failure of the operation and the German success at cutting XXX Corps' corridor of advance both demonstrated the risks Anglo-Canadian forces courted when Montgomery abandoned his innate caution and his emphasis on flank security.[47]

Surprise

In Northwest Europe, Montgomery also placed great emphasis on the tactical achievement of that standard military principle, surprise, which he believed was "always possible and must always be sought."[48] The attainment of surprise represented one motive behind his utilization of the alternate-thrusts approach discussed in the previous chapter. Montgomery hoped that by attacking first in one sector and drawing off enemy forces, this would facilitate the success of a surprise attack in another sector that would consequently face weakened opposition. To achieve tactical surprise, Montgomery placed strong emphasis on the use of deception techniques within the operations that the 21st Army Group undertook.[49] Anglo-Canadian forces widely used deception methods in Normandy, albeit not always with marked success. Montgomery's employment of deception techniques improved gradually during the campaign culminating in "Veritable," the greatest success story using such methods. In this operation, Allied use of the most stringent and sophisticated security and deception arrangements ensured that the Germans remained virtually unaware of the concentration of 250,000 Anglo-Canadian troops in the Groesbeek-Nijmegen area.[50] There seems to have been an element of revenge in the Allied deception effort prior to the "Veritable" offensive: It represented a deliberate response to the successful German deception scheme, "*Wacht am Rhein*," used in their December 1944 Ardennes counteroffensive.

Flexibility

Though Montgomery's preference for a master plan and tight control of operations suppressed operational flexibility, he still emphasized flexibility of force structure within his operational methods. This form of flexibility constituted another adjunct of concentration, because "true concentration implies the power of flexibility." Indeed, Montgomery believed that the relationship between the two was "the vital key to effective operations."[51] This form of flexibility manifested itself in Montgomery's policy of avoiding fixed corps compositions, separate armored and infantry corps, and distinct armored/tank formations. Instead, all corps staffs had to be proficient at handling any type of division.[52] Having a flexible corps composition facilitated Montgomery's desire to maintain balance: It made it easier for him both to redeploy divisions in response to the changing operational situation and to vary corps composition to match their particular task. O'Connor's VIII Corps, for instance, comprised entirely of armor at "Goodwood," fielded mixed divisions for "Epsom" and deployed mainly infantry for the twinned Operations "Nutcracker" and "Mallard," the November 1944 British attempt to clear the enemy salient on the west bank of the Maas around Venlo.

The drawback of a such a policy, as O'Connor observed to Montgomery, was that in a fixed corps, divisions became experienced in cooperating with their supporting armored or tank brigades, and the efficiency engendered by this familiarity was lost with flexible corps composition.[53] Montgomery was not unsympathetic to this point, and in the 21st Army Group he attempted to keep old cooperation associations together as much as possible; the teeing up of the XXX Corps for "Veritable" saw three of the four main assault divisions supported by armor with which they already had had a long association.[54]

Cooperation

Montgomery also regularly stressed that proper cooperation was essential if the Anglo-Canadian forces were to fight effectively in the field. His conception of cooperation encompassed both interservice and interarm varieties. The army could only reach its full potential on the battlefield with full cooperation from the navy and particularly the air force. The greatest example of the power of effective interservice cooperation was the D-Day landings, one of the greatest amphibious assaults in history. The other aspect of cooperation was interarm cooperation. Montgomery stressed to his subordinates the need for both realistic combined-arms training and for an effective combined-arms tactical approach based around solid infantry and tank cooperation that was tied in appropriately to the mechanics of tactical fire-plans. Despite the widespread recognition of these requirements within the senior command echelons of the 21st Army Group, Anglo-Canadian infantry/tank cooperation proved rather deficient during the first few weeks in Normandy.[55] Gradually, this cooperation improved, partly through increased tactical experience and partly through modification of divisional force structure to produce better integrated all-arms combat teams.[56]

Simplicity
Montgomery also placed great emphasis on the need for simplicity in the planning of military operations. He believed that simplicity was one of the "fundamental principles that really matter" in achieving success.[57] Plans had to remain simple, because the more complicated a plan, the greater the chance that things would go wrong. Simplicity was also important because Montgomery wanted all the soldiers participating to fully understand their own individual part in the bigger operation: This would, he felt, improve both troop morale and efficiency. The one example that vindicated this belief in simplicity was Simonds' August 1944 "Totalize" offensive, where a complicated corps plan hindered rather than facilitated successful development of the attack through the depth of the German defenses.

The Assimilation of Combat Lessons
One of the most emphasized elements in Montgomery's thought was the need to learn from combat experience. A large part of his conflict with the War Office and Home Forces during 1942–44 centered on the identification and then assimilation of the correct lessons of his experience in North Africa. Montgomery argued, in typically patronizing style, that the doctrinal statements emanating from the War Office in this period did not equate to the realities of modern war that recently had been discovered in battle in North Africa. In Northwest Europe, Montgomery remained slightly more interested in the assimilation of tactical lessons than operational ones. Initially, this might seem surprising, but it arose principally because Montgomery believed after Alamein that he had developed an effective operational doctrine. He utilized this operational technique virtually unchanged for the remainder of the war; and this fact could be interpreted by the cynical as suggesting that Montgomery never learnt from his mistakes.

This chapter has examined the remaining four fundamental tenets and seven ancillary characteristics of Montgomery's "Colossal Cracks" operational technique. This completes this study's comprehensive examination of both the characteristics of, and the factors influencing, Montgomery's operational approach. Having established the factors that influenced his conduct of the 21st Army Group in Northwest Europe, this analysis now turns to examine the contribution that his subordinate army commanders made to the campaign.

CHAPTER 6

Dempsey and the Second (British) Army

> I defy anyone to get any colour into Dempsey. So far as I am
> aware, as Monty's instrument, he has no story of his own.
> —LHCMA, JNP/II/3/250A,
> JOHN NORTH TO CAPT W. MILES, 3 OCT 1953[1]

> The notion . . . that D[empsey] was simply M[ontgomery]'s poo-
> dle is clearly quite inaccurate.
> —CCA, RLEW/7/7, LEWIN'S NOTES—TALK WITH DEMPSEY, 4 NOV 1968

This chapter and the next one examine the contribution made to the conduct of the Northwest Europe campaign by the two armies permanently
under the command of the 21st Army Group—the Second (British) and the
First Canadian. Lieutenant-Generals Miles Christopher Dempsey and Henry
Duncan Graham Crerar respectively commanded these formations. The contribution made at army level to the overall operational approach of the 21st
Army Group was determined by the following three interconnected aspects:
the operational function of an army; the relationship between army group
and army; and the extent to which these armies implemented or modified
army group operational methods. This study will now examine each of these
aspects with regard to Dempsey and the Second (British) Army.

For the Normandy campaign, the First United States Army also served
under Montgomery's operational command. However, in reality, Montgomery
held a very loose rein on the commander of the First Army, General Omar N.
Bradley. In this case, the politics of inter-Allied cooperation compelled Montgomery to treat Bradley differently from Crerar and Dempsey. For though
Bradley's Army developed its operations broadly within the framework of
Montgomery's overall theater strategy for Normandy, the latter sought to persuade Bradley to conduct his operations in particular ways rather than formally to control him through directives.[2] Montgomery informed Brooke on
27 June 1944, for example, that though he had tried very "hard" to get
Bradley to thrust toward Coutances simultaneously with his completion of the
capture of Cherbourg, the American commander did not "want to take the

risk."[3] Hence, the First United States Army remained a quasi-autonomous subordinate command within Montgomery's army group, and this distinguished it from the more orthodox subordinate roles assumed by both Crerar's and Dempsey's Anglo-Canadian Armies.

During July and early August 1944, the ever increasing American numerical strength within the Allied forces deployed in Normandy compelled Montgomery to accept certain key politico-military developments, not least those that related to the Allied command structure. At the beginning of August, the 12th United States Army Group became operational with Bradley being promoted to command it. There now existed the awkward situation of one army group commander (Bradley) serving under the command of another (Montgomery). Furthermore, the time was drawing near when Eisenhower would take over the office of Land Forces Commander from Montgomery, in accordance with the intentions stated during the pre-invasion planning. Given these facts, during August the grip that the British Commander-in-Chief exerted over the Americans grew steadily weaker; the increasing communication difficulties Montgomery experienced as the American forces swarmed out of the Avranches bridgehead, only served to exacerbate his dwindling control of Bradley's forces. Then, on 1 September 1944 Eisenhower became the dual Supreme Allied and Land Forces Commander, and Montgomery reverted to being just an army group commander, with merely the two Anglo-Canadian armies under his command, in a theater that now also fielded two American army groups. In the light of these factors, this study will not examine the contribution that the First United States Army made to the manner in which the 21st Army Group conducted this campaign.

THE FUNCTION OF AN ARMY IN NORTHWEST EUROPE

An army is a higher formation in the military chain of command below that of army group and above that of corps. The composition of an army is not fixed, and its only permanent establishment is its headquarters staff. To this is added several corps, typically between two and four in total, according to the operational situation. An army also has under its command various army troops—independent artillery, armor, armored car, engineer, signal, transport, and service units—that army headquarters allocates to support corps for specific tasks as required by operational needs.

In Northwest Europe, when the 21st Army Group decided that a particular operation was required, it issued a directive to its subordinate army commands setting out in broad terms their respective tasks. On 4 August 1944, for example, the army group set the First Canadian Army the task of launching "a strong attack from the Caen sector towards Falaise on night

7/8 August."[4] The Canadian army's fulfillment of this task became Operation "Totalize." These tasks were allocated to armies within the context of army group operations as a whole. After studying the problem, each army headquarters would issue its own operation instruction to its subordinate corps. This set out the army's task in greater detail, and specified the particular task to be carried out by each subordinate corps. The army plan, however, left the precise methods by which the corps accomplished these tasks to be worked out in the plan subsequently drawn up by corps. Hence, it was the corps headquarters that drew up the detailed tactical—or lower operational—plan for how a particular operation would be conducted, and not the army headquarters. However, the latter did set criteria within which the corps had to develop its detailed plan. For instance, in "Totalize," the First Canadian Army instructed the II Canadian Corps that its plan should both achieve surprise and address the problem of maintaining the momentum of the penetration as the attack developed.[5]

The theme of the relationship between levels in the chain of command weaves itself through many of the issues that this study examines. One fundamental principle of many armies, including the British, is that a higher formation, once it has set a mission, should leave its subordinate formation to decide which methods it will use to achieve that task. This analysis assesses the extent to which higher formations maintained this principle under the pressures of war. This chapter demonstrates that British and Canadian higher commands tended to impinge upon the freedom of their immediate subordinate formations to plan the methods to be used to accomplish the tasks set them from above. This tendency to "overcontrol" subordinates is the subject of debate in the modern British army as it wrestles with the doctrinal tenets of maneuver warfare, particularly that of mission command.[6] In Northwest Europe, "overcontrol" resulted from the following four attitudes held by higher commanders: their lack of confidence in their subordinates; their supreme faith in their own abilities; their desire to help newly promoted—and thus inexperienced—corps and divisional commanders master their new responsibilities; and their desperate concern to see operations develop that not only achieved success but did so with tolerable casualties.

In Northwest Europe, a British or Canadian army headquarters performed seven main operational/tactical roles: It allocated resources to support corps in their operations; it helped establish the necessary administrative and logistical infrastructures and organize the relevant preparations to enable its subordinate corps to launch their operations; it negotiated with Allied air commands for the provision of strategic bombing attacks in direct support of the land operation; it arranged on a daily basis tactical air support for operations; it coordinated the actions of its corps if the operation constituted a multicorps affair; once the corps battle was underway, army commanders influenced the operation by their commitment of army-level reserves; and last, an army commander could intervene directly at key moments in the corps battle if he felt the operational situation demanded, or justified, such intervention. On balance, an army's contribution to a corps-level operation lay more in the preparation phase than in the execution of the battle.[7]

DEMPSEY'S ROLE IN NORTHWEST EUROPE

This analysis now examines the contribution that Dempsey, the commander of the Second (British) Army, and his staff made to the manner in which the 21st Army Group conducted this campaign. It also explores Dempsey's relationship with Montgomery, and analyzes the extent to which he shared his superior's operational methods. These analyses show that although Montgomery circumvented "Bimbo" Dempsey, as he was known according to an army sobriquet of obscure origination, the latter was not simply the colorless cipher that the existing literature has portrayed him as being.[8]

The dearth of extant archival material that relates to Dempsey constitutes a serious methodological problem for any analysis of his role in this campaign. Such archival scraps that do exist include his 1944–45 diary—simply a basic narrative of his daily activities, the operational papers of the Second Army, and fragmentary comments made by his colleagues. Indeed, principally as a result of this paucity of documentary evidence, Dempsey has remained the forgotten commander of the campaign.[9] His absence from the 1991 book, *Churchill's Generals*, is highly significant, as is the fact that to date there has been no major biographical work on him; an ignominy that is only shared, amongst the senior Anglo-Canadian commanders in the theater—those at or above corps level—by Bucknall and Crocker.[10] The enduring feature of the campaign's historical literature has been an obsession with Montgomery, a focus that was encouraged by the Field Marshal himself; incredibly, his account of the campaign only mentions Dempsey just six times, and none of these entries is substantial.[11] Several historians have recognized the need to remedy this historical oversight, but such intentions have fallen flat due to the dearth of documentary material available.[12] However, with careful use of the wide range of snippets of material relating to Dempsey, an attempt to systematically examine Dempsey's role in Northwest Europe can now be made.

Another key reason for Dempsey's historical obscurity emanates from his personality. Dempsey, a career infantryman, was an efficient, calm, charming, and wholly unperturbable commander, who possessed a legendary ability to read ground from a map.[13] But Dempsey also was an extremely quiet, introverted, and unassuming soldier, who shunned publicity; he simply got on with his job effectively and with the minimum of fuss.[14] Given the subordination of the introverted Dempsey under the command of the glory-grabbing Montgomery, it is not surprising that Dempsey's profile among the British general public in 1944–45 remained very low indeed. The unassuming Dempsey proved the perfect foil for the egotistical Montgomery, and one is compelled to ponder to what extent this influenced the Field Marshal's selection of Dempsey as his subordinate for this campaign. Dempsey's public prominence reached its—still lowly—heights in 1945, on the crest of victory in Europe. After the war, however, his limited reputation dwindled rapidly, in part because Dempsey refused to enter into public debate over the campaign. His firm determination not to contradict the Montgomery line, and his disinterest in self-promotion, did nothing to bolster the public's paltry interest in him; he remained the forgotten victor of what was, for the Western Allies, the decisive campaign of the Second World War in Europe.[15]

Another methodological problem that dogs any examination of Dempsey's contribution to this campaign revolves around the obfuscating features of his relationship with Montgomery. The closeness of their working relationship makes it extremely difficult to trace the authorship of a particular operational decision. This problem is greatly exacerbated by their practice in Northwest Europe of working entirely on verbal orders. Montgomery's directives were merely the subsequent "confirmation of our conferences and discussions."[16] Montgomery later confirmed that the only written order he gave Dempsey in Normandy was "the one for the record" about "Goodwood."[17] This reliance on verbal orders attests to the smoothness and mutual confidence of their operational relationship; but this also muddies analysis.

These problems of interpretation are compounded by the fact, as Dominick Graham has observed, that an almost symbiotic relationship existed between the two commanders.[18] They had worked so long together that they thought along very similar lines and often anticipated each other's reactions and decisions. Though this symbiosis hypothesis is both eminently plausible and a useful explanatory tool, it is impossible to prove. Acceptance of this hypothesis plausibly explains a notable feature in the two commanders' documentary record of the campaign: sometimes, both their contemporary records claim authorship for the same decision. Montgomery informed O'Connor on 19 June 1944, for instance, that he had "told Bimbo to chuck" an intended operation by O'Connor's corps east of the Orne; yet the day before, Dempsey noted in his diary that he "had told" Montgomery that he had concluded that this attack was "too risky" to undertake.[19]

This notion of a symbiotic relationship proffers two possible explanations for the contradictions inherent in the disputed authorship of this decision, and similar ones that also exist: that both men either reached independently the same conclusion or together reached a mutual conclusion. If one rejects this symbiosis hypothesis, there still exist other plausible explanations for this contradiction; that the glory-grabbing Montgomery, as the superior officer, was claiming credit for Dempsey's decisions; or that the down-trodden Dempsey, tiring of his superior's interference, was claiming (at least for posterity) credit for decisions reached by Montgomery. From what is known generally of these two commanders and the context of this campaign, all of these explanations are plausible. Whatever the truth behind these confusions— and history may never know—the crucial point is that these uncertainties make it difficult to make a conclusive assessment of Dempsey's role in the campaign. Reaching definitive conclusions about his role remains problematic when the authorship of key decisions may now never be attributed precisely. Moreover, to date historians have often assumed that Montgomery was the real author of these disputed decisions; and hence, to date these confusions have both contributed to the consignment of Dempsey's historical profile to oblivion and fueled the consuming fascination with Montgomery. But it may be the case that some decisions that appear to have been made by Montgomery were in fact inspired by Dempsey; but proving this assertion beyond reasonable doubt is fraught with significant difficulties.

Dempsey was in every sense Montgomery's right-hand man. He had been one of Montgomery's students at the Staff College, Camberley, in 1930–31, and the latter had requested personally that Dempsey assume command of the XIII Corps in December 1942. Yet Dempsey was not Montgomery's initial choice to command the Second (British) Army in the 1944–45 Northwest Europe campaign. Originally, Montgomery intended that another of his favored protégés—Oliver Leese—who had taken over the Eighth Army after Montgomery returned to England to command the 21st Army Group, should command the Second Army with O'Connor replacing Leese in Italy.[20] Montgomery hoped that alongside Leese would be Dempsey as commander of the First Canadian Army, because Dempsey had served both successfully and popularly with the Canadians in 1940 as the BGS(Ops) of the new Anglo-Dominion VII Corps.[21] In these considerations, Leese had a slight advantage over Dempsey in that he already possessed a modicum of experience as an army commander in the field whereas the latter had none. However, Montgomery's plan fell through after being blocked by Brooke. The CIGS both refused to allow Leese's abilities to be withdrawn from the Italian theater and recognized that Canadian political requirements demanded that the Canadian General Henry Crerar head the First Canadian Army, not a British commander.[22] Subsequently, Montgomery without hesitation selected Dempsey to command the Second (British) Army. At the time, the military thinker Liddell Hart and the radical tanker General Percy Hobart both enthusiastically welcomed this appointment.[23]

Montgomery and Dempsey worked very well side by side. The latter commander was—like Leese, Horrocks, Simonds, de Guingand, Belchem, and Richardson—one of "Monty's men," in that they had hitched their careers to the Montgomery flag and that the Field Marshal had nurtured their abilities and careers. Dempsey nailed his flag firmly to Montgomery's post after the war, refusing to contradict his superior's disingenuous accounts of the campaign. Dempsey also unobtrusively defended the Field Marshal's battlefield reputation from criticism both at home and particularly in America. In 1968, Dempsey told Lewin—while requesting that his information not be conveyed to Liddell Hart—that "since the war [Montgomery] has been his own worst advertising agent. I would not attempt to defend that. It is an anathema to me. But I will do anything I can to help you establish his genius as a commander in the field."[24]

Such loyalty may have been misplaced given that in 1946 Montgomery treated the faithful de Guingand with shameful insensitivity when he casually informed his former chief of staff that he would not now be made VCIGS as Montgomery had previously indicated.[25] Dempsey' postwar loyalty owed much to Montgomery's shielding of him from criticism during the campaign, especially over the failure of "Goodwood." Montgomery also exerted a remarkably strong influence over all the former "Monty men" long after the war had ended.[26] Dempsey's fidelity also may have been counterproductive in the sense that his determination not to contradict Montgomery's obvious massaging of the historical facts reinforced increasing American alienation with British accounts of the campaign. Indeed, the nationally orientated historical debate that raged during the 1950s and 1960s served both to increase these confusions rather than clarify them and to hinder objective analyses of Montgomery's generalship not excessively focused on his personality. Furthermore, Dempsey's loyalty to Montgomery also was misplaced both in that his superior never gave Dempsey the credit he rightly deserved for the important role he played in the campaign and because such fidelity also proved personally damaging to Dempsey's historical reputation.

Dempsey the Cipher
To date, the campaign's historical literature has portrayed Dempsey the army commander as just a cipher who simply passed on Montgomery's orders to his highly capable corps commanders, and who made little contribution himself. This view asserts that Montgomery "commanded an Army Group as he did an Army"—or to be more precise, the Eighth Army.[27] This view argues that Montgomery circumvented Dempsey by frequently dealing directly with his corps commanders. Ronald Lewin noted that when he asked O'Connor "what did [Dempsey] personally contribute, beyond being a 'usual channel'

between Mont[gomer]y and his very able corps commanders, there was really no answer."[28] The fact that Dempsey has had such sparse historical investigation justifies further examination of Dempsey's actual contribution to the conduct of this campaign.

An army commander can contribute personally to the conduct of a campaign in several ways. One such aspect was theater strategy, traditionally the preserve of the theater or army group commander, but where army commanders might exert some marginal influence. Given Montgomery's personality, command style, and operational methods, it seems highly unlikely that Dempsey exerted any significant influence on the higher strategical direction of the campaign. General Horrocks, the commander of the XXX Corps, did not believe that "Dempsey was much involved with the higher planning of the Normandy campaign," for which Montgomery "relied almost entirely on his own judgement." Indeed, Horrocks recalled only one instance during the entire campaign—in October 1944—"when Montgomery ever consulted me about future operations."[29]

Such a view is reinforced when one recalls that Montgomery was infamous for not changing his mind once he had reached a decision on some strategic matter—as was demonstrated egregiously by Montgomery's decision to go for Arnhem in "Market-Garden."[30] Indeed, in Normandy, only Montgomery's decisions altered the proposed sequence of operations he had envisaged to fulfill the theater strategy he had established. On 8 July 1944, for instance, he instructed Dempsey to shift the center of gravity of the Second Army to the attack by the VIII Corps west of the Orne, this taking "priority over the advance east of the Orne" that had been the intended development of operations.[31]

Whereas the higher strategic conduct of a campaign remained the domain of Montgomery, one might expect that the objectives of specific operations would only be decided after closer discussion between Montgomery and Dempsey. At times, however, this seems not to be the case. In Operation "Market-Garden," the final decision to go for Arnhem—instead of for Wesel as Dempsey favored—remained Montgomery's decision alone. David Belchem, the army group's BGS(Ops), later observed, "there was no question of going to Arnhem. Dempsey and Browning arrived" early on 10 September "to finalize their master plan for Wesel." But Montgomery "greeted them" with "we are going to Arnhem," even though he knew that "all of us from Dempsey downwards were against Arnhem."[32] Dempsey recollected that he telephoned Montgomery that morning and arranged a meeting to decide what objective they should set. Dempsey arrived "convinced that we should go to Wesel," but when he got to the caravan, "Montgomery was standing at the door with a telegram from the War Office in his hand" about the V2 rocket threat. Dempsey believed that this message "decided the question," because Montgomery had not "really made up his mind on Arnhem before he got this telegram."[33] Montgomery clearly overrode the advice not only of his staff but also of the army commander responsible for the operation. In his diary, Dempsey observed that the enemy was doing "all he can to hold" Arnhem. Consequently, Dempsey pondered, "Are we right to direct Second Army to Arnhem or would it be better to hold a firm left flank along the canals and strike due east" in conjunction with the First United States Army?[34] Dempsey's willingness both to carry out an operation that he personally felt was suspect and to accept Montgomery's dismissal of his opinions suggests that Dempsey remained subservient to his forceful superior.

An army commander also contributed to the conduct of the campaign in other ways. Dempsey's key function was the day-to-day coordination and supervision of his subordinate corps and the operations these undertook. This is the sphere in which Dempsey might justifiably be expected to have made a highly significant contribution to the overall operational conduct of the Northwest Europe campaign. Yet Dempsey's subservience to his superior, as illustrated in the Arnhem incident, prompts consideration of whether Montgomery bypassed Dempsey (just as he did with Crerar) through dealing directly with Dempsey's corps commanders. At least in the case of O'Connor, Montgomery made clear his policy that corps commanders could pass over their army commander to discuss matters directly with him. On 11 July 1944, O'Connor wrote to Montgomery, "You did tell me to ring you up or write to you on tactical questions when I am in doubt, which I often am! And so I am doing so now."[35] O'Connor informed D'Este that Montgomery often visited him and sometimes issued new orders on the spot, whereas at other times Dempsey would issue subsequently orders that confirmed what Montgomery had asked O'Connor to do.[36]

At first sight, O'Connor's case might seem to be a special one, since the VIII Corps commander had been in an Italian prisoner of war camp for two years, and naturally was rusty on the latest tactical methods. It had been for this reason, as well as on grounds of age, that Montgomery had been unhappy at O'Connor's appointment to command the VIII Corps in Northwest Europe; Montgomery also simply did not want another corps commander who was not a "Monty man" because he always remained suspicious of independently minded commanders whose careers he had not personally nurtured or whom he had not inculcated with his techniques. But such concerns do not justify Montgomery's interference in a problem that ought to have been dealt with by O'Connor's immediate superior—Dempsey. It is possible, however, that Montgomery anticipated that O'Connor, the firm-minded victor of Beda Fomm in early 1941, might resent being nursed operationally by his erstwhile subordinate—Dempsey. If this had been the situation, with O'Connor being a unique case, Montgomery's interference with Dempsey's handling of the Second Army might have been more defensible.

Montgomery's bypassing of Dempsey, however, does not seem to be restricted to just the special case of O'Connor. Both Lewin and D'Este concluded that Montgomery regularly bypassed his army commanders.[37] Dempsey was also bypassed in Montgomery's dealings with Horrocks, with the latter recollecting that although "Dempsey was told what Montgomery was doing" during the advance into Belgium and in "Market-Garden," he doubted "whether Dempsey had been told beforehand when Montgomery came up to see me just prior to my last battle . . . the seizure of Bremen."[38] Equally, it was Montgomery, rather than Dempsey, who ultimately made major operational decisions, such as the withdrawal of the 1st Airborne Division from the Oosterbeek bridgehead during Operation "Market-Garden."[39]

O'Connor's frankly astounding 11 July 1944 missive to Montgomery illustrates well that the latter bypassed Dempsey. In this semi-official letter, O'Connor asked Montgomery's opinion on two projected operations, which Ritchie's XII Corps would undertake when they had taken over the frontage of O'Connor's VIII Corps. The latter stated that Dempsey had accepted his recommendation that the next attack should aim to capture the high ground west of Evrecy. However, Dempsey refused to accept O'Connor's further argument that the Evrecy operation had to be "preceded by an operation to capture the high ground about Noyers." O'Connor then explained his proposed preliminary operation, the tactical reasons behind it, and Dempsey's grounds for rejecting it. If he undertook the Evrecy operation before the Noyers one, O'Connor insisted, the former "might possibly be a failure." O'Connor then asked Montgomery to "consider the matter."[40]

Clearly, O'Connor unofficially had referred to Montgomery a disagreement between him and Dempsey over projected operations that were going to be carried out not by him but by a third party, Neil Ritchie. Even if one acknowledges that O'Connor knew the terrain better than Ritchie, this seems a strange state of military affairs. One is led to ponder to what degree Montgomery's willingness to interfere in Dempsey's handling of his corps commanders damaged the army commander's authority with these subordinates or encouraged them to refer matters direct to Montgomery. Unfortunately, no written reply by Montgomery exists in the relevant archives, and one is forced to surmise that in all probability any response was given verbally and will not ever be known.

Further evidence of Montgomery's close grip on Dempsey's handling of O'Connor is to be found in the case of Operation "Dreadnought." During mid-June 1944, prior to the "Epsom" offensive, Montgomery had contemplated an attack, "Dreadnought," from the bridgehead beyond the Caen canal that sought to outflank Caen from the east. O'Connor made a negative appreciation on the planned operation, which he sent, as requested, to Montgomery rather than to Dempsey. Montgomery replied that he had reconsidered the operation after O'Connor's "very clear exposition" of the difficulties involved and had "told Bimbo to chuck" the attack in favor of an operation toward Evrecy.[41] Again, this operation demonstrated the possible symbiosis that existed between Montgomery and Dempsey—or their mutual desire to claim responsibility for decisions. In 1946 Dempsey confirmed to Chester Wilmot his diary entry of 18 June 1944 that he had informed Montgomery of his decision "to cancel the proposed attack by 8 Corps from the airborne bridgehead."[42] Whether the decision to abandon "Dreadnought" was made by Dempsey or by Montgomery, or the two together, remains a mystery.

The evidence presented indicates that Montgomery bypassed Dempsey in dealing directly with the latter's corps commanders. It is significant, however, that Dempsey offered no criticism of this meddling by his superior. It is not entirely clear whether this acceptance stemmed from a general deference to Montgomery's will, or whether Dempsey tolerated this interference because he recognized Montgomery's undoubted operational qualities and subordinated personality issues to the crucial requirement of producing a battlefield performance capable of defeating the *Westheer*. D'Este has suggested that in Normandy Dempsey became increasingly frustrated with the stalemate in the bridgehead, with Montgomery's excessive grip on the Second Army, and with his correspondingly low profile within the 21st Army Group. Brigadier Williams recalled that Dempsey "would deliberately sit up as high as possible in his staff car so that the troops would recognize him."[43] Moreover, the practice of Montgomery's liaison officers to report directly back to the Field Marshal, ignoring regular command channels, not only annoyed many commanders but sometimes upset "even the impeccable" Dempsey.[44] Whatever the reasons behind Dempsey's stoic acceptance of Montgomery's interference, this acceptance constituted a crucial element in the efficiency of the two commanders' working relationship, a partnership on which much depended if the Allies were to defeat Germany.[45] Is this picture, however, of Dempsey being bypassed by a superior who often dealt directly with his corps commanders really the whole story? To leave the analysis at that would lead to a significant undervaluation of Dempsey's overall contribution to the campaign.

Dempsey the Significant Contributor

There is other evidence, however, that indicates that Dempsey did make a significant individual contribution to the conduct of this campaign. D'Este concluded that Dempsey had "a far stronger personality" than that "suggested by his public image."[46] Moreover, Dempsey did contribute to the higher direction of the campaign. Even if his influence on Montgomery's theater strategy in Normandy remained negligible, Dempsey and his army staff played a substantial role during the pre-invasion planning in fleshing out the final "Overlord" plan from the broad framework for the Normandy campaign produced by the 21st Army Group.

At times during the campaign, moreover, Dempsey exerted a marked influence on the sequence of operations developed in pursuit of this strategy and on the conception of particular operations. The build-up schedule constituted a fundamental part of both Montgomery's strategic plan for Normandy and of the sequence of operations he envisaged to fulfill this plan. The fact that Dempsey's opinions resulted in alterations to the build-up schedule attests to the influence he exerted on his superior. On 26 June 1944, at a Second Army staff conference, Dempsey stated that he now wished that the II Canadian Corps Headquarters should be landed before the troops of the 2nd Canadian Division, reversing the sequence originally timetabled in the build-up program. Dempsey then simply requested that Montgomery "approve this arrangement."[47]

Dempsey influenced individual operations most significantly in "Goodwood"—the Second Army's all-armored assault on 18 July 1944 that sought to outflank Caen from the east. This attack was conceived by Dempsey, who sold it to a reluctant Montgomery. Dempsey told Liddell Hart in 1952 that it was "my suggestion that I could break out."[48] At the army group conference of 10 July 1944, when "Goodwood" was proposed, the ambitious Dempsey attempted to convert Montgomery to a significant change in the theater strategic plan for Normandy, which shifted the main breakout role away from the Americans and to the British. At this conference, Dempsey recollected, he "suggested to Monty—when talking in private—that I should make the breakout, and could do so. But Monty did not favour such a change of aim."[49] Dempsey was more frustrated with the slowness of the advance in Normandy than his superior.[50] It is unclear to what extent this frustration reflected the fact that the constricted lodgment area facilitated Montgomery's stifling control of Dempsey's activities as commander of the Second Army. In Dempsey's mind a successful "Goodwood" would alleviate the burden of the grip Montgomery currently exercised over him. Despite Montgomery's refusal to allow Dempsey's proposal to alter his master plan, it is significant, however, that a few days after this conference, Brigadier Richardson's army group G (Plans) section began study on an operation, "Lucky Strike," that allocated the British by far the greater role in a breakout toward the Seine.[51] While Montgomery refused to sanction this fundamental alteration to his Normandy strategy, he acquiesced in the launching of

"Goodwood"—an attack for which Dempsey, privately, appears to have entertained the highest hopes for a decisive British breakout.

Another example of the significance of Dempsey's contribution during the Normandy campaign concerned Operation "Bluecoat." On 25 July, Montgomery instructed Dempsey to carry out an operation to help the American "Cobra" offensive, which would "have no geographical objective" but would divert German forces away from the Americans. The next day Dempsey informed his superior that he had selected the Caumont sector for this operation: Dempsey alone made this significant decision.[52] In contrast, moreover, to the evidence that Montgomery often bypassed Dempsey, the Second Army commander's diary reveals that he was actively involved in the daily business of supervising his corps commanders. Dempsey's diary indicates that he remained in very frequent contact with his corps commanders, usually twice daily in Normandy, and that in most cases Montgomery was not present at these meetings. Quite correctly, Dempsey was in contact with his corps commanders far more frequently than he was with Montgomery. This diary also shows that he was intimately involved with the corps commanders' planning of operations; therefore, cases like Operation "Dreadnought," where the Field Marshal and O'Connor appear to have marginalized Dempsey, constituted the exception rather than the rule.[53]

The picture of Dempsey being circumvented frequently also sits uneasily with the fact that Dempsey was clearly a competent army commander who often displayed "fingertip feel" over his battles. It is an army commander's privilege, if not duty, to intervene in his corps commander's battle if he thinks that the latter has missed a tactical opportunity. Where this stopped being appropriate intervention and became "overcontrol" of subordinates is a moot point. Dempsey displayed the authority and keen grasp of the operational situation not only to intervene when he felt this necessary, but to do so without prior reference to Montgomery. On 12 June 1944, for example, Dempsey intervened crucially to shift the weight of Major-General Erskine's 7th Armored Division to the west prior to their advance on Villers Bocage, in order to take advantage of a thin point in the German front. In 1946, Dempsey recounted how he "went to see Erskine—gave him his orders and told him to get moving and that I would tell the corps c[omman]d[e]r what he was doing."[54] Thus, Dempsey also bypassed his subordinate corps commanders to deal direct with divisional commanders. This crucial intervention permitted the strategically significant British advance to Villers Bocage—a beneficial development sadly marred by the débâcle of the forced retreat inflicted by Michael Wittmann's Tiger tanks.

In Normandy, the close control that Dempsey exercised over his corps commanders during the break-in phase of operations, particularly with regard to the deployment of reserves, further demonstrated his "fingertip feel." This suggests that Montgomery's bypassing of Dempsey was limited in both frequency and in context. Dempsey, for instance, moved his tactical headquarters up to that of O'Connor during Operation "Goodwood," in order "to control" the operation if the enemy collapsed as expected.[55] If enemy resistance had disintegrated Dempsey wished "to be forward" so that he "could take over and direct the exploitation."[56] This was not the behavior of an army commander who was routinely circumvented. Similarly, in "Bluecoat," Dempsey situated his tactical headquarters less than a mile away from the tactical headquarters of the two corps involved in the operations.[57] Presumably, the purpose of this move was to help Dempsey exert a firm grip on his subordinate commanders. Furthermore, it is significant that Dempsey's tactical headquarters were located further forward than those of Lieutenant-General Hodges, the commander of the First United States Army after Bradley had been promoted to army group command.[58] Finally, during Operation "Charnwood," Dempsey only permitted his subordinate corps commander, John Crocker, to pass his reserves, the 3rd (British) Division's rear brigade plus the 33rd Armored Brigade, through his left-hand assault forces after receiving Dempsey's express permission.[59] Clearly, Dempsey often gripped firmly his subordinates.

Dempsey's close control of the break-in phase of offensives also reflected his general policy of keeping reserves under his own army control instead of releasing them to corps commands. On 11 June 1944 Dempsey received indications that German armor was preparing to attack the vulnerable eastern flank of the bridgehead from where the panzers could roll up the entire Allied lodgment area. Dempsey ordered Crocker to place all his armored reserves on the dominating high ground at Colomby-sur-Thaon—terrain so critical that Dempsey called it "the heart of the British Empire." The army commander instructed Crocker "not to move his armor from it except on orders from me."[60] Similarly, on 30 June 1944, Dempsey informed Bucknall, the commander of the XXX Corps, that while Bucknall's reserve division would remain under his corps command, he would "position it at Bayeaux and not move it without" Dempsey's authority.[61] Once again, in the midst of the crisis during "Market-Garden," when German forces had cut the axis of advance of the XXX Corps, Dempsey instructed Ritchie's XII Corps to place a brigade group at Zon that could not be moved "without orders from me."[62] Brigadier Pyman, the Second Army's Chief of Staff, was much impressed by Dempsey s determination personally to control these reserves, and his resistance to the repeated pleas of corps commanders to have them released to their own control.[63] When the evidence presented here is considered as a whole, it is clear that Dempsey was a competent army commander who gripped his subordinates during break-in operations and who possessed sufficient confidence to intervene directly in file corps battle. This side of Dempsey is hard to reconcile with his image as a mere cipher of Montgomery.

Analyzing Montgomery's opinion of Dempsey provides evidence that supports both seemingly contradictory views of Dempsey's role in this campaign. Montgomery respected and trusted Dempsey's ability, as indicated by the smoothness of their working relationship both in Italy and in Northwest Europe, Montgomery told Oliver Leese on 24 July 1944 that Dempsey was a "first class" army commander, and in 1969 he told the historian Ronald Lewin that Dempsey could "always be relied on."[64] Montgomery's favorable opinion of Dempsey, however, resulted in part from the latter's compliant acceptance and tolerance of his superior's interference. The clearest operational manifestation of the trust Montgomery placed in his subordinate was his deliberate delaying of the date at which Crerar's First Canadian Army became operational in Normandy.[65] Rather than have troops serve under the suspect generalship of Crerar, Montgomery preferred to permit Dempsey to control as many as five corps—a heavy burden, even with Montgomery's nursing grip, for an accomplished army commander.

Montgomery the ruthless military professional, however, also remained aware that Dempsey had never commanded an army before and hence was likely to experience teething troubles adjusting to this new level of command. On 10 June 1944, Montgomery wrote to de Guingand that his time was "fully occupied" as he had "two army commanders who have never commanded armies in battle before."[66] Montgomery obviously felt it necessary to nurse the two commanders until they adjusted to the task of commanding an army. Similarly, Montgomery observed in his letter to Leese of 24 July that both Bradley and Dempsey were "very inexperienced on the air side, but are anxious to learn and are doing so."[67] As the arrangements for tactical air support were made primarily at army level, rather than at corps level, Dempsey had little practical experience of such matters to draw upon.

Montgomery recognized that in addition to Dempsey's inexperience, the Second Army staff also possessed little practical experience of running an army. Only on 27 November 1944 did Dempsey reveal to the staff at the Second Army's main headquarters how anxious he remained prior to D-Day about their inexperience. He doubted whether his staff would "produce the goods at once," because many of them had "never been to war before," and because it remained unclear if they could cooperate effectively with 83 Group RAF.[68] During the course of the campaign, however, growing practical experience gradually honed the Second Army staff into an efficient, experienced organization, and this development facilitated Anglo-Canadian successes on the battlefield. In summary, therefore, Montgomery held a slightly ambivalent opinion of Dempsey's operational ability that recognized both the latter's strengths and weaknesses; this ambivalence mirrors the curiously contradictory contribution Dempsey made to the campaign.[69]

Another important aspect of the conduct of the Northwest Europe campaign was the making of appointments. Dempsey made only a limited contribution on such matters, which were monopolized by Montgomery who devoted a lot of his attention to them.[70] Dempsey's marginal role in appointment matters reinforces the image of Dempsey as subservient to Montgomery. Dempsey's contribution contrasted with that of Crerar who dominated Canadian appointments in the theater—but only because political realities forced Montgomery to accept the national sensibilities of the Anglo-Canadian military relationship. Dempsey's subservience to his superior on appointments was evident in the case of General Allan Adair, the commander of the Guards Armored Division. In February 1944, Montgomery concluded that Adair lacked sufficient drive to command the division in the forthcoming invasion of France and wanted him removed. On 19 February, Dempsey faithfully informed O'Connor, who had just taken over the corps that deployed Adair's division, of Montgomery's view and asked him to write an unfavorable report on Adair.[71] Since O'Connor remained "less in awe" of Monty than most, and "certainly not in awe of Dempsey his former subordinate," the corps commander refused to make such a report.[72] O'Connor argued justifiably that he had had insufficient time to form a valid opinion of Adair and hence could not write an unfavorable report; as a result Adair commanded the division during the campaign.

At the time, O'Connor consistently professed a high opinion of Adair, possibly due to his sensitivity to the political power of the Guards lobby; but in 1975 he admitted that Adair "was not really a flyer."[73] This latter view was shared by other commanders within the 21st Army Group, like "Pip" Roberts who felt that he would have succeeded if he had undertaken "Market-Garden" instead of Adair.[74] Indeed, a strong sense of the "Gentleman-Amateur" comes through from Adair's own memoirs.[75] Given Montgomery's intense resentment of having his will thwarted, O'Connor's technically correct actions scarcely endeared him to a Montgomery who had not wished to have the elderly O'Connor command a corps in the 21st Army Group in the first place. In this affair, Dempsey's loyalties were firmly with the wishes of Montgomery, rather than with the strict military correctness of O'Connor.

O'Connor clashed with Montgomery yet again over appointments in September 1944. Montgomery had met the aging general Silvester commanding the American 7th Armored Division that was serving temporarily under O'Connor's corps command. Montgomery requested that Eisenhower dismiss Silvester, without even discussing the matter with O'Connor.[76]

This behavior so infuriated the latter that he tendered his resignation.[77] Although Dempsey persuaded O'Connor to retract his resignation, this was the final straw in the strained relations between Montgomery and the corps commander, and the former allowed O'Connor to be poached for the vacant army command in India. On 28 September 1944, Montgomery cryptically told Brooke "the VCIGS will tell you what I said about O'Connor, and if by chance you took [him] for Egypt then I would ask you to let me have Browning for 8 Corps."[78] Montgomery's request for the dashing, politically powerful, yet operationally inexperienced "Boy" Browning, then the commander of the British airborne corps, is baffling. It is inconceivable that a commander as consumed with operational efficiency as Montgomery would seriously have wanted the inexperienced Browning as a corps commander, because he must have been aware of Browning's culpability in the failure of the airborne landings at Oosterbeek-Arnhem in "Market-Garden." Perhaps this request reflected political considerations in a war that Montgomery believed would be over in a few weeks.[79] O'Connor believed that Dempsey secretly supported his position over Silvester, as evidenced by the fact that both commanders wrote letters of condolence to Silvester while Montgomery did not. However, O'Connor felt that there was little either of them could do because "we carried no weight with Monty." O'Connor recalled that on the one occasion after the war when Montgomery referred to the matter, he stated that in his opinion Dempsey and O'Connor "had said far too much" in Silvester's favor.[80] These command squabbles illustrate the minimal influence Dempsey exerted on his superior on such matters.

Another example of the marginal contribution that Dempsey made on such matters concerned Major-General "Pip" Roberts, commander of the 11th Armored Division. Roberts was unhappy with the GSOI who had replaced Brian Wyldbore-Smith and asked O'Connor to speak to Dempsey. Both the latter commanders relied that they could do nothing as Montgomery himself had appointed the officer. Roberts persisted with his complaint, going over the heads of O'Connor and Dempsey to speak directly to Montgomery, who agreed to replace the officer with Roberts' preference.[81] Similarly, in October 1944, Montgomery visited Lieutenant-Colonel Michael Carver, and they discussed who should assume command of one of the latter's battalions. Despite the Field Marshal's initial reservations about Carver's choice, Montgomery personally saw to it that Carver got the man he wished.[82] Equally, O'Connor failed to secure for Brigadier Combe an appointment in the theater because Montgomery was "adamant" about age limits for commanders—a concern that was later to cost O'Connor his corps command.[83]

After the war, Montgomery recounted an incident concerning Horrocks, which again reveals Dempsey's limited contribution to appointments.

Horrocks had reported to Montgomery that he was dissatisfied with his Chief Signals Officer and wanted another. After discussing the matter with the army group's senior Signal Officer, Montgomery appointed a replacement. Horrocks, however, refused to accept the new man and threatened to resign. Montgomery telephoned Dempsey, who remained determined not to become involved; it was, he said, a technical matter beyond his competence. Montgomery refused to alter his decision and eventually compelled Horrocks to take the new man.[84]

There is, however, some contrary evidence that Dempsey did exert some influence on appointments within the 21st Army Group. Lewin noted that Dempsey had told him that Montgomery "never sacked any" of his officers unless the army commander had "so recommended."[85] Brigadier Pyman also believed that it had been Dempsey's decision that Bucknall be sacked—a view Dempsey subsequently affirmed to Chester Wilmot in 1946.[86] Thus, though it is problematic to be definitive about Dempsey's contribution to appointments within the 21st Army Group, the balance of evidence seems to suggest that Montgomery monopolized this area, at least with regard to British—as opposed to Canadian—appointment matters.

SECOND (BRITISH) ARMY'S CONDUCT OF THE CAMPAIGN

This study now examines briefly the extent to which Montgomery's operational methods were either duplicated or modified at the level of the Second Army. This analysis utilizes the same categorization used to investigate Montgomery's operational technique to demonstrate that the methods used by the Second Army reflected strongly those of Montgomery. That this was so was not surprising given the following factors: that the Second Army Headquarters had been created out of Montgomery's Southeastern command and already had absorbed many of the Field Marshal's techniques by late 1942; that Dempsey had worked so long and closely with Montgomery; and that the latter remained so determined to instill his approaches throughout the 21st Army Group.[87]

Dempsey displayed the same prominent concern about the morale of his troops as his superior. On 18 October 1944, in the midst of the sodden gloom of the autumn, Dempsey gave a morale-boosting address to the men of the 7th Armored Division. Dempsey stated with regard to their next operation that the division "will do it 100%—that I know: just as you have always done."[88]

Dempsey's rhetoric was intended to bolster the morale of these war-weary veteran troops. In reality, however, Dempsey felt that the division was "lacking in drive," at least during "Goodwood" if not elsewhere as well.[89] The sparse documentary record that concerns Dempsey, however, does not reveal the same extreme emphasis on the maintenance of morale that can be discerned from an examination of Montgomery's thoughts and actions in Northwest Europe.

Dempsey also shared his superior's overwhelming concern with avoidance of heavy casualties. Selwyn Lloyd, the Second Army's Colonel GS (in effect, the deputy Chief of Staff), observed that Dempsey's "experience in the First World War" had made him "determined to have no unnecessary casualties."[90] Brigadier Pyman concurred, remarking that Dempsey was "by nature, merciful to a fault."[91] It was avoidance of infantry casualties that shaped Dempsey's "Goodwood" plan, with its heavy reliance on armored formations instead of infantry ones. This consideration also prompted Dempsey to halt the operation soon after it became clear that a major breakthrough was unlikely.[92] Dempsey remained acutely aware of the infantry reinforcement situation throughout the campaign; on 15 August 1944, for instance, he informed O'Connor and two of his divisional commanders of the severity of the situation.[93] Similarly, in October 1944, Dempsey instructed that Operation "Nutcracker," which sought to clear the German salient at Venlo on the west bank of the Maas, had to be carried out "slowly and in considerable strength, to ensure complete success with as few casualties as possible."[94]

Dempsey also shared his superior's cautious operational methods and displayed a similarly healthy respect for German abilities, especially in the counterattack. Dempsey, like Montgomery, desired the provision of maximum possible fire support at every opportunity, and emphasized in particular the employment of tactical air power. The day before "Goodwood" was due to commence, Dempsey noted that the operation was "entirely dependent on the weather, and if the air cannot take part the operation will have to be cancelled."[95] Similarly, on 4 October 1944, Dempsey noted that the forthcoming Operation "Gatwick," due to commence on 10 October, would "be postponed from day to day if the weather does not allow the air to function."[96]

This caution reflected Dempsey's fear of German counterattacks because his methods sought to offer no opportunities for the Germans to catch British units and formations off-balance or without adequate firepower support and inflict morale-damaging local defeats on them. This study already has noted Dempsey's concern to anticipate the expected German counterattack on the eastern flank in the days after D-Day. Furthermore, his policy of holding reserves under army control also reflected his fear of German counterattack. Both of these approaches were very close to what Montgomery meant by balance: the art of arranging unit dispositions in such a manner that any enemy move had been anticipated and hence could be swiftly dealt with. Dempsey displayed this attitude during "Epsom" when the VIII Corps had managed to get a foothold on the strategic Hill 112, Though Dempsey recognized that to hold Hill 112, his form would elm have to hold Evrecy and Hill 113, he had insufficient troops to take hold these objectives because he "was convinced that the vital spot to hold was the Rauray gap." For he had calculated that this "was where the Germans would strike," and hence "concentrat[ed] everything to give the Germans a sound beating when they came in there," as they duly did.[97]

Generally, Dempsey's caution proved justified in that it prevented the Germans being presented with opportunities to use their undoubted tactical abilities to inflict local defeats on Anglo-Canadian forces. During "Epsom," both Dempsey and O'Connor rightly remained "anxious to strengthen and widen the bridgehead over the Odon before letting 11th Armored Division push on," as both feared that "too deep and narrow an advance" would enable the Germans to cut off the Allied salient with counterattacks from either flank."[98] Dempsey's caution, therefore, also manifested itself in his concern over exposed flanks—a consideration shared by Montgomery. As the advance of the XXX Corps on the northern sector of the early October "Gatwick" offensive would create an ever-lengthening, exposed northern flank, Dempsey instructed it both to advance on only a very narrow (one divisional) front and to deploy the bulk of its strength to protect this elongating flank.[99]

Though Dempsey shared his superior's caution, and perhaps occasional overcaution, he also carefully weighed the necessities of caution against other valid operational considerations. Like Montgomery, Dempsey could also be bold—could demand boldness from his subordinates—when he felt that this was required: Whether his subordinate commanders could deliver advances commensurate to Dempsey's bold demands was another matter. The army commander, for example, stressed the need for such urgency during Operation "Bluecoat," when he informed Bucknall, the commander of the XXX Corps, that "time was of the utmost importance."[100] Indeed, in the aftermath of the failure of "Bluecoat," Dempsey sacked Bucknall on the grounds that the corps commander allegedly had failed to inject sufficient urgency into his subordinates.

Dempsey clearly also shared that British doctrinal emphasis on extreme concentration that remained so prevalent in Montgomery's offensive operational methods and that contrasted with American techniques. On 13 June 1944 Dempsey noted in his diary that it was "clear now that Caen c[oul]d only be taken by a set piece assault and we did not have men or ammunition for that at the time."[101] Dempsey commented on the first abortive American drive on St Lô that "Bradley had obviously made his task more difficult by trying to buck the whole line instead of concentrating on punching a hole in one important sector."[102] Dempsey's emphasis on concentration was reflected in the Second Army's policy of meeting all resource demands made by its subordinate corps. According to Brigadier Stone, the Second Army's Chief Engineer, Dempsey had instructed his staff "to meet all demands" for men or stores made by corps "at once and without discussion."[103]

Dempsey's headquarters displayed a reliance on massively concentrated firepower that mirrored, if not exceeded, that emanating from the 21st Army Group. On 21 June 1944 Major-General Graham, the army group's chief administrative officer, commented that "the demands of Second Army for ammunition" were "fantastic" and "out of proportion to the real needs."[104] The conference the Second Army staff held on 27 October 1944 to discuss the projected "Gatwick" offensive illustrates the extent to which Dempsey's command desired to blast its way forward by weight of gunfire. This conference produced a carefully calculated requirement for 1,112 artillery guns for the operation—more than three-quarters of all the artillery pieces in the entire 21st Army Group. If the "Gatwick" fire-plan had been carried out according to this scheme, it would have been the largest Anglo-Canadian fire-program in the entire Northwest Europe campaign.[105]

Dempsey's methods also reflected Montgomery's concept of balance. Dempsey's control of reserves, engendered by his fear of German counterattacks, enabled him to deal quickly with any enemy countermoves before they could achieve significant success. Furthermore, Dempsey's conduct of the Second Army in Normandy revealed his utilization of a technique similar to Montgomery's concept of forcing the enemy off balance. One of Dempsey's motivations for "Goodwood" was what he called "tennis over the Orne." This involved striking "first on one side of the Orne and then on the other" to force the enemy to move reserve armor across the river, which permitted the British "to hit them with our air forces in the process of crossing when they were particularly vulnerable."[106] The Second Army could then exploit this opportunity by undertaking a major offensive.

In the early phases of the Normandy campaign, Montgomery remained critical of Dempsey's abilities—or rather his lack of experience—on air support matters. The fact that Montgomery's army group staff included senior officers like de Guingand, Belchem, and Richardson, who had gained considerable practical experience of such matters with the Eighth Army in North Africa, served to reinforce Montgomery's critical views. Given that air matters were coordinated principally at army level, the fact that Dempsey had previously only commanded a corps meant that he possessed little relevant experience. On 7 July 1944, for example, Montgomery told Brooke that "Dempsey and his staff do not know a very great deal yet about how to wield air power; and Dempsey himself has slipped up once or twice in the matter." Montgomery reassured the CIGS, however, that he was both "watching over this very carefully" and that he was confident that Dempsey would soon "get the form," even though at present he was too impatient.[107]

One of these "mistakes" appears to have been the manner in which the Second Army staff planned a proposed attack in early June to outflank Caen in conjunction with a drop of the 1st Airborne Division. On 11 June 1944, de Guingand informed Montgomery that he was "not very happy with the way in which planning was undertaken in Second Army."[108] The latter, he explained, had commenced detailed planning on the assumption that the use of the airborne division was definite, even though Leigh-Mallory, the Air Commander-in-Chief, had not yet approved its deployment. Leigh-Mallory's subsequent rejection of the plan as being potentially too costly in casualties, substantiated de Guingand's concerns. Consequently, all the staff work devoted to the plan proved to have been wasted. Dempsey was keen to get on with the difficult task of forging a way inland, although Montgomery's accusation that Dempsey was rushing his fences may reflect the accuser's great caution as much as Dempsey's impatience.

For the first few days of the Normandy campaign, Montgomery relied on de Guingand to supervise the arrangements for tactical air support. The latter, who had the necessary experience of air matters, headed the 21st Army Group Main Headquarters back at Southwick near Portsmouth. This arrangement initially proved necessary as the bridgehead was insufficiently large for the Allies to establish the headquarters of the Tactical Air Forces on French soil; as soon as this had been accomplished, de Guingand handed over air support arrangements "to the armies to control."[109] Similarly, in mid-June 1944, Montgomery sent Brigadier Richardson, his BGS(Plans), who now had relatively little work to do once the fighting had started, to act as a BGS(Air) at Dempsey's Second Army headquarters. According to Richardson, the lack of experienced staff officers from the Mediterranean campaigns at the Second Army joint army/air headquarters—together with the "unhelpful influence" of the tactical air commander "Mary" Coningham—had resulted in "co-operation [that] was ineffective."[110] Moreover, Dempsey not only shared his superior's appreciation of the power of Allied tactical air forces on the battlefield, but concurred with the Field Marshal that it was essential that land/air arrangements be directed at army level, and not at lower commands.[111]

Dempsey shared the conservative operational outlook demonstrated by Montgomery, for example, in his suspicion toward the British army's most secret weapon, the Canal Defense Light (CDL) tank.[112] Dempsey also proved reluctant to acquiesce to O'Connor's repeated demands for the introduction of armored personnel carriers (APCs). In July 1944 O'Connor had requested that surplus self-propelled artillery chassis be converted to

APCs for "Goodwood," but Dempsey turned him down. Only later, some time after Simonds had demonstrated the value of newly converted Canadian APCs during "Totalize," and after consistent demands from O'Connor, did Dempsey agree to seek Montgomery's permission to raise an APC regiment for the Second Army.[113]

Dempsey's military outlook also shared that sense of superiority often typical of the British officer in its suspicion of American military abilities. During the late August 1944 advance to the Seine, Dempsey—in an interview with the *Daily Telegraph*—blamed the Americans for delaying his advance by crossing over into the British sector. In reality, Montgomery had approved such a maneuver, and it was he who had to apologize to Bradley for Dempsey's lack of tact—an extremely ironic incident given that officers like de Guingand regularly had to apologize to the Americans for Montgomery's tactless comments. The frictions that existed between Dempsey and the Americans, however, were worn down during the rest of the campaign by his prolonged close cooperation with the First United States Army on his right flank.[114]

DEMPSEY'S HANDLING OF THE SECOND (BRITISH) ARMY

This analysis now briefly assesses Dempsey's conduct of the Second Army. Despite Montgomery's interference, Dempsey clearly proved a capable army commander who often displayed "fingertip feel" for the battle, who intervened when necessary, and who gripped his corps commanders during the break-in phase of offensives. Initially, however, Dempsey seems to have experienced major problems adjusting to his new level of command. His planning of the western outflanking attack on Caen in conjunction with the airborne drop was premature. His choice of ground for "Goodwood"—though understandable given the strategic context—was in tactical terms extremely flawed, because the constricted front only permitted O'Connor to commit his armored divisions into the assault one after the other. This was a major factor in the failure of the operation, as was the failure to deploy sufficient infantry to adequately support the armor. Dempsey's failure to appreciate these flaws constitutes a significant error in his generalship. Indeed, Dempsey admitted in 1946 that "Goodwood" was "not a very good operation tactically, but strategically it was a great success, even though we did get a bloody nose."[115]

In Normandy some dissatisfaction with the Second Army emanated from its subordinate corps. Dempsey's severest critic was Bucknall—notably after the latter had been relieved of his command. Probably with a good degree of ill feeling, Bucknall appealed vigorously against his dismissal and criticized the tasks the Second Army had set his corps. During the planning of "Bluecoat," Bucknall—after "weeks of study"—presented sound tactical reasons why the operation should be undertaken on different axes by just one corps instead of two, but Dempsey rejected this. To Colonel Browns, Bucknall wrote bitterly on 17 August 44 that Dempsey's "Bluecoat" plan was "untidy in conception" as it meant "launching my corps" across "difficult bocage country" on "a frontal assault" of the "heavily defended" Mont Pinçon feature. Bucknall insisted that his sacking was "grossly unfair" and then detailed what he believed to be Dempsey's motivations for this decision. During "Epsom," "Goodwood," and "Spring," Bucknall alleged, the Second Army "had launched formations badly to attack and even under the heaviest heavy bomber support the attacks eventually petered out untidily and expensively." He believed that "Dempsey could not afford the shadow of a fourth check" and had sacked him as a "scape-goat" to explain away the failure of the operation.[116]

Although this is neither objective nor conclusive evidence of Dempsey's failures, it illustrates poignantly both the frictions that existed between commanders at different levels in the command hierarchy and how their respective command functions influenced different appreciations of the operational situation that faced them. Despite this criticism, the evidence of the campaign as a whole indicates that Dempsey proved a competent commander who, not surprisingly, experienced initial difficulties as an inexperienced army commander—difficulties that ultimately he went a long way toward mastering.

To conclude, while this examination has demonstrated that historians can tackle the fallacy of Dempsey's historical obscurity, it also has revealed that a precise assessment of Dempsey's contribution to the operational conduct of the Northwest Europe campaign remains problematic. Dempsey's role clearly was more significant than the existing literature has indicated. Yet an assessment of how significant his contribution was depends fundamentally on an analysis of his role vis-à-vis Montgomery. Such an assessment, however, is obfuscated by the closeness and symbiotic nature of the two commanders' relationship, and by the ambiguities in the historical record; for together these factors confuse definitive appreciation of the authorship of crucial decisions.

The balance of the evidence leads to the slightly ambiguous conclusion that although Miles Dempsey's role as an army commander remained somewhat restricted due to his superior's interference, he was by no means the colorless cipher as suggested by much of the campaign's historical literature. The two faces of a seemingly Janus-like Dempsey do not sit together at all well; the image of Dempsey the introverted, subservient cipher, sidelined as Montgomery dealt direct with his corps commanders, rankles with the picture of Dempsey, the architect of "Goodwood," the competent commander with fingertip feel, willing to intervene with and firmly grip his corps commanders' break-in operations, and to keep tight control of reserves. Undoubtedly the reality of Dempsey's role in the campaign lies in some uneasy combination of these two contradictory images. Perhaps the latter picture may have been closer to the true Dempsey. That the former image has to date dominated the historical literature is due to Montgomery's suppressing influence on his subordinate's personality and to Dempsey's stoic toleration of the interventions of his superior, a forbearance based on Dempsey's recognition that Montgomery possessed an ability in the operational art of war that only was equaled by very few commanders in the British army of 1944.[117]

These ambiguities and uncertainties may be rather unsatisfactory, yet they serve to illustrate that this analysis is merely the start of the process whereby Miles Dempsey is rescued from an undeserved historical oblivion. Ultimately it seems unlikely that historians will ever pin down precisely Dempsey's contribution to the conduct of this campaign, given that the emergence of significant new documentary material relating to Dempsey is now unlikely. Dempsey's counterpart—the other army commander within the 21st Army Group—Henry "Harry" Crerar, also remains a "forgotten victor" of the campaign. However, there is not the same dearth of documentary evidence that relates to Crerar as there does with Dempsey. And it is to Crerar, and the First Canadian Army, that this study now turns.

CHAPTER 7

Crerar and the First Canadian Army

This chapter examines the contribution made by the First Canadian Army to the manner in which the 21st Army Group conducted the Northwest Europe campaign. This army was commanded by Lieutenant-General—from November 1944, General—Henry D. G. Crerar. To recapitulate, the contribution made at army level to the operational approach of the 21st Army Group was determined by the following: the functions of an army; the relationship between army group and army; and the extent to which army group operational methods were implemented at the level of army. The last two of these aspects are now examined with regard to Crerar's First Canadian Army.

CRERAR'S OPERATIONAL APPROACH

This analysis briefly explores, within the context of an army's operational functions, Crerar's operational approach in Northwest Europe. Three factors ensured that in this campaign Crerar's operational methods mirrored those of Montgomery: The latter was determined to disseminate his methods; Crerar had already been inculcated with Montgomery's approach back in 1942 as the latter's subordinate in Southeastern Command; and the British army had developed a broad doctrinal consensus from its experiences in the western desert.[1] The operational style of General Crerar and the First Canadian Army are now examined using the same categorization that was used earlier to analyze Montgomery's and Dempsey's approaches.

Crerar's operational methods, like Montgomery's, displayed strong concern to maintain the morale of his troops. His own cautious approach mirrored Montgomery's fears that setbacks would have an adverse impact on troop morale. For example, on 13 September 1944 Crerar told Montgomery of his concern that the morale boost gained by the recent rapid success at Le Havre "should not be more than lost by an unsuccessful attack on the next objective, Boulogne." To avoid this, Crerar ordered Simonds to take "more time, if necessary, in order to ensure a decisive assault."[2]

Crerar was also as concerned as Montgomery about avoiding heavy and unnecessary casualties. Crerar's 22 July 1944 Tactical Directive, his first instruction after assuming command in Normandy, stated that his "tactical methods" sought to both "defeat the enemy" and "spare us needless casualties."[3] Similarly, Crerar reported to Colonel Ralston, the Canadian Minister for National Defense, that Simonds had used novel methods in Operation "Totalize" to penetrate the strong German defensive position "without heavy casualties."[4] On occasion, this concern made the First Canadian Army reluctant to accept that impending operations would be difficult; its planning of operations to clear the Scheldt estuary, for example, was permeated with the expectation that the Germans would withdraw from Zeeland after only token resistance.[5]

The fact that Crerar was a career gunner may explain why he was as wedded to a doctrine of massive firepower as was Montgomery. In his 22 July directive, Crerar emphasized the need to employ "preliminary, prolonged, and overpowering fire" to avoid unnecessary casualties.[6] Like Montgomery, Crerar's Great War experiences as a gunner staff officer exerted a strong influence on his Second World War methods. Major-General Vokes, commanding the 1st Canadian Infantry Division, recounted that at a 1944 Eighth Army tactical conference in Italy, Crerar stunned those present by stating that they "should adopt [1918] Flanders tactics." According to Vokes, the conference chairman, Lieutenant-General Oliver Leese, "was too polite to tell" Crerar that "he was old fashioned."[7] Montgomery concurred with Vokes's assessment and confided spitefully to Brooke that Crerar had "gained the idea that all you need is a good fire-plan, and then the Germans all run away!!"[8]

Throughout the campaign, the First Canadian Army's operations displayed a reliance on firepower equal to that of Dempsey's Second (British) Army. The stated administrative policy of the 21st Army Group was immediately and unquestioningly to allocate the resources that each army requested they needed; arguments concerning "overinsurance" in resource requests would be settled after the battle had been fought. However, 21st Army Group suspended this policy temporarily after it received the First Canadian Army's 24 September request for the artillery ammunition it required for their Scheldt operations. The Canadian request provoked Colonel Oliver Poole, the Army Group's Colonel Q(Plans) to accuse the Canadians of seeking a degree of "administrative security" unjustified by the circumstances—in other words, "overinsurance."[9] The First Canadian Army stated their initial logistic requirement as 9,000 tons daily, falling to 6,000, whereas Second (British) Army requested 7,700 tons per day. However, at that time Dempsey's army had priority for resources while they undertook the crucial "Market-Garden" operation. This fact, plus the extant deficiency in logistical stocks and infrastructure that prevented daily supply from meeting demand, led Colonel Poole to conclude that Crerar's demands were excessive. Consequently, while the 21st Army Group allocated to both Dempsey's army and the headquarters, line of communication, all the resources they demanded,

Crerar's command only received 53 percent of the logistic tonnage it had requested.[10]

Crerar, however, was not just an old-fashioned Great War "weight of gun-fire" general, in that Vokes seems to have misunderstood Crerar's advocacy of Great War gunner techniques. In Normandy, Crerar stressed the use of surprise as well as firepower; he advocated "obtaining maximum surprise by eliminating prolonged preliminary bombardment" prior to the attack, and "substituting for it really overwhelming fire, from the air if possible, as the advance to close with the enemy commences."[11] It appears that by 1918 Flanders tactics Crerar actually meant the use of tactical surprise achieved by attacking without preliminary bombardment, rather than, as Vokes perceived it, just crude "weight of gunfire" methods.

Before Operations "Totalize" and "Veritable," Crerar stressed the need to gain tactical surprise as an alternative to simple reliance on overwhelming preliminary bombardment.[12] Simonds, as acting army commander, issued similar orders for Operation "Switchback," the 6 October 1944 attack on the Breskens Pocket.[13] These two methods—surprise and preliminary bombardment—were not opposites, but rather different emphases within a broadly similar approach. Seeking surprise, therefore, did not indicate abandonment of firepower doctrine; instead it meant the development of a more sophisticated, flexible, firepower-reliant operational approach. In this respect, Crerar's gunner thinking was relatively progressive. The flexible artillery tactics he advocated in August 1944 were subsequently adopted by the 21st Army Group as its firepower doctrine evolved during the next six months of combat. It was in the light of these recommended methods that Crerar was to claim somewhat exaggeratedly—but not without some justification—that his was the inspiration behind the novel methods used by Simonds in "Totalize."[14]

The impact of Crerar's relatively progressive firepower thinking remained limited, however, because these ideas remained rather theoretical and because he exerted only moderate influence on the genesis of operational fire-plans. Although Crerar had advocated a surprise attack for "Veritable" supported by barrage without preliminary bombardment, the fire-plan actually utilized saw the greatest preliminary bombardment of the campaign. This fire-plan was the brainchild of Horrocks, the commander of the XXX Corps, and of Brigadier Rawlins, his Corps Commander, Royal Artillery [CCRA]. Superficially, it appears that Rawlins sacrificed surprise in favor of the crude, devastating weight of shell of "a typical Monty set-up" with "bags of guns crammed on a narrow front."[15] Horrocks, though concerned over loss of surprise, appreciated that the sodden, restricted "Veritable" battlefield permitted him "no room for manoeuvre and no scope for cleverness," which left him compelled to simply "blast" his "way through."[16] Though Horrocks sacrificed tactical surprise by using preliminary bombardment, the Allies had already achieved operational surprise through extensive deception and security efforts that concealed the Allied buildup. Moreover, even though the fire-plan developed for Operation "Veritable" sacrificed surprise, it remained a progressive, ingenious, flexible one with excellent target discrimination.[17] This example attests to the ability of a capable corps commander, like Horrocks, to get his own way at Crerar's expense in planning the detailed corps battle.

Crerar's determination to tackle the tendency toward tactical overreliance on artillery firepower also suggests that he was not simply an old fashioned gunner general. On 5 August 1944, he admonished Canadian infantry to "drive on" just by "use of their own weapons," criticized the idea that sustained infantry advances were "impossible" without "colossal" artillery or aerial support, and observed that the Germans had repeatedly disproved this notion. Hence, though Crerar remained as wedded to firepower doctrine as any of the senior commanders in the 21st Army Group, he was not one of the most backward in terms of his tactical ideas.

Crerar and the First Canadian Army displayed an enthusiasm for use of aerial bombardment in direct support of land operations equal to that of Montgomery and Dempsey. Such assistance was pivotal to the operational plans for "Totalize," "Tractable," "Infatuate," and "Veritable." The similar attitude held at army group no doubt encouraged this enthusiasm within Crerar's staff. The 21st Army Group was keen to allocate its subordinate armies as many resources as possible, and usually initiated the first contacts with air commands over potential use of bombers; this encouraged both its subordinate armies not only to seek, but often to expect, the use of bombers in their operations.

In Normandy, another factor encouraged the First Canadian Army to seek extensive use of aerial bombing: Crerar remained enthusiastic to use such support because this was one tactical area that army could control as opposed to corps. Typically, the authority of an army commander was required to successfully negotiate with senior Allied air commanders for the provision of strategic bombing support. Crerar's concerns at being outshone by the tactically more capable Simonds reinforced his determination to utilize bomber support. Arranging this support ensured that Crerar and his army headquarters retained a key role in the operations of Simonds' II Canadian Corps toward Falaise. This remained the only practical way in which Crerar could compete with his tactically more capable subordinate.[18]

THE RELATIONSHIP BETWEEN ARMY GROUP AND THE FIRST CANADIAN ARMY

A key factor determining the contribution made by each army command to this campaign was its relationship with army group. As has been observed, the personalities and relationships of higher formation commanders remained crucial because executive power in headquarters was vested in the commander. This personality element was particularly prominent within the 21st Army Group because of the forcefulness of Montgomery's will and his resultant strong influence on his subordinates. Even though the current operational situation overwhelmingly influenced the way in which the army group treated its subordinate armies, the relationship between Montgomery and his commanders sometimes also exerted a major influence. In this relationship, the army group constituted the dominant partner, because it allocated tasks and resources to these army commands. Hence, the limits of what each army could achieve were determined substantially by prior decisions at army group allocating tasks and resources to these armies.

The evidence demonstrates that there existed significant differences in Montgomery's relationship with Crerar and the First Canadian Army on the one hand and with Dempsey and Second (British) Army on the other. Of the two armies, Second (British) Army enjoyed a more favorable relationship with army group. The role that the First Canadian Army played in the campaign was determined principally by the Montgomery-Crerar relationship. Though the cooperation between the two remained generally good, serious rents ran through the fabric of their relationship. One source of tension resulted from Montgomery's belief that Crerar was not up to the job of a field army command in such a vital campaign. This study now assesses the factors that lay behind the formation of this opinion.

Montgomery made clear his poor opinion of Crerar's abilities to those in whom he confided. While there is no reason to doubt that Montgomery meant what he said about Crerar, it should be remembered that the Field Marshal held forceful opinions, which often he expressed in extreme language; regularly he castigated as "useless" those who failed to impress him. This should be considered when Montgomery's opinions of his fellow commanders are examined. In December 1943, Montgomery made clear to the CIGS his negative appreciation of Crerar's ability. In July 1944 he reiterated this opinion, and stated that Crerar "will be quite unfit to command an Army" because he was "very prosy and stodgy."[19] Crerar's activities as an army commander during the Normandy campaign did little to alter Montgomery's poor opinion of his abilities. On 8 October 1944, while Crerar was on sick leave in England, Colonel Ralston conferred with Montgomery and noted that the latter felt Crerar to be "adequate but not a ball of fire," as an army commander, and certainly "not in the same parish" as Simonds.[20] Crerar, who became aware of Montgomery's hostility long before the D-Day landings, also noted the continued decline of their relationship as the Normandy battles unfolded. On 21 August 1944, Major-General Kitching, whom Simonds had just dismissed as the commander of the 4th Canadian Armored Division, recalled Crerar comforting him with the words, "It may not be long before Montgomery tries to remove me."[21]

Montgomery's poor opinion of Crerar resulted primarily from the fact that they were very different sorts of soldiers. Crerar did not fit Montgomery's conception of what a field commander should be. Montgomery was a decisive, inspirational, highly experienced officer dedicated to field command; Crerar was a ponderous, uninspiring, administratively focused general, who had never commanded a large formation in the field. Crerar, an excellent staff officer, was a skilled political player driven by "overweening ambition."[22] He had only assumed command of the I Canadian Corps through a series of chance circumstances, and though he wished desperately to lead this corps in active operations in Italy, events brought him back to England for "Overlord" before he could fulfill this wish.[23] Earlier he had rejected Montgomery's suggestion that he accept a demotion to command a division in Italy to gain vital operational command experience.[24]

Crerar did not command, as Montgomery conceived the word, because he was neither decisive nor able to grip his subordinates.[25] In September 1944, for instance, when discussing the impending operations to clear the Scheldt estuary, Crerar told Montgomery that his comments were only "tentative because my staff have not yet had adequate opportunity to analyze, and present to me, the various issues involved."[26] In contrast, Montgomery and Simonds made their decisions and then set the staff to work out the details. According to senior Canadian officers, Crerar was also too cold, aloof, humorless, "reserved, and self conscious" to be able to inspire his command.[27] He was also too pedantic to be inspirational—for instance, insisting in the field in Italy on proper paperwork and strict adherence to dress codes; his own written reports stood out for their prolixity.[28] In Northwest Europe, Brigadier Beament recalled seeing Lieutenant-Colonel Anderson, the army's G(Operations) first grade staff officer [GSOI(Ops)], returning despondently from a morning conference with Crerar because the general had spotted an incorrect map reference in Anderson's report of the previous night.[29] Crerar was hardly following Montgomery's maxim that commanders avoid detail and concentrate on the essentials. In late September 1944, Crerar's ponderous *modus operandi* was highlighted when Simonds made an "electrifying" impact on the army staff after he temporarily replaced the sick Crerar.[30]

Montgomery also believed that Crerar was a poor judge of men. On 7 July 1944 the Field Marshal informed Brooke that in Normandy, Major-General Keller, the 3rd Canadian Infantry Division commander, "has proved himself quite unfit to command a division." Montgomery went on to deride as "absurd" Crerar's earlier suggestion that Keller should be the next Canadian general to obtain a corps command.[31] Montgomery's concern with Crerar's judgment reflected his cognizance of the latter's growing antipathy toward Simonds. To Montgomery this feud represented an example of allowing personal feeling to get in the way of operational judgments—a weakness the ruthless Field Marshal fought to contain. Hence, even though Montgomery had "great personal affection" for Crerar, he refused to let this influence him into making "unsound" judgments of the Canadian General's military capabilities.[32]

Not only was Crerar an unsound judge of men, according to Montgomery, but he sometimes handled his subordinates badly. Crerar quarreled with Lieutenant-General Crocker, the commander of the I (British) Corps, within a day of the First Canadian Army becoming operational in Normandy. This prompted Montgomery to comment spitefully to Brooke that Crerar "thinks he is a great soldier, and he was determined to show it the moment he took command at 1200 [hours] 23 July. He made his first mistake at 1205 h[ou]rs; and his second after lunch."[33] Montgomery also believed that Crerar lacked patience and that he was not calm in the midst of a battle. For instance, during "Totalize"—the first battle fought in Normandy by Crerar and the First Canadian Army—Montgomery commented to Brooke that Crerar not only was "so anxious that he worries himself all day," but also failed to realize that "battles seldom go completely as planned."[34]

Montgomery's poor opinion of Crerar, however, was formed not just from operational considerations but also from political ones—or, more precisely, from the area where the operational and political realms of military decision-making blended together. For it was also Crerar's staunch defense of both the Canadian army's national interests and his own authority in overseeing these rights that prompted Montgomery's hostility toward him.[35] Crerar insisted on being a Canadian army commander instead of the compliant clone of a British commander that Montgomery wished him to be; as Brigadier Elliot Rodger, Simonds' Chief of Staff, commented, Crerar strove to ensure "that Canada is 'done right by' as far as it is humanly possible."[36]

By 1944, it had long been established that Canadian forces serving with the British army had the right, as a last resort, to refer any matter concerning them to the Canadian Government. Prior to D-Day, Crerar's position was that, as senior combatant officer of the Canadian forces in Europe, he had an inalienable responsibility to the Canadian government for all Canadian troops overseas.[37] Montgomery had already clashed with Crerar—then commanding the I Canadian Corps—on this issue in July 1942 over the Dieppe raid, which Canadian formations under Montgomery's command were to undertake. Crerar requested that he be present at 11th Fighter Group Headquarters, "the only place in England from which the operation could be effectively influenced once it had been launched."[38] Montgomery refused on the grounds that no commander could share his responsibility with, nor abrogate it to, another commander. Crerar refused to accept this denial of what he saw as his inalienable responsibility. Standing his ground, he warned Montgomery, his superior, that he would raise the issue at "the highest political levels" where, he added confidently, "the decision would go against" Montgomery; consequently, the British commander backed down.[39] Crerar later told Colonel Stacey, the Canadian official historian, that he had discerned then a pattern that was to be often repeated: Montgomery would "always go through a yellow light: but when the light turned red, he stopped."[40]

By 1944, while both the War Office and Montgomery accepted the Canadian right of referral, the key issue was which officer should exercise this right. Montgomery maintained that the proper channel for this right was the Chief of Staff at Canadian Military Headquarters [CMHQ] in London, Lieutenant-General Stuart. CMHQ dealt with the War Office, while the First Canadian Army dealt with British operational commands; there remained, however, a continuing debate on the precise relationship between these two Canadian commands. Montgomery remained concerned that Crerar's defense of Canadian national military autonomy would be detrimental to the conduct of operations. Moreover, if Montgomery accepted that Crerar was the correct channel for this referral, it followed that Crerar had responsibility for Canadian forces within the 21st Army Group but outside Crerar's First Canadian Army. The units concerned were the 3rd Canadian Infantry Division and the 2nd Canadian Armored Brigade, both serving under the I (British) Corps in Dempsey's Second (British) Army and earmarked for the D-Day assault. Montgomery drew encouragement for his resistance to Crerar's demands from his 18 May 1944 meeting with the Canadian Prime Minister, Mackenzie King, who assured the British commander that he would not allow political considerations to undermine operational ones.[41] An arrangement where Crerar exercised the right of referral affronted Montgomery's narrow military mind as an incorrect command organization; how could Crerar, a subordinate, have a responsibility that circumvented his superior, Montgomery, in dealing direct with the Canadian government concerning troops outside's Crerar's command?[42]

As often before, however, Montgomery could not shift his thinking from its narrow operational focus to contemplate the politico-military, Imperial, and inter-Allied dimensions of military decision-making—failings that both Crerar and Brooke recognized.[43] In the months preceding "Overlord," Montgomery argued when denying Crerar's exercise of the right of referral that the Canadian "would be treated by him as any other [subordinate] army commander."[44] Crerar rightly denounced this spurious assertion with the statement, "I do not think, for a minute, that Monty assumes the same attitude to, and powers over, Bradley . . . as he does in respect to Dempsey." Crerar reasoned correctly that the responsibility for exercising this right of referral should be his rather than Stuart's, because only the senior Canadian operational commander within the 21st Army Group would "directly bear the result of any decisions" made on how these forces were employed.[45]

Through defending his right to exercise this power of referral, Crerar also sought to maintain his own power base within the Canadian army, particularly against encroachment on his powers by Stuart at CMHQ. However, Crerar also remained genuinely concerned to protect the constitutional position of the Canadian army. Crerar, when defending Canadian interests, resolutely stood his ground against the forceful Montgomery; whereas Stuart, in contrast, admitted that he found it impossible to do so. Indeed, Crerar consistently defended Canadian army interests throughout the war. In early 1944 he systematically chipped away at the reluctance of Leese, the Eighth Army commander, to group all Canadian formations in Italy under their own national corps headquarters. Montgomery's well-known egotism, pride, and dislike of not getting his own way made him resent being stood up to in this manner by a commander like Crerar whose Dominion status afforded protection against Montgomery's disapproval.[46] Montgomery did not tolerate dissent among his subordinate commanders, and in autumn 1944 allowed O'Connor to be poached to become an army commander in India after the latter had questioned his demand for the summary dismissal of the American General Silvester.[47] Much of Montgomery's bad feeling toward Crerar, therefore, was simply a result of pique, of wounded vanity.

This simmering dispute with Montgomery in the months preceding "Overlord" was finally resolved to Crerar's satisfaction after he discussed the matter with Brooke on 10 June 1944, Crerar noted that Brooke, clearly annoyed at Montgomery's inability to grasp the wider aspects of senior field command, had responded that "notwithstanding anything Monty might say," Crerar "was bound to be responsible to the Canadian government, in the last resort, for the operational employment of all Canadian troops in the 21st Army Group."[48] Brooke's unwavering patronage of Montgomery throughout the war, therefore, was not merely a blinkered one; Brooke was prepared to show his protégé the red light when the latter overstepped the mark.[49]

Although Crerar strove to establish in principle the constitutional relationship between the British and Canadian armies, he did not believe that this principle would actually be required; this debate "remained academic and theoretical."[50] This is significant, because it was easy—as Montgomery did—to interpret Crerar's determination to establish the letter of the law as an indication that he remained only half-heartedly committed to military cooperation with the British. The great irony, however, was that nothing could be farther from the truth. For despite appearances, Crerar remained determined to fully cooperate with the British. Crerar's determination to do so was illustrated in his May 1944 correspondence with senior Canadian officers over what scenarios would justify the withdrawal of Canadian forces from their cooperation with the British. Crerar's 19 May 1944 instructions from the Canadian Chief of the General Staff, Lieutenant-General Murchie, stated that Canadian forces might be withdrawn from cooperation with the British after consideration of the following: whether these forces had been given a task that was not "a practicable operation of war," or one that "with the resources available" was not "capable of being carried out with reasonable prospects of success," or one where "the extent of prospective losses" did not match "the importance of the results prospectively to be achieved."[51] Crerar's utter conviction to cooperate fully was attested by his response that on occasions "it may be necessary" for Canadian forces "to attempt the seemingly 'impracticable'" for the benefit of the wider campaign.[52] One wonders if there were any British commanders who would have gone so far as to state that they were prepared to attempt an operation that was clearly "not on" on the grounds of its wider benefit for the campaign.

That Crerar and other senior Canadian officers in the theater remained committed to full cooperation, even when given tasks beyond their resources, proved evident during the Scheldt operations; here Montgomery allocated them a task in terrible sodden conditions that was beyond their resources.[53] Unfortunately, Crerar's constant defense of Canadian national interests obscured from the British his real desire to cooperate fully, and hence served to undermine the very Anglo-Canadian cooperation for which he strove. The irony of this situation was compounded by the fact that Crerar's defense of Canadian interests remained largely unnecessary; the constitutional fallback positions for which he fought were never actually needed in Northwest Europe.[54]

This Canadian determination to cooperate fully was manifested frequently on the battlefields of Europe, and typically the cooperation between the British and Canadians forces in both Italy and Northwest Europe proved excellent.[55] This good cooperation resulted partly from the last four years of training together in the United Kingdom, which had allowed both sides to adjust to each other's idiosyncrasies and become comfortable in their cooperation.[56] It also resulted from the fact that First Canadian Army Headquarters was Anglo-Canadian in composition. After the dispatch of the I Canadian Corps to Italy, manpower constraints meant that the First Canadian Army's continued existence remained practicable only as a hybrid Anglo-Canadian entity. As a result, and in order to improve cooperation, both governments agreed prior to "Overlord" that up to 50 percent of the army's staff appointments could be filled by British officers. In practice, however, the actual figure did not rise above 15 percent, and all the senior appointments remained in Canadian hands.[57]

At times, however, there existed considerable tensions in the Anglo-Canadian relationship. There was some validity to Canadian accusations that the British sometimes displayed an attitude of "colonial" superiority toward their Dominion allies.[58] Leese's criticisms of Lieutenant-General Burns in Italy, and his suggestion that the latter's I Canadian Corps be disbanded, prompted an unusually bitter complaint from Crerar to Stuart that "the Englishman's traditional belief in the superiority of the Englishman" meant that "no Canadian or American" commander, unless they possessed "phenomenal qualities," was "ever rated as high as an equivalent Britisher."[59] British commanders found the existence of Canadian higher formations, with their corresponding national requirements, a military inconvenience that limited British operational flexibility.[60] Equally, Canadian defense of their military autonomy was fueled by fears that the British would use Canadian forces piecemeal as they had been in the 1941 War Office Exercise "Victor."[61]

In the light of these factors, it is pertinent here to consider whether Montgomery's judgment on Crerar was fair. In general, the Field Marshal's judgment on military appointments was highly regarded by his colleagues. Crucially, many commanders recognized Montgomery's judgments as being relatively objective in that he placed greater emphasis on ability to do the job than on the regimental traditions and interests, or on the patronage system of "the old boy network" that pervaded the British army. Montgomery's formation of his opinions, however, had serious weaknesses: He made judgments quickly, and once made, little changed them; he had several fixations such as weeding out elderly commanders; he rarely gave officers a second chance if they initially failed to live up to his expectations; and he trusted only those whom he had taught and whose careers he had himself nurtured. Given these factors, Montgomery clearly was not immune to making mistakes with appointments. Not surprisingly, therefore, there was no truly objective voice assessing the abilities of senior commanders in the British army during the last eighteen months of the Second World War.

Was Montgomery's opinion that Crerar possessed limited operational abilities a fair assessment? Notwithstanding the fact that Montgomery's dislike of Crerar stemmed from the politico-military disputes previously discussed, his opinion on Crerar's operational abilities was broadly correct, if slightly exaggerated; the political disputes probably reinforced Montgomery valid operational suspicions of Crerar. The Field Marshal, however, believed these two aspects to be inextricably interconnected. Montgomery judged that Crerar's national approach impinged on his capability to make objective operational decisions. Crerar's operational handling of the First Canadian Army was at best merely competent—but what else could be expected from a commander who had not commanded a large formation in the field? It is Crerar's handling of the First Canadian Army in Northwest Europe that this study now assesses.

From December 1941 until October 1943 Crerar was de facto commander of the I Canadian Corps in the United Kingdom under the then Lieutenant-General Montgomery's Southeastern Command. The most striking aspect of the correspondence between Crerar and Montgomery during this period is the extent to which the Canadian parroted Montgomery's advice when issuing his own policy guides.[62] Many of these stand out for their banality rather than their incisiveness. Moreover, when Montgomery gave his opinion on some matter, notably appointments, Crerar frequently replied that this advice merely confirmed his own opinions on the subject; this was stated so regularly that one becomes skeptical of the veracity of these responses.[63] An examination of this correspondence reveals that the flow of operational ideas was primarily one way—from Montgomery to Crerar—despite the latter's efforts at the time to play up his contribution to this debate.[64]

Crerar's operational abilities in this campaign remained limited firstly because he rejected Montgomery's quite correct maxim that operational command in war was a "full time job for one man."[65] Crerar was not, indeed could not be, dedicated full time to operational matters, because he also had administrative responsibilities as the senior Canadian officer overseas. Throughout the latter half of the war, Crerar sought to maintain a firm grip on this administrative authority, zealously fending off the encroachments of Stuart's CMHQ in London. For Crerar's administrative role was the power base behind his Canadian army career, particularly his grip on appointments that enabled him to act as a "kingmaker."[66] Crerar could not be a dedicated operational commander, and it is hard to imagine how any field commander who was also senior Canadian officer overseas could be dedicated wholly to operations, unless (like Simonds) he was prepared substantially to sacrifice Canadian interests in favor of Allied operational requirements.[67] It was again ironic that Crerar, despite his willingness to cooperate, failed to see the adverse impact his administrative position had on the strict operational aspects of this cooperation.

That Crerar was not a full-time operational commander is revealed by an analysis of the nonoperational matters with which he dealt during the campaign. Although Crerar did delegate some of his administrative responsibilities to Stuart once the First Canadian Army became operational in France, Crerar retained extensive commitments on general Canadian army matters while commanding the First Canadian Army in the field.[68] In the month of August 1944, during Operations "Totalize" and "Tractable," Crerar received, dealt with, or issued fifteen pieces of substantial correspondence on non-First Canadian Army operational matters; this figure excludes his work on general appointment issues. In September 1944, during operations to open up the channel ports and the Scheldt, Crerar dealt with twenty-nine such pieces of correspondence. For perspective in June 1944, before the First Canadian Army became operational in the field, Crerar dealt with fifty such communications.[69] Crerar's administrative commitments remained onerous even during the burden of commanding an army in vitally important active operations. In stark contrast, Dempsey had no such commitments, not even formal appointment responsibilities, which were dominated by Montgomery.[70] Consequently, according to Bill Williams, Montgomery "correctly" felt that Crerar was "more of a Quartermaster-General than a Field Commander."[71]

Crerar's operational judgment and decisions also proved not always completely sound. Evidence for this may be discerned by comparing his views on the recommendations made by the G(Plans) section at the First Canadian Army with those of Simonds. It is widely accepted that Simonds was one of the most effective corps commanders in Northwest Europe, who possessed penetrating operational judgment. If Crerar and Simonds disagreed on the merit of these G (Plans) recommendations, one might conclude that Crerar's decisions on practicalities—rather than the generalities—lacked the perceptive grasp that Simonds displayed. Crerar's First Canadian Army G (Plans) section drew up appreciations of imminent and future operations to help the army commander formulate his plans. Headed by Lieutenant-Colonel Pangman, this G (Plans) section produced a prolific amount of work in Northwest Europe. However, on at least two occasions, Simonds—when his opinion had been requested by Crerar—savagely criticized recommendations made by Pangman that Crerar previously had endorsed. First, in September 1944, during the planning phase of operations to clear the Scheldt estuary, Simonds produced a bitterly critical appreciation that represented "one of the most striking and original tactical statements of the campaign."[72] In it Simonds savaged Pangman's assumption that the Canadian forces could liberate the Breskens pocket, the German-held southern bank of the Scheldt estuary, without meeting any significant enemy resistance.[73]

The second occasion concerned the plans drawn up between November 1944 and January 1945 for an intended future attack, code-named "Siesta," an operation that the campaign's historical literature has all but ignored. The plan for "Siesta" involved a single divisional attack from the eastern flank of the "Island"—the area between Arnhem and Nijmegen bordered by the rivers Neder Rijn in the north and Waal in the south and by the Pannerden Canal in the east. The objective of "Siesta" was to advance the Allied eastern flank to the line of the Pannerden Canal, thus securing a frontage that could be more economically held and that, by securing the lock gates, prevented the enemy from deliberately flooding the "Island." Terrain conditions and other operational requirements meant that the Canadians postponed the operations several times and ultimately decided that it should be canceled.[74]

Initially, in late November, Crerar had informed Montgomery that Canadian troops had to complete "Siesta" before "Veritable" could "be prepared."[75] This was an erroneous judgment, as was subsequently demonstrated by the success of "Veritable" in February 1945 despite the fact that "Siesta" had not been undertaken. By January 1945, with the preparations for "Veritable" almost complete, Pangman presented another appreciation of "Siesta" that recommended that the operation be carried out before or during "Veritable," and Crerar accepted this advice. Simonds rejected Pangman's argument that "Siesta" afforded significant flank protection to "Veritable." Simonds also contradicted Pangman by stating that the enemy's deliberate flooding of the "Island" benefited the Canadian defense as much as that of the Germans. Simonds concluded that it was only necessary to undertake "Siesta" in the spring when dry terrain made the threat of German attack both significant and imminent. Although Crerar previously had recognized this point, he still concluded that "Siesta" should be carried out immediately to coincide with "Veritable." At a conference on 22 January 1945 Horrocks concurred with Simonds' view, and consequently Crerar scrapped the project. Simonds' position, when compared with that of Crerar and Pangman, is convincing: He rightly believed that "Siesta" constituted an unnecessary diversion that did not facilitate the real business in hand, Operation "Veritable."[76]

In contrast to the First Canadian Army, there is no extant documentation that confirms the existence of a G (Plans) section at Second (British) Army, despite Montgomery's recommendation on 31 January 1944 that each army should have one.[77] This makes the question of why Pangman was so prolific more interesting. Lieutenant-Colonel Anderson, a close friend of Pangman, felt at the time that the latter anticipated future operations and prepared appreciations in advance in case Crerar required them, and the existing documentation suggests that this was often the case.[78] However, at other times Pangman's appreciations were drawn up on the direct orders of either Crerar or his army Chief of Staff, Brigadier Churchill Mann.[79] This suggests that Crerar relied heavily on these G (Plans) appreciations in forming his opinions and decisions. This fits the often stated view that Crerar (unlike Simonds) did not conceive his own plans but relied on his staff to do so.[80]

Crerar's operational decision-making also was complicated by his defense of Canadian national interest, and this caused Montgomery great concern. Crerar remained determined to keep Canadian formations under their national command—an inconvenience for Montgomery in his efforts to maintain balanced dispositions. After the war, Montgomery complained that when the II Canadian Corps had become widely stretched in the early Scheldt operations, Crerar proved reluctant to transfer the 2nd Canadian Division on its far flank to the adjacent I (British) Corps; in contrast, Simonds recognized this operational need immediately.[81] Crerar also proved reluctant initially to have the British XXX Corps spearhead the "Veritable" attack, even though its future role in the Rhine crossing meant that it had to be deployed on the southern sector of Crerar's frontage, which constituted the only sensible axis of advance for "Veritable." Indeed, Crerar only abandoned his policy of "keeping Canadian formations together" on 16 January 1945, and instead allowed them for the first time to "be moved, to meet op[erational] requirements, irrespective of any 'national' aspects."[82]

At times Crerar also displayed a less-than-perfect grasp of the operational context in which Canadian operations were undertaken. For instance, in late November 1944 Montgomery first broached the subject of an operation akin to the canceled early October "Gatwick" offensive. This plan involved an attack from the Nijmegen bridgehead towards the southeast, and this eventually became Operation "Veritable." On 28 November Crerar replied to Montgomery that it was not "practicable to initiate any such operation at this time."[83] The Field Marshal's exasperated response reiterated that this was a long-term plan that he never intended to carry out in the immediate future.[84] With hindsight, it is hard to comprehend how Crerar could think that Montgomery could order such an operation to be launched immediately at a time so obviously unsuited for its undertaking. Perhaps Crerar had the recent "Market-Garden" scenario in his mind, during which Montgomery—hoping to seize a golden strategic opportunity to exploit enemy weakness—atypically ordered an operation to commence despite the existence of an inadequate administrative situation. However, by late November the theater situation was far different from that of early September; dismal weather, waterlogged terrain, strained logistics, fragile morale, and a largely revitalized enemy force all precluded a full-scale army group offensive. Crerar ought to have recognized that this situation was obvious to Montgomery.

There also were other examples when Crerar's operational handling of the First Canadian Army remained weak. John English criticized Crerar's failure to intervene directly in the conduct of "Totalize." In contrast, in mid-June Dempsey intervened decisively to shift the axis of advance of the 7th Armored Division toward Villers Bocage in order to exploit a weak spot in the German front. Crerar erred in not overruling Simonds' understandably cautious decision to wait for the second bombing run despite the swifter-than-expected success of the first phase of "Totalize." It was not surprising that Crerar failed to recognize this decisive moment. He lacked the "finger-tip feel" for the battle that a commander as skillful as Montgomery or Dempsey possessed, and "simply did not know [operationally] as much as Simonds." As a result Simonds lacked "the usual counsel, help, and coercion that might have been received from an army headquarters," and thus "could not have been more alone."[85]

Montgomery felt that although Crerar handled the Seine crossings well, his conduct of operations during the rapid advance to the Scheldt area in Holland left much to be desired. [86] It is surprising that during the 1944–45 campaign the often scathing Montgomery seldom criticized openly the performance of his subordinate commanders in either his own contemporary notes or in his confidences to Brooke and Simpson. This restraint was due both to the abilities of these subordinates and to Montgomery's concerns to sustain morale. In contrast, he freely castigated officers in other commands such as SHAEF, Bomber Command, Allied Armies Italy, and the United States armies. Montgomery did not record in ink any criticism of the commanders involved in the partly unsuccessful "Market-Garden" offensive, and virtually the only corps commander to receive open criticism during the campaign was Bucknall when he was dismissed.

It is, therefore, striking that one of Montgomery's rare criticisms to Brooke on his senior subordinates alleged that Crerar's operations "since crossing the Seine have been badly handled and very slow."[87] This message was written under the very rare War Office "Guard" security classification, the existence of which has not been yet brought out in the campaign's literature. The "Guard" classification was reserved for use by only the highest British commanders relating "messages of far reaching importance or controversial matters which must never be known to the United States."[88] Even the existence of the "Guard" procedure was never to be disclosed to the Americans. Montgomery used it for his correspondence with Brooke and Simpson when castigating Eisenhower during the lengthy dispute on theater strategy and command.[89]

As one of very few examples in the campaign of direct criticism made by Montgomery of his senior subordinates, this comment seems particularly significant. Paul Dickson has interpreted this particular criticism as the product of Montgomery and Crerar's serious disagreement of 2–3 September 1944. The Field Marshal clashed with Crerar on the second after the latter ordered the Canadian 2nd Infantry and 4th Armored Divisions to halt, the former at Dieppe to absorb over 1,000 reinforcements. Crerar ordered the halt even though Dempsey's forces were over 100 miles ahead of the Canadians and still advancing. That evening Montgomery, newly promoted to Field Marshal, became irritated by Crerar's sluggishness and signaled that both Crerar's armored divisions should "push forward with all speed" and that he did "not consider this" a time for any division "to halt for maintenance."[90] An irked Crerar responded testily that the halt was "quite essential" and that Montgomery could "be assured that there is no lack of push or rational speed" in the First Canadian Army.[91] Crerar pointed out that the narrowness of his front prevented him deploying more than two divisions abreast, and thus the halt had no real impact on the Canadian advance. Yet Crerar misunderstood that his superior actually had objected to the halting of one of Crerar's armored divisions, not the halt of the 2nd Infantry Division at Dieppe. Crerar, again, seems to have been somewhat out of touch with his superior's thinking.[92]

The next day Montgomery summoned Crerar to an operational conference, but Crerar had already arranged to attend the ceremony honoring the Canadian casualties of the 1942 Dieppe raid. Through signals error, the fact of Crerar's absence was not conveyed to Montgomery, who waited in vain for Crerar to turn up.[93] It seems that Crerar deliberately ensured that no messages preventing him from attending the ceremony reached him.[94] During a stormy meeting later that evening, Montgomery indicated with the words "Our ways must part" that Crerar was to be removed.[95] However, when Crerar stated that he would raise the matter with higher authority—the Canadian government and the Joint Chiefs of Staff—Montgomery precipitously backed down. A few days later the Field Marshal wrote a sickly note of apology; once again the light had changed from yellow to red.[96] At that moment, Montgomery "would have been happy to replace Crerar whom he had never wanted as one of his army commanders, but he was not prepared to risk a political row" in doing so.[97] The souring of the relations between the two commanders was probably a combination of these two disputes, which exacerbated Montgomery's earlier suspicions arising from Canadian failures in the hot August days in Normandy.[98]

One cannot be certain whether the interpretation of Dickson, whose work appears favorably disposed toward Crerar, is correct. However, these disagreements, for which both commanders must accept some responsibility, made Montgomery more critical of Crerar. The Canadian attributed the fact that his superior lately had been "pretty trying" to Montgomery's loss of overall control of land forces and his promotion to Field Marshal, which both "accentuated" his "mental disturbance [sic]."[99] As Montgomery had long held adverse views of Crerar in private, it is likely that this disagreement merely prompted him to be less restrained in stating his opinions to Brooke. This quarrel did not cause the rift between these two commanders but triggered the long-standing underlying tension that existed between them.

Crerar's handling of the first part of the Scheldt operations again demonstrated his ponderous style. This period witnessed a protracted series of planning conferences that achieved little on the ground.[100] Moreover,

Dempsey felt that Crerar's forces undertook sluggishly the essential prelimi-
naries to these Scheldt operations, the clearance of the channel ports.[101]
Given the modest German garrison at Le Havre, the British hoped that the
Canadians would avoid repeating the methodical style of operation that
David Strangeways reported they had utilized at Rouen. According to de
Guingand, after Strangeways had reached a Canadian brigade that claimed
to be unable to advance due to stiff opposition, he "got tired of waiting and
drove" into Rouen without meeting a single German.[102] There was an understandable lack of enthusiasm within Crerar's Army for the impending operations in the Scheldt, which clearly would be a dismal slog through appalling
conditions of mud and flooding in a strategic backwater. Crerar appeared
unable to inspire his army to rise fully to this dreadful challenge.[103] In contrast, the arrival of the "gung-ho" Simonds as acting army commander on 26
September (due to Crerar's illness) changed all this; his immediate impact
was like "a breath of fresh air."[104]

On 22 October 1944, Crerar—now recovered from his illness—informed
Simonds that he would reassume command on the last day of that month.
However, on 24 October Brooke, in compliance with Montgomery's request,
asked Crerar not to return from sick leave until after Simonds had completed
the Scheldt operations. The pretext was that Montgomery did not want the
disturbance that would result from a change of command in the middle of a
particular set of operations. However, the real reason was that Montgomery
simply wanted to keep Crerar away and give Simonds his head.[105] Charles
Foulkes, promoted to acting commander of the II Canadian Corps in
Simonds' place, later told Stacey that he recollected Montgomery telling him
that Crerar would not be returning.[106] Crerar recognized the personal slight,
yet nevertheless on 25 October acquiesced to the British request.[107]

The nature of Crerar's resumption of command was as surprising as the
absence of attention to this event in the campaign's literature is curious.
Incredibly, although Crerar returned to army headquarters on 7 November
1944—the date given in the historical literature as his resumption of command—he did not take command of the First Canadian Army for a further
two days; for no less than forty-eight hours Crerar had to watch Simonds, his
erstwhile—and again soon to be—subordinate, perform Crerar's own responsibilities. Why this was so remains shrouded in uncertainty.[108]

One must be careful, however, not to exaggerate Crerar's operational
failings. On the whole his command of the First Canadian Army in Northwest Europe was competent—perhaps more so than some had expected.
Montgomery recognized back in 1942 that Crerar had his merits, praising his
handling of the troops under his command during several exercises. Equally,
there is evidence to support Crerar's assertion during the "Overlord" plan-

ning that it was he who drew Montgomery's attention to the threat of a German counterattack against the eastern flank of the Normandy bridgehead.[109] Moreover, Crerar supervised the preparations for "Veritable" capably, even if the presence of corps commanders as able as Simonds and Horrocks helped ensure that potential mistakes were kept to a minimum.[110]

Crerar also deserves some credit both for his emphasis on achieving surprise by abandoning preliminary bombardment, and on maintaining the momentum of Allied penetrations. While it is undeniable these were the broad parameters within which Simonds drew up his "Totalize" plan, Crerar went too far in claiming the credit for the innovative approach used in this operation; this was manifestly the product of Simonds' fertile mind. This claim echoed Crerar's 1942 assertions that Montgomery's advice merely confirmed the opinions he already had reached. It also mirrored his exaggerated claims that the success of "Overlord" was due largely to training exercises like "Pirate" that utilized the lessons learned by the Canadian sacrifice at Dieppe.[111] However, Crerar's exaggerated claims should not distract attention from his real contributions to the campaign. Crerar's emphasis on surprise resulted partially from his creditable determination to study both German views of Allied techniques and the tactics the enemy developed to counter them.[112] Though Montgomery was a didactic general who placed great weight on assimilating the lessons of combat experience, in this campaign he appears to have given relatively little attention to German tactical views.[113]

On balance, Crerar's conduct of the First Canadian Army in Northwest Europe was competent, rather than poor; he was probably "a better general than Montgomery was prepared to admit."[114] Brooke's profession before "Overlord" that he had "full confidence" in Crerar was proved correct.[115] Furthermore, Crerar's weaknesses did not exert a great impact on the campaign, for his subordinate corps commanders—Crocker and Simonds—remained very capable. Major-General Vokes believed that though Crerar lacked field command experience, he made "quite a successful Army commander" because he acted merely as "chairman of the board" by holding his experienced subordinates on a loose rein.[116]

Prior to "Overlord," however, Crerar was the only realistic choice for command. In operational terms he was an improvement on McNaughton who, though a genius at administration, was a poor field commander—as Exercise "Spartan" showed—who neglected training for the impending Second Front.[117] Consequently, in late 1943 Brooke, abetted by Ralston, engineered the demise of McNaughton for the make of the success of the D-Day invasion.[118] In the vacuum formed by McNaughton's departure there was no Canadian officer matching Crerar's stature, and his only serious rival—

Simonds—was too inexperienced to assume an army command; by the end of Normandy this position had, however, completely changed.

Some key similarities existed between the situation facing Crerar and that of Burns's I Canadian Corps in Italy. Initially Burns's experienced divisional commanders—Hoffmeister and Vokes—had reasonable confidence in their superior, despite his inexperience, as long as Burns held them on a loose rein permitting them to fight their own battles. However, British criticism of Burns revolved around the fact that he would not command or grip his subordinates. To protect Burns from Leese's criticism, Stuart advised him to "exert his power of command" and to "express his personality more."[119] It was, therefore, ironic that Burns, in endeavoring to exert his will on his subordinates, not only failed to gain the confidence of Leese, but also lost the confidence of his subordinates. The latter development ended Canadian resistance to British criticism of Burns, who was consequently replaced in November 1944. Indeed, Vokes's perceptive observation that "command is often not what you do but the way that you do it" seems to have been the crux of Burns's problems in Italy; the dour corps commander—sardonically nicknamed "smiler"—was "not a member of the 'club' and made no attempt to be."[120]

The critical issue, however, is whether Montgomery's limited faith in Crerar's abilities—irrespective of whether this was justified—affected the manner in which the 21st Army Group conducted the campaign. Did Montgomery's concerns influence the tasks and resources Montgomery allocated to Crerar's Army during the campaign? In general the Field Marshal treated the First Canadian Army less favorably than Dempsey's Second (British) Army. This was at least partly due to Montgomery's distrust of Crerar, although he was equally suspicious of the majority of Canada's inexperienced senior formation commanders—with the exception of Simonds.[121] On 8 October 1944 Ralston discussed with Montgomery who might be appointed commander of the First Canadian Army if both Crerar and Simonds became casualties. Montgomery replied that there was not "any Canadian" in whom he had "the necessary confidence" and that he could only suggest "one of the Corps Commanders in Second [British] Army."[122]

It is interesting to speculate which British corps commander Montgomery would have suggested. From hindsight Horrocks may seem the best candidate, yet in 1969 Montgomery stated that he would "never have given him an army."[123] Montgomery also had informed Brooke in 1945 that "Crocker would not command an army in the field."[124] The performance of the XII Corps' commander, Ritchie, had been competent rather than spectacular, so his chances of promotion seemed slim.[125] At this time O'Connor's relationship with Montgomery was no longer at its height but was not yet completely

soured. It seems plausible that O'Connor may have been promoted, especially as Montgomery considered him rather old to be a corps commander.

Montgomery's concerns over the abilities of senior Canadian commanders mirrored Lease's attitude in Italy during 1944. Leese was reluctant to
make use of the I Canadian Corps, because Burns lacked both "tactical
sense" and the "power of command," Leese remained loathe to place experienced British formations under Burns's corps command, yet this formation lacked sufficient Canadian forces to reach full combat power without
British reinforcement. The choice facing Leese was slack; to give the corps
"a task beyond the powers of the Commander" or one "below the capacity of
the troops."[126]

In Normandy, Montgomery's limited faith in Crerar prompted him to
keep the First Canadian Army back in England. The Field Marshal confided
to Brooke that he was keeping Crerar "out" of the battle "as long as I can,"
allowing Dempsey's Second (British) Army to control no less than five
corps.[127] There were sound operational reasons for this, because the con-
fined area of the lodgment area could take an additional corps headquarters
but could not accommodate the ancillary troops associated with an army
headquarters. However, Montgomery also manipulated this valid reason as a
justification for keeping Crerar out of the battle.

Montgomery's distrust of Crerar's abilities also influenced the tasks he
set the latter's command. On 11 July 1944 Brooke informed Montgomery
that Canadian opinion left him no choice but to accept that Canadian forces
would all have to serve under their national army and be commanded by a
Canadian. Brooke made clear, however, that Montgomery should "keep
[Crerar's] army small" and give it "the less important jobs."[128] On 22 July,
the day that the First Canadian Army became operational in France, Montgomery responded to Brooke that he would only give Crerar "tasks within
his capabilities."[129]

Given Montgomery's attitude, it appears curious that in August 1944 the
First Canadian Army assumed a spearhead role by undertaking Operations
"Totalize" and "Tractable." It was other operational circumstances, rather
than faith in Crerar, that prompted Montgomery's choice. With the Americans advancing swiftly in Operation "Cobra" and threatening to outflank the
German forces from the south, it became imperative for the 21st Army
Group to rapidly advance southeast to meet the Americans near Trun, sur-
rounding the German forces in the Falaise pocket. This objective necessitated an immediate attack from the Caen area down the main road to Falaise.
Simonds' II Canadian Corps held this part of the front. Before Crerar's Army
became operational, Simonds' Corps served under Dempsey's Second
(British) Army, spearheading the advance south from Caen in Operation

"Spring." Once the First Canadian Army became functional, Montgomery had to bow to the demands of nationality and place Simonds' Corps under Crerar's Army command. Hence, Montgomery had to assign Crerar's army the vanguard role—despite his limited faith in its commander—because Simonds' II Canadian Corps held the sector where an attack was immediately required. The failure of Crerar's army to seize Falaise in "Totalize" and "Tractable" exacerbated Montgomery's existing misgivings about Crerar's abilities. Given the Field Marshal's high regard for Simonds, he was likely to place any blame for these failures, perhaps unfairly, on Crerar. However, these failures had as much to do with Simonds' corps plan, despite its commendable tactical innovations, and with troop performance, than with failings at army headquarters.[130]

A lack of faith in a subordinate was a prime factor in the phenomenon of "overcontrol" by higher commanders. One might fully expect, therefore, that Montgomery gripped Crerar more firmly than he did Dempsey. The evidence, however, suggests that Montgomery gripped both commanders equally firmly (albeit for different reasons). Despite Montgomery's faith in Dempsey, the closeness of their working relationship and the latter's bountiful tolerance meant that Montgomery was able to interfere in the running of the campaign at army level. Moreover, Dempsey, though highly competent, had no previous experience of army command and needed help initially to adjust. In general, Montgomery devoted equal amounts of attention to each army commander in proportion to the importance (as he perceived it) of the operations then being carried out.[131] But Montgomery's preference for the Second Army meant that it was given more significant tasks and therefore more frequently received Montgomery's focused attention.

Montgomery's doubts about Crerar's capabilities also prompted him to firmly grip the Canadian army commander. On 21 August 1944, Major-General Kitching recalled that Crerar had complained to him that "he was having trouble" with Montgomery who kept phoning Crerar with new instructions.[132] Furthermore, Crerar's limitations and political sensitivity to Montgomery's operational demands, exacerbated Montgomery's tendency to circumvent Crerar and deal directly with Simonds. Crerar told Kitching that when he "was not available," Montgomery "dealt with Simonds directly."[133] Brigadier Beament also formed the impression that Montgomery sometimes bypassed Crerar and dealt directly with Simonds.[134] Equally, according to Brigadier Belchem, for a few days during "Veritable" Montgomery sat next to Horrocks at the XXX Corps' Tactical Headquarters, while Crerar merely looked on and "virtually played no direct role in the proceedings."[135]

John English has hinted that had the First Canadian Army performed better in Operations "Totalize" and "Tractable," it might have spearheaded the 21st Army Group's advance into Germany. Yet irrespective of the success of these operations, it seems unlikely that Crerar's Army would have spearheaded the advance into Germany. Any advance southeast or east by Simonds' Corps toward the upper Seine would have widened the exposed eastern flank held by the I (British) Corps. Any continuance of an advance spearheaded by Simonds' Corps would have required the transfer of some or all of the Second (British) Army from the western flank, behind the First Canadian Army's frontage, onto the eastern flank. A redeployment as fundamental as moving one army behind another was impracticable after active operations had commenced. The only moment that this was feasible was once the Falaise pocket had been liquidated. However, given Montgomery's well-known loathing for crossed lines of communication—which restricted administrative efficiency—it was extremely unlikely that any such maneuver would have been attempted after D-Day. Rather than Simonds continuing to spearhead the advance, it would have been operationally more sensible for the most easterly corps of the Second Army to continue the advance after taking over the frontage of Simonds' Corps, thus allowing the latter to be deployed to cover the extending vulnerable eastern flank; if done, this would result in no crossing of liner of communication.[136]

With the benefit of hindsight, it is clear that the future long-term role of the First Canadian Army was, inadvertently, preordained when in January 1944 Montgomery assigned it to the eastern sector. This pre-invasion planning envisaged that Crerar's army would cross the Seine, capture Le Havre, capture the other channel ports, and advance up the sodden left flank into Zeeland. The pre-invasion planning envisaged this sequence of operations because it was the logical operational repercussion or being assigned the eastern sector of the lodgment area.[137]

Montgomery's limited faith in Crerar's Army also contributed to him making one of the most egregious mistakes of the campaign—the failure to rapidly open the port of Antwerp to Allied shipping through clearing the German-controlled Scheldt estuary. The Allies captured the Antwerp docks intact on 4 September 1944, yet failed to clear the Scheldt estuary until early November. After the breakout from Normandy and rapid advance through Belgium, Montgomery became obsessed with the Ruhr, Germany's industrial heartland lying east of the River Rhine. The deployment of Dempsey's army in the eastern half of the sector held by the 21st Amy Group, when combined with Montgomery's predisposition toward Dempsey, reinforced the Field Marshal's strategically correct focus on this glittering prize to the east. However, Montgomery's distrust of Crerar's army on his left (western) flank encouraged Montgomery's focus on the Ruhr to escalate from appropriate strategic vision to a fixation. Consequently, on 13 September 1944 Montgomery ordered Crerar's depleted command simultaneously to clear both the channel ports and the Scheldt estuary, while Dempsey's reinforced forces meantime attempted to "bounce" the Rhine in Operation "Market-Garden." When this operation failed, Montgomery immediately reconstituted the Second (British) Army so that it could launch Operation "Gatwick," an eastward thrust intended to reach the Rhine near Krefeld.[138]

Montgomery had given the First Canadian Army a task impossible to achieve with the inadequate resources he had allocated to Crerar. Consequently, the Canadians struggled slowly in mud and flooded polders to clear the Scheldt. Inexcusably, though Montgomery fully recognized Antwerp's enormous logistical significance, his Ruhr fixation made him slow to shift the main weight of the 21st Army Group to the task of clearing the Scheldt. Despite clear orders from Eisenhower and the exhortations of Admiral Ramsey, the Allied Naval Forces Commander, Montgomery did not deploy the full weight of his army group to clear the Scheldt until 16 October 1944.[139] The six-week delay before opening Antwerp constituted the gravest of errors, as some of Montgomery's peers recognized at the time.[140] With hindsight, it is clear that Montgomery should have rapidly opened the Scheldt by using the full power of his army group, before turning east. After the war, in an extremely rare example of honest self-appraisal, Montgomery was humble enough to concede that he had made a serious mistake.[141]

Planning Dilemmas over "Veritable"

Examination of the circumstances surrounding the planning and execution of Operation "Veritable," the 8 February 1945 assault from the River Maas towards the Rhine, sheds further light on the impact that the relationship between the 21st Army Group and the First Canadian Army exerted on the overall conduct of the campaign. For the campaign's historical literature has not yet observed the startling extent to which Montgomery was prepared to deny the operational logic of the situation facing him in his attempts to get the Second (British) Army to undertake "Veritable" instead of Crerar's army.

To understand this complicated episode, regard has to be paid to the interrelationship between the geography of the "Veritable" attack and the overall disposition of forces within the 21st Army Group (see map essay). During the initial planning in October and November 1944, the First Canadian Army held the northern part of the army group's front from the North Sea at Walcheren due east along the River Maas up to the east side of the Nijmegen bridgehead near Gennep. Dempsey's Second (British) Army faced east holding a front from Gennep running approximately north-south along the Maas until they met American forces near Geilenkirchen.

In early October, Montgomery had wanted Second Army to carry out Operation "Gatwick," a precursor of "Veritable," but developments prevented Dempsey from undertaking this offensive. In November, planning commenced on "Veritable" (or "Valediction" as it was then termed) for which Montgomery had earmarked Dempsey's army; Crerar's army was merely to provide protection for the northern flank of Dempsey's advance.[142] Given the restricted geography of the area, there was barely sufficient space for the Second Army to concentrate for the offensive and to build up the logistical infrastructure so vital for a successful advance. Crucially, to be able to do so, Dempsey's assault forces would also have to control the "Island" bridgehead immediately to the west and north of the area of the proposed offensive. The "Island," however, was the most strategically important piece of ground within the army group's entire front because it contained the bridgehead over the River Waal, which could serve as a launching point for an easterly advance into Germany. The Allies, therefore, had to hold the "Island" in considerable strength.[143] Unfortunately the "Veritable" attack frontage was adjacent to the vital "Island" bridgehead, and this constricted geography complicated the planning of this offensive.

Dempsey's Second Army, however, could not concentrate sufficient troops for "Veritable" in the Groesbeek area, hold the "Island" strongly, and defend the southern half of its front from south of the "Veritable" area down to the interarmy group boundary. It had too few forces, even with reinforcement, to hold such a long front including the vital "Island" bridgehead. Giving the Second Army sufficient forces for these tasks would have meant allocating virtually all of the army group's resources to Dempsey, leaving the First Canadian Army emasculated. If Montgomery had commanded two solely British armies, he may well have opted for this course of action; but to Crerar and the Canadian government it would be politically unacceptable to have the First Canadian Army stripped bare. However, even if the latter had been done, any eastward advance by the Second (British) Army would only increasingly expose its already dangerously stretched southern flank; its penetrative power would dissipate gradually as forces were redeployed to protect this lengthening flank. As a result, it looked increasingly as if Dempsey's army could not undertake the offensive.

To enable the Second (British) Army to concentrate for "Veritable" without dangerously thinning its southern flank, Montgomery then suggested that Dempsey share the defense of the "Island" with Crerar's army. This would shorten Dempsey's front and hence permit both concentration and security for the sector south of the "Veritable" assault frontage. However, it soon became clear that the cramped geography and limited communication routes in the "Island" rendered it impracticable to divide defense of the "Island" between two separate armies with their respective administrative infrastructures. This area was scarcely able to support the administrative networks of two corps of the same army, let alone two corps from two different

armies. Therefore, Montgomery ultimately recognized that there was no way
that the Second (British) Army could concentrate its forces at Groesbeek for
"Veritable," hold part of the "Island," and maintain the security of its defensive southern sector down to Geilenkirchen.[144]

The army group staff prepared these convoluted arguments for Montgomery; to so professional a commander as the Field Marshal, the implications of these appreciations must have been clear. Clearly, Montgomery's
suspicion of Crerar's abilities led him to explore several impracticable alter-
natives that would allow Dempsey's army to undertake Operation "Veritable." Sound operational reasoning, however, also influenced Montgomery's
desire that the Second (British) Army undertake this offensive rather than
Crerar's forces. Firstly, if Crerar's army undertook "Veritable," it would be
advancing southeast from the eastern end of its north-facing front; every
mile it advanced eastward would lengthen its exposed north-facing flank.
Because this flank was already thinly held, albeit facing similarly stretched
enemy forces, Crerar's army was in danger of becoming unbalanced. In fact
this situation was similar to that facing the Canadians in Normandy after the
closing of the Falaise pocket, but transposed through 90 degrees. Consequently, if Crerar's army undertook "Veritable," there might be a limit to
how far east it could advance; its offensive strength would be increasingly
weakened by dispersion to protect this lengthening northern flank.

Given that the Second Army was deployed facing east on a front running north-south, it made better sense for it to advance east or southeast,
and for the Canadians to advance north or northeast. Yet, despite this, the
other considerations explained previously prevented Dempsey from carrying out "Veritable." There was only one satisfactory answer to these conflicting operational considerations, and that was the one eventually adopted;
despite Montgomery's suspicions of Crerar, the latter's army would have to
be massively reinforced by British troops so that it could undertake "Veritable," leaving an emasculated Second (British) Army in static positions for
the first time, planning the future assault crossing of the River Rhine. All factors considered, the only sensible course was to allocate the task of undertaking "Veritable" to the First Canadian Army; Montgomery's tardiness at
conceding this attests to his suspicions of Crerar's abilities.

To summarize, it can be seen that Crerar was a competent army commander, but not much more than that. He was too concerned with nonoperational matters, too inexperienced, too weak a field commander, and too
determined to protect Canadian interests to gain Montgomery's confidence.
This was so, despite Crerar being fully inculcated with the Field Marshal's
operational methods. However, these weaknesses exerted only a limited
adverse impact on the campaign because Crerar held both of his two capable corps commanders on a loose rein.

Both the operational factors observed here and the national aspects of inter-Commonwealth military cooperation, permeated the relationship between Crerar and Montgomery. As a result, Montgomery and the 21st Army Group treated Crerar's First Canadian Army differently than Dempsey's Second (British) Army. The Field Marshal held back Crerar's army headquarters during the first six weeks of the Normandy campaign. In the Scheldt, Montgomery allocated it too large a task for its limited resources, and consequently the Field Marshal failed to ensure that Antwerp was opened quickly to Allied shipping. In "Veritable" Montgomery struggled hard to evade the operational logic that indicated he should allocate the offensive to the Canadians. The relationship between Crerar and the First Canadian Army on the one hand and Montgomery and his army group on the other clearly impacted on the manner in which the 21st Army Group as an institution conducted the Northwest Europe campaign.

CHAPTER 8

Conclusions

This work has systematically analyzed the operational methods used by the 21st Army Group in the 1944–45 Northwest Europe campaign, methods encapsulated by Montgomery's term "Colossal Cracks." The technique utilized by Montgomery and the 21st Army Group involved large set-piece battles based on concentration of force, massed artillery firepower (supplemented by strategic aerial bombing when possible), and integrated use of tactical air power. The army group only commenced these set-piece battles after careful preparation and massive concentration of resources, and then conducted these operations cautiously and methodically, with great regard to the logistical situation. "Colossal Cracks" constituted an attritional method based on copious matériel, particularly massed artillery firepower. This technique eschewed operational maneuver—at least until the combat power of the *Westheer* had been seriously denuded; once this point had been reached, the Allies would utilize their superior mobility—engendered by their dominance of the skies—to conduct successful mobile operations that would secure ultimate victory.

This analysis has demonstrated that Montgomery and his army commanders—Crerar and Dempsey—conducted this campaign in a highly competent manner. Montgomery's generalship in this campaign—that is, his handling of the 21st Army Group—remained more effective than some historians have previously recognized. The hypothesis that underpins and justifies this reassessment of the manner in which the 21st Army Group conducted this campaign is that although historians to date have produced good partial examinations of the methods used by this formation, they have not produced an entirely satisfactory comprehensive analysis of all the characteristics comprising the "Colossal Cracks" approach. Such a systematic examination is necessary because the individual aspects of this approach are all interrelated. The validity of some of the criticism of Montgomery made by historians remains limited because these criticisms only relate to individual aspects of his operational approach; such critics have failed to relate these aspects to the rest of the factors that comprised his operational methods. Too often historians have criticized Montgomery's caution, for instance, without adequate consideration of how this aspect related to all the other components of his operational approach, but especially to his morale and casualty concerns.

Within the body of historical literature written on the campaign, there still is lacking a wholly adequate comprehensive examination of the manner in which Montgomery and the 21st Army Group conducted the campaign. This absence has resulted from six interconnected causes: that historians have focused excessively both on Montgomery's personality, especially his flaws, and on his significance within the campaign; that to date this body of literature has lacked a systematic examination of the various aspects of Montgomery's operational approach; that scholars have overemphasized theater strategic issues and neglected the operational level; that historians have given insufficient consideration to the real situation facing the 1944 British army; that scholars have not fully appreciated the appropriateness of Montgomery's methods to achieving British politico-Imperial war aims; and that historians have criticized Montgomery personally both for operational techniques shared by his subordinates and for failures as attributable to these subordinates as to himself.

This analysis has established a fuller picture of the manner in which the 21st Army Group conducted this campaign by examining the two most senior command levels within this formation and the relationships that existed between them. This study has argued that historians cannot achieve a full understanding of the activities of the 21st Army Group by focusing solely on Montgomery, as so much of the campaign's historical literature has done. Historians only can obtain such an understanding by analyzing this formation's two most senior command levels and the interconnections that existed between them. A particular 21st Army Group style for conducting the campaign emerged both from the methods of these commanders and from the interactions between them. The excessive focus on Montgomery has been misleading because this has reinforced the belief that he was the prime impulse on events. Although Montgomery's role remained crucial, his subordinate army commanders also made key contributions to the manner in which the 21st Army Group handled the campaign.

This analysis also has demonstrated that by winter 1943–44 Montgomery's subordinates at army level had already assimilated the basic techniques of the "Colossal Cracks" approach, and to some extent had done so independently of Montgomery's influence. The British army's doctrinal development during 1941–44, based on the experiences of combat in North Africa, had developed along similar lines to that of Montgomery. After he assumed command of the 21st Army Group, both Montgomery's desire for grip and his predilection for such methods reinforced powerfully the extent of consensus concerning operational technique that already existed within this formation. Hence, Montgomery did not impose an alien doctrine on this formation.

This study also has demonstrated that the maintenance of morale and casualty conservation constituted the paramount influences on the manner in which Montgomery and the 21st Army Group conducted this campaign. Furthermore, this analysis has illustrated that the campaign's historical literature to date has given insufficient consideration to these two interconnected concerns. This work has argued further that it is impossible for historians to fully comprehend the performance of Anglo-Canadian forces in Northwest Europe without appreciation of these factors. The constant need for senior commanders within the 21st Army Group to nurture the relatively fragile morale of their conscript soldiers strongly influenced their utilization of a cautious, firepower-laden, attritional operational approach. These commanders could only expect so much sacrificial heroism from Britain's civilian, mass-conscript forces. Moreover, given wider inter-Allied considerations, the fact that the 21st Army Group could field just a modest number of divisions alongside an ever-growing American force made it essential for Montgomery to keep all his formations fit for combat in the long term; he had to get the best out of his limited manpower resources. The best way for senior commanders within the 21st Army Group to get the best out of their civilian troops despite the terrible demands of combat was to allocate them the maximum possible level of support in terms of machines—that is, of matériel. Indeed, Montgomery rightly recognized that, despite massive Allied numerical superiority in matériel, the key to the eventual defeat of the *Westheer* was to nurture the relatively fragile morale of the conscript soldiers fielded by the 21st Army Group into an adequate, but sustained, combat performance. What really mattered in Britain's contribution to the Allied defeat of the *Westheer* was how effectively in the long-term these civilian troops used this mass of machines.

The necessity for the 21st Army Group to avoid excessive casualties in the campaign strongly influenced its reliance on massive firepower. Casualty conservation proved essential for Montgomery because the 1944 British army was suffering from a chronic manpower shortage, particularly in the case of rifle infantry reinforcements. Moreover, Britain's most senior commanders of the Second World War had been profoundly moved by the slaughter of the Great War and remained determined to avoid this scale of blood-letting during the 1939–45 conflict. The casualty- and morale-conscious senior commanders within the 21st Army Group sought to sustain the fighting power and integrity of their formation—a force which constituted Britain's last uncommitted field army—until this force had defeated the enemy. In this manner Britain would secure her politico-Imperial war objectives. These aims sought a high military profile for Britain's limited—and diminishing—forces within a larger Allied effort that eventually would defeat the enemy without incurring a bloodbath of the last of Britain's fit young men. If the British army defeated the enemy in such a manner, this would ensure a prominent British influence on the emerging postwar political structure of Europe. This objective had been a major motivation that reinforced Britain's decision to go to war in September 1939 to defeat the continuing Nazi aggression in Europe.

Much of historians' criticism of Montgomery and the 21st Army Group has focused on the relatively poor Combat performance of Anglo-Canadian forces, despite their marked numerical in matériel, in comparison with the skilled and effective *Westheer*. Some of this criticism is perfectly valid. Yet it is not in the least surprising that at the tactical level the 1944 British army could not match the *Wehrmacht*, one of the most efficient military forces in history. Four groups of structural factors shed light on why this was so: that the 1944 British army was a mass-conscripted civilian army, based on a tiny peace-time nucleus; that many of its regular officers possessed Empire-wide experiences of peace-time soldiering and training that had scarcely prepared them for a technologically advanced major European war; that its personnel came from a society that lacked a pronounced martial tradition, and consequently many of its personnel lacked the fanaticism that characterized sizable numbers of the German Armed Forces; and finally that whereas the desperate German need to avoid Götterdämmerung powerfully reinforced their battlefield resolve during 1944–45, this situation simply did not exist for Anglo-Canadian troops.

Many historians critical of Anglo-Canadian performance in Northwest Europe also have given insufficient consideration to the interconnections that existed between the operational and tactical levels. It was not necessary for the 21st Army Group to strive to compete tactically with the German army in order to defeat the latter. Nor was such an approach appropriate either to British war aims or to the nature of the resources available to Britain. Even though the operational methods utilized by the 21st Army Group remained crude, they nevertheless constituted an appropriate way of securing British war aims given the relatively fragile nature of the resources available. These war aims did not seek to produce the most impressive British combat performance but rather to defeat the German army with the relatively limited manpower now available by relying on matériel. These British campaign objectives sought not only to achieve a high national military profile within the victory attained over the enemy by a larger Allied force, but to do so without incurring a massive bloodletting of British youth. The real task facing senior British and Canadian commanders in Northwest Europe was not to attempt to match the virtuosity of the best German commanders, but eventually to achieve victory by doing what the British army did best: to gradually grind down the enemy into a virtual submission by an attritional war based on Allied numerical superiority in machines. As long as Anglo-Canadian forces avoided presenting the enemy with any opportunities to inflict on them tactical setbacks, then overall Allied numerical superiority would eventually succeed—through simple attrition—in bringing the *Westheer* close to defeat. This was the inexorable dynamic of *Matérielschlacht*. Of course, in Northwest Europe, once protracted attritional warfare had depleted the fighting power of the *Westheer*, the Allies would translate this combat potential into ultimate victory over their enemy by unleashing their armored formations in large-scale mobile operations.

It is fair to argue that prior to D-Day, the British and Canadian armies might have done more to improve the tactical training of the soldiers fielded by the 21st Army Group; in particular, to instill in them more effective tactical flexibility and use of initiative. It is debatable, however, whether there existed enough time, or sufficient expertise within the army, to train personnel—some of whom were then being drawn from the bottom of the manpower barrel—to a significantly higher level of tactical effectiveness. In reality, however, what the British army needed to achieve for the Northwest Europe campaign was to train its soldiers to an adequate level of tactical competency, sufficient to permit them to exploit the devastation that massed Allied firepower inflicted on the enemy. For the 21st Army Group eventually would achieve victory over the *Westheer* not through tactical excellence but rather through crude techniques and competent leadership at both the operational and tactical levels.

Some historians' criticism of the poor tactical combat performance of Anglo-Canadian forces, moreover, has given insufficient consideration to the strong influence that British operational technique exerted on their activities at the tactical level. The "Colossal Cracks" operational approach stifled tactical initiative, flexibility, and tempo. The availability of massive firepower within the 21st Army group still would have stifled tactical performance to some degree even if better training had produced tactically more effective troops. Such copious firepower support inevitably created a tactical dependency on it amongst other combat arms. The availability of large amounts of highly effective artillery assets made it possible for British troops to capture enemy positions devastated by artillery fire without having to aggressively fight their way forward using their own weapons. The existence of such resources enabled troops to achieve their objectives while minimizing unnecessary casualties. Given that even soldiers determined to do their duty still desperately wish to return home alive, it seems unlikely that more effective training would have done much to lessen the adverse impact that this firepower-reliant operational technique exerted on the tactical combat performance of Anglo-Canadian troops.

This study's examination of Montgomery's two subordinate army commanders, Dempsey and Crerar, has highlighted the extent to which their operational methods mirrored those of Montgomery. A strong degree of consensus existed within the senior Anglo-Canadian commanders on what techniques should be utilized to undertake effectively major operations. This analysis also has demonstrated that Montgomery tended to "over-control" both his army commanders, though each for different reasons. The Field Marshal gripped Dempsey because his focus on Second (British) Army operations, the closeness of their working relationship, and Dempsey's stoic tolerance of his superior's interference all encouraged Montgomery to do so. The campaign's historical literature universally has portrayed Dempsey as being a mere cipher of Montgomery. However, the fading of Dempsey's reputation into historical oblivion is undeserved. Dempsey made a more significant contribution to the campaign than historians previously have recognized. Unfortunately, the nature of the Montgomery-Dempsey relationship has obfuscated historical analysis, particularly as both commanders have claimed authorship of the same key decisions. Consequently, historians now may never establish precisely Dempsey's role in the campaign. However, despite this imprecision, this study nevertheless has demonstrated that Dempsey exerted a greater influence on the way on which the 21st Army Group conducted the Northwest Europe campaign than scholars to date have recognized.

In contrast, Montgomery gripped Crerar because he justifiably remained both suspicious of the latter's operational abilities and concerned that Crerar's defense of the Canadian army's national interests would undermine the operational conduct of the campaign. This latter concern reflected Montgomery's narrow focus on the purely operational aspects of the campaign and the inability of his decision-making to embrace fully the wider politico-military aspects of inter-Allied cooperation in the theater. This failing, as well as Montgomery's arrogance and colonial superiority, dogged Anglo-Canadian cooperation in Northwest Europe. The objective weaknesses in Crerar's generalship, however, did not exert a serious deleterious impact on the campaign because he held both of his capable corps commanders—Crocker and Simonds—on a loose rein, permitting them to fight relatively unhindered their respective corps battles.

This study's examination of the army level of command also has demonstrated first the extent of consensus that existed within the 21st Army Group concerning operational technique, and second how the relationships between these commanders influenced the conduct of the campaign. This study has demonstrated the validity of the argument that historians can only obtain a full appreciation of the manner in which the 21st Army Group conducted the campaign by combining an examination of the methods used by its senior commanders with an analysis of the relationships that existed between them.

In summation, therefore, this study has examined the way in which Montgomery and the 21st Army Group conducted the 1944–45 Northwest Europe campaign. It has demonstrated that this conduct was not only both highly competent and appropriate but also more effective than some scholars have acknowledged. As a whole, "Colossal Cracks" remained an appropriate operational technique given British politico-Imperial war aims and the real capabilities of the rather fragile and limited resources available to the 1944 Anglo-Canadian army relative to that of the *Westheer*. Serious inherent drawbacks existed in this crude operational technique, not least the limitations on tactical mobility caused by the vast devastation massive firepower inflicted on the battlefield; this restricted Allied exploitation of the fleeting tactical opportunities that arose out of the use of this firepower. However, when historians consider all pertinent factors, it is clear that the advantages of "Colossal Cracks" undoubtedly outweighed the disadvantages. It is undeniable that many of the senior commanders within the 21st Army Group could not match the capabilities of their adversaries. Yet, these commanders sensibly stuck to what they—and especially their civilian troops—did best. They stuck to conducting the campaign through the utilization of firepower-reliant, attritional warfare—at least until the *Westheer* had been so weakened that large-scale Allied mobile operations could achieve decisive victory.

The "Colossal Cracks" approach relied on the British army's strengths, notably its artillery and its ability to call down the awesome power of the Allied tactical air forces. This operational technique also helped British forces avoid presenting the enemy with opportunities to make use of their tactical abilities on the counterattack to inflict setbacks on Montgomery's forces, Moreover, the fact that Anglo-Canadian troops only attacked when they were in as favorable position as possible to do so successfully nurtured the relatively fragile morale of these civilian troops. This method represented an appropriate use of the limited manpower resources available. For "Colossal Cracks" allowed the 21st Army Group to wear down enemy assets and liberate territory without having to do so predominantly by sustained individual combat. In this way, Montgomery's forces avoided sustaining both severe casualties and significant morale degradation. Only after these methods had significantly denuded the combat power of the *Westheer* would Montgomery run the risks involved in seeking to achieve final victory. In this final bid for ultimate success, the forces deployed by the 21st Army Group would attempt to tactically outperform their depleted enemy through implementation of highly effective, large-scale, mobile operations. Above all, both the morale and casualty concerns inherent within the "Colossal Cracks" approach ensured that the 21st Army Group secured Britain's 1944–45 war aims. Using this operational technique, the 21st Army Group emerged in May 1945 intact and undiminished in size after making a significant contribution to the Allied defeat of the *Westheer* in Northwest Europe.

"Colossal Cracks" clearly represented a winning method, even if it was not a flawless one; it was a double-edged and rather fragile sword. Yet it had taken truly heroic efforts to get the British army from the depths of despair in 1940 after Dunkirk to a point in 1944 where it could, using these methods, defeat the skilled *Wehrmacht*—without incurring a bloodbath—within a larger Allied effort. For the British army by June 1944 there simply had not been enough time, and probably insufficient ability and experience within its senior echelons, to overcome the weaknesses inherent in the "Colossal Cracks" approach. On D-Day and after, the 21st Army Group had to do its best with whatever weapon, unpromising or not, that the British army had managed to forge. Overall, this technique represented the most appropriate weapon the British, army could develop in the circumstances. And it would prove to be enough, albeit just enough, to defeat the enemy and secure British war aims. The 21st Army Group emerged intact in early May 1945 after making a significant contribution to the Western Allied effort in defeating the Nazi canker. For the British army of mid-1944 there was no more viable alternative weapon than "Colossal Cracks" that realistically could have been forged by D-Day.

Notes

CHAPTER 1

1. This study focuses only modestly on events after the March 1945 Allied crossing of the Rhine, when the German army ceased to oppose effectively Montgomery's forces.

2. For convenience, this work refers to Montgomery in the text as "the Field Marshal," even though he only attained this rank on 1 Sept 44, and as BLM in notes.

3. Generals Omar N. Bradley and Jacob L. Devers respectively commanded the 1st (later retitled 12th) and 6th U.S. Army Groups.

4. Public Record Office [henceforth PRO], WO205/174, Conference Minutes [henceforth Conf Mins], 24 May 44; WO171/103, (War Diary, General Staff (Operations) Branch, HQ 21st Army Group, May 1944) [(WD G(Ops) 21AG May 44)], Memorandum [Memo], de Guingand to Supreme Headquarters, Allied Expeditionary Forces [SHAEF], 30 May 44.

5. On the linked issues of command and theater strategy, see (for example) G. E. Patrick Murray, "Eisenhower and Montgomery, Broad Front versus Single Thrust; The Historiography of the Debate Over Strategy and Command, Aug 44 to April 45," Ph.D. Diss., Temple Univ., 1991 [henceforth "Historiography"]; this has now been published as *Eisenhower versus Montgomery: The Continuing Debate* (New York; Praeger, 1996). See also N. Gelb, *Ike and Monty: Generals at War* (London: Constable, 1994), 345–53, 374–77.

6. J. J. B. Mackenzie and Brian Holden Reid, eds., *The British Army and the Operational Level of War* (London: Tri Service Press, 1988), i.

7. John A. English, *The Canadian Army and the Normandy Campaign: A Study in the Failure of High Command* (London: Praeger, 1991), xiii.

8. Narratives include the official British account: Maj L. F. Ellis, *Victory in the West*, 2 vols., History of the Second World War, UK Military Series (London: HMSO, 1962–68)—noted edition PRO, CAB101/29-30. Other early accounts include: H. C. O'Neill, [Strategicus, pseud.], *The Victory Campaign, May 1944–August 1945* (London: Faber & Faber, 1947); M. Schulman, *Defeat in the West* (London: Martin Seeker & Warburg, 1947); H. Darby and M. Cunliffe, *A Short History of 21 Army Group* (London: Gale & Polden, 1949); C. Wilmot, *The Struggle for Europe* (London: Collins, 1952); J. North, *Northwest Europe* (London: HMSO, 1953); H. Essame and E. Belfield, *The North-West Europe Campaign 1944–45* (Aldershot, Gale & Polden, 1962).

9. English, *Canadian*, 159–60.

10. R. A. Doughty, *The Seeds of Disaster*, x–xi, cited English, *Canadian*, 159, n. 1.

11. Hence "[I] concentrate great strength at some selected place and hit the Germans a colossal crack;" Department of Documents, Imperial War Museum [IWM], Montgomery Papers [BLM/], 126/35, M535, Letter [Ltr] Montgomery [henceforth BLM] to Chief of the Imperial General Staff [CIGS], 17 Nov 44.

12. This study does not analyze the role of the First U.S. Army in Normandy because it remained in practice a largely autonomous command despite its technical subordination to Montgomery within the 21st Army Group.

13. S. A. Hart, "Corps Command in Northwest Europe, 1944–45," unpublished paper, 1999. The British and Canadian higher formations that served in Northwest Europe were titled: the Second (British) Army; the I (British) Corps; the VIII and the XII Corps; the First Canadian Army; the I and the II Canadian Corps. PRO, WO179/2609, (WD G(PI) FCA 44), July Diary, Minutes of Chief of Staff's Conference [CoS Conf], 23 July 44, entry 254.

14. BLM's critics include: John Ellis, *Brute Force: Allied Strategy and Tactics in the Second World War* (London: Deutsch, 1990); R. W. Thompson, *Montgomery the Field Marshal: A Critical Study* (London: Allen & Unwin, 1969); M. Blumenson, "The Most Over-rated General of World War Two," *Armor* (May–June 1962): 4–10; T. Copp and R. Vogel, "'No Lack of Rational Speed': 1st Canadian Army Operations, September 1944," *Journal [Jnl] of Canadian Studies* 16, nos. 3–4 (Fall-Winter 1981): 145–55; Maj-Gen J. F. C. Fuller derided "Colossal Cracks" as "asinine," *The Second World War: A Strategical and Tactical History* (London: Eyre & Spottiswoode, 1948), 304.

15. Such as Nigel Hamilton's favorable biography *Monty*, 3 vols: vol. 1, *The Making of a General 1887–1942*; vol. 2, *Master of the Battlefield 1942–1944*; and vol. 3, *The Field Marshal 1944–1976* (London: Hamish Hamilton, 1982–86). See S. T. Powers, "The Battle of Normandy: The Lingering Controversy," *Jnl of Military History [J.Mil.H]* 56 (July 1992): 455–71, 464–65.

16. See, for example, Darby, *Short.*

17. Thompson, *Montgomery*, 20–21, 218.

18. This focus is the product of the copious extant source material on the issue: BLM's correspondence with Alan Brooke, the Chief of the Imperial General Staff [CIGS], and with General Simpson, the Director of Military Operations [DMO]: Liddell Hart Centre for Military Archives, King's College London [LHCMA], Alanbrooke Papers [AP/], /14; IWM, BLM-Simpson Correspondence Papers [MSC].

19. See, for example, R. Clark, *Montgomery of Alamein* (London: Phoenix, 1960), 74; Murray, "Historiography," passim; Dominick Graham and Shelford Bidwell, *Coalitions, Politicians and Generals* (London: Brassey's 1993), 226–54.

20. Murray, "Historiography," passim.

21. Ellis, *Brute*, 375–83; Thompson, *Montgomery*, 19, 173–74, 213, 321.

22. A. Moorehead, *Montgomery* (London: Hamish Hamilton, 1946), 183; J. C. Smuts, *Jan Christian Smuts* (London: Cassell, 1952), 454.

23. M. Howard, in R. H. Kohn, ed., "The Scholarship on World War II: Its Present Condition and Future Possibilities," *J.Mil.H* 55, no. 3 (July 1991): 365–94.

24. Carlo D'Este, *Decision in Normandy* (London: Collins, 1983), 258–59; C. P. Stacey, *Official History of the Canadian Army in the Second World War*, vol. 3, *The Victory Campaign* (Ottawa: The Queen's Printer, 1960), 284–85, 385–86, 630–33.

25. Gelb, *Ike*, 377; Thompson, *Montgomery*, 16; Powers, "Normandy," 471.

26. Howard, in Kohn, "Scholarship," 379.
27. Ministry of Defence, Design for Military Operations. The British Military Doctrine (London: HMSO, 1996).
28. Howard, in Kohn, "Scholarship," 378–79. Quotations from British sources retain their original (British) english idiom.
29. Thompson, *Montgomery*, 218.
30. Moorehead, *Montgomery* (1946); Clark, *Montgomery* (1960); R. W. Thompson, *The Montgomery Legend* (London: Allen & Unwin, 1967), and *Montgomery* (1969); R. Lewin, *Montgomery as Military Commander* (London: Batsford, 1971); Brian Montgomery, *A Field Marshal in the Family* (London: Javelin, 1973); A. Chalfont, *Montgomery* (London: Weidenfeld & Nicolson, 1976); Hamilton, *Monty* (1982–86); R. Lamb, *Montgomery in Europe 1943–45: Success or Failure?* (London: Buchan & Enright, 1983); T. E. B. Howarth, ed., *Monty at Close Quarters* (London: Leo Cooper, 1985); Alistair Horne and Brian Montgomery, *The Lonely Leader: Monty 1944–1945* (London: Macmillan, 1994).
31. Thompson, *Montgomery*, 321.
32. Moorehead, *Montgomery*, 208.
33. Thompson, *Montgomery*, 292, 322.
34. Carl von Clausewitz, *On War*, Michael Howard and Peter Paret, trans. (Princeton, N.J.: Princeton University Press, 1976), (orig. 1832), 100–112; B. H. Liddell Hart, *Great Captains Unveiled* (London: Blackwood, 1927).
35. J. Dalgleish, *We Planned the Second Front* (London: Gollancz, 1946), 22.
36. T. N. Dupuy, *A Genius for War: The German Army and General Staff, 1807–1945* (London: Macdonald & Jane's, 1977), 5, emphasis in original.
37. Similarly, the Allies won in Italy through "a modest series of victories;" Brian Holden Reid, "The Italian Campaign 1943–45," in John Gooch, ed., *Decisive Campaigns of the Second World War* (London: Frank Cass, 1990), 137.
38. Brian Horrocks, *Corps Commander* (London: Sidgewick & Jackson, 1977), 29–30; Omar Bradley concurred (*A Soldiers Story* [New York: Holt, 1951], xi–xii).
39. Richard Lamb, "Rude but Effective," *The Spectator* (28 May 1994): 40.
40. Churchill College Archive, Cambridge [CCA/], Ronald Lewin Papers [RLEW/]; LHCMA, Maj John North Papers [JNP/]; LHCMA, Liddell Hart Papers [LHP/]. See also Capt B. H. Liddell Hart, *The Other Side of the Hill* (London: Cassell, 1951); *The Tanks*, 2 vols. (London: Cassell, 1959); *History of the Second World War* (London: Cassell, 1970). Lewin, *Montgomery*; North, *Europe*.
41. Brian Holden Reid, ed., *The Science of War: Back to First Principles* (London: Routledge, 1993), 1–2.
42. E. N. Luttwak, "The Operational Level of War," *International Security* 5, no. 3 (Winter 1980–81): 61–79.
43. Horrocks, *Corps*, 31; E. R. Snoke, *The Operational Level of War* (Fort Leavenworth, Kans.: Combat Studies Institute, 1985), v.
44. Harold S. Orenstein, trans., *The Evolution of Soviet Operational Art, 1927–1991*, Vol. 1 (London: Frank Cass, 1995), passim.
45. "For the British army doctrine at any level above the tactical has always been an anathema," Mackenzie and Reid, *British*, 10.
46. An early example of this literature is Maj. G. L. Scott, "British and German Operational Styles in World War Two," *Military Review* 65 (Oct 1985): 37–41.
47. Luttwak, "Operational," 61. (Grand Tactics): English, *Canadian*, xiii.

(1961); C. B. MacDonald, *The Siegfried Line Campaign* (1963); H. M. Cole, *The Ardennes: Battle of the Bulge* (1965).

67. English, *Canadian*, xv; D'Este, *Decision*, 254–55.
68. F. W. Winterbottom, *The Ultra Secret* (London: Weidenfeld & Nicolson, 1974); Ronald Lewin, *Ultra Goes to War* (New York: McGraw-Hill, 1978); R. Bennett, *Ultra in the West* (London: Hutchinson, 1979); C. Cruikshank, *Deception in World War Two* (Oxford: O.U.P., 1979); F. H. Hinsley, *British Intelligence in the Second World War*, 4 vols. (London: HMSO, 1982–88).
69. See PRO, CAB106/962, 21AG Report "Market-Garden."
70. Howard, in Kohn, "Scholarship," 379–80.
71. Max Hastings, *Overlord: D-Day and the Battle for Normandy* (London: M. Joseph, 1984); D'Este, *Decision*; Lamb, *Montgomery*; English, *Canadian*.
72. See, for example R. Miller, *Nothing Less than Victory: The Oral History of D-Day* (London: Penguin, 1994), and J. E. Lewis, ed., *Eye-Witness D-Day* (London: Robinson, 1994).
73. English, *Canadian*.
74. Howard, in Kohn, "Scholarship," 378–79.
75. Hastings observed that much of the debate about Normandy "focussed solely upon the generals, as if their making a decision ensured its effective execution" (*Overlord*, 369).
76. For these manpower issues see John Peaty, "Manpower and the 21st Army Group," working drafts for Ph.D. Diss., Univ. of London, currently in progress. On comparative tactical innovation see Hart, "Learning." Previously, the only significant comparative work on this campaign was John Keegan, *Six Armies in Normandy* (London: Jonathon Cape, 1982).
77. Kohn, "Scholarship," 365.

CHAPTER 2
1. The British and Canadian official histories devote only modest attention to morale or manpower problems. (Manpower): Ellis, *Victory* 1:132–33, 308, 453; 2:141–42, and 158–59; Stacey, *Victory*, 284–85, 385–86, 630–33. Recent works have focused a little more on these factors, including: D'Este, *Decision*, 252–71, 282–84; Hastings, *Overlord*, 180, 372–73.
2. LHCMA, AP/7/3/12, War Office Exercise "Evolution," Aug 46, pp. 3, 7, 39–40.
3. Grigg, *Prejudice*, 422.
4. See John Baynes, *Morale* (London: Cassell, 1967); John Ellis, *The Sharp End: The Fighting Man in World War Two* (London: David & Charles, 1982); Richard Holmes, *Firing Line* (London: Jonathon Cape, 1985); John Keegan, *The Face of Battle* (London: Jonathon Cape, 1976); Lt-Col J. H. A. Sparrow, *Morale* (London: War Office, 1949); David French, "'Tommy Is No Soldier': The Morale of Second British Army in Normandy, June–August 1944," *Journal of Strategic Studies* 19, no. 4 (December 1996): 154–178.
5. Clausewitz, *War*, 97, 184–85.
6. ("Big"): IWM, BLM/[no #], Address to the Middle East Staff College, Haifa, 21 Sept 42 [Haifa]; draft in IWM, Belchem papers; also quoted Stephen Brooks, ed., *Monty and the Eighth Army* (London: Bodley Head, 1991), 54–55. ("Chief"): IWM, BLM/74, Notes on Planning the Campaign, /5, Mansion House Speech, 24 March 44, p. 1 [Mansion]. See also BLM/90/1, Address to Staff College, 7

Jan 44, para 7 [Addrs Stf Col]; BLM/90/3, Talk to Generals, 13 Jan 44; IWM, BLM/90/5, Speech to Railwaymen at Euston, 22 Feb 44 [Euston]; BLM/90/9, Speech to Staff, 28 March 44, para 5.

7. IWM, BLM/161, BLM's *Morale in Battle: An Analysis*, April 46, para 59, emphasis in original, [*Morale*].

8. LHCMA, AP/7/3/12, "Evolution," Aug 46, p. 7.

9. Thompson, *Montgomery*, 23–24.

10. Respectively: IWM, BLM/74/5, Mansion, p. 1; BLM/90/5, Euston.

11. Horne and Montgomery, *Lonely*, xix–xxii; Gen F. Morgan, *Peace and War* (London: Hodder & Stoughton, 1961), 155; North, *Europe*, 34.

12. Clark, *Montgomery*, 60; Hugh Essame, *Patton: A Study in Command* (London: Batsford, 1974), 135; G. Picot, *Accidental Warrior* (Lewes, England: Book Guild, 1993), 24–25.

13. LHCMA, AP/3/B/XII, Notes on My Life, entry 27 June 1944 [Notes]. IWM, BLM/72, Personal Diary, p. 8, para 26, entry 20 Feb 44.

14. LHCMA, AP/3/B/XII, Notes, 27 May 44; Winston S. Churchill, *The Second World War*, Vol. 5. (London: Cassell, 1952), 514–15.

15. LHCMA, AP/3/B/XII, Notes, 5 June 44. The Assistant CIGS (Ops) also agreed: Maj-Gen. J. N. Kennedy, *The Business of War* (London: Hutchinson, 1957), 325–26.

16. IWM, BLM/74/5, Mansion.

17. Picot, *Accidental*, 45.

18. Michael Howard, "Monty and the Price of Victory," *Sunday Times*, 16 Oct 1983, 42; Hastings, *Overlord*, 14. See also Grigg, *Prejudice*, 423.

19. ("Best"): IWM, BLM/74/5, Mansion. ("Finest"): BLM quoted in Howard, "Price"; Howard observed that "even at its best the army remained a fragile instrument."

20. Howard, "Price." Dominick Graham observed that Allied morale "never ceased to cause its commanders anxiety" (*Coalitions*, 211).

21. Hamilton, *Monty*, Vols. 1 and 2, passim.

22. LHCMA, Maj-Gen. Francis W. de Guingand Papers [DGP] /IV/1/14-24, BLM's messages.

23. Hastings, *Overlord*, 372.

24. Picot, *Accidental*, 24–25.

25. PRO, AIR37/784, Leigh Mallory Diary, p. 94, entry 29–31 July 44.

26. Hastings concluded that "when Allied troops met Germans on anything like equal terms" during Normandy, "the Germans almost always prevailed" (*Overlord*, 369).

27. IWM, BLM/41/5, Some Notes on Morale in an Army, Aug 43 [Notes].

28. CCA, P. J. Grigg papers, 11/1, BLM Lecture, St Andrew's Univ, 15 Nov 45, p. 13, para 11 [St Andrew's].

29. LHCMA, Gen R. N. O'Connor papers [OCP/] 5/4/22, Ltr O'Connor to Lt-Gen P. Neame, 19 Aug 44.

30. PRO, CAB106/1060, Reports on Normandy by Brig Hargest, 25 June 44 [Hargest].

31. Charles Richardson, *Flashback. A Soldier s Story* (London: Kimber, 1985), 121.

32. IWM, BLM/161, *Morale*.

33. IWM, BLM/ [no #], Haifa.

34. Horne, *Lonely*, xxii.
35. BLM stated, "We British are a martial but not a military race" (CCA, Grigg Papers, 11/1, Guildhall Address, 18 July 46). His troops were "indeed ordinary men" (Picot, *Accidental*, 45).
36. English, *Canadian*, passim.
37. The resilience of German morale has fascinated scholars: E. A. Shils and M. Janowitz, "Cohesion and Disintegration in the *Wehrmacht* in World War Two," *Public Opinion Quarterly* 12 (1948): 280–315; W. V. Madej, "Effectiveness and Cohesion of the German Ground Forces in World War II," *Journal of Political and Military Sociology* 6 (1978): 233–48; Omer Bartov, *Hitler's Army: Soldiers, Nazis, and War in the Third Reich* (Oxford: Oxford Univ. Press, 1991). Though Bartov examined the impact of Nazification on the morale of the Ostheer, historians have ignored the *Westheer* until recent research demonstrated that it was more Nazified than was previously thought: R. Hart, "Learning." (German discipline): Col. Hans von Luck, *Panzer Commander* (London: Praeger, 1989), 198–200.
38. Dupuy, *Genius*, 5, emphasis in original.
39. Hastings, *Overlord*, 15, 370.
40. This poor performance is evidenced by the high surrender rates in Operation "Veritable:" PRO, WO171/4130, (WD GS 31D 45), Intelligence Summary [IS] 242, 16 March 45; WO171/3957, (WD GSIa SBA Feb 45), IS 595, 11 Feb 45.
41. Hastings, *Overlord*, 372.
42. Michael Howard, "How Will History Judge Montgomery's Generalship?," *The Times*, 25 March 1976.
43. National Archives of Canada [NAC], Crerar Papers, Vol. 2 [CP/2], [file] 1-0-2, fll, Ltr Keller to Crerar, 22 April 44; 1-0-2-1, RFK3, Mess Keller to Crerar, 7 June 44; PRO, CAB106/1060, Hargest, Notes to D+10.
44. French, "Tommy," 164.
45. Horrocks, *Corps*, 34.
46. (Bocage): Hastings, *Overlord*, 43, 175–77, 181–93, 288–89. (Sniping): R. Wingfield, *The Only Way Out* (London: Hutchinson, 1955), 62–63.
47. PRO, CAB106/106, Hargest, Opn 20 June 44.
48. Picot, *Accidental*, 83.
49. For the keenness of fresh formations, see PRO, CAB106/1060, Hargest, notes 25 June 44.
50. PRO, CAB106/1060, Hargest, notes 21 June 44.
51. J. B. Salmud, *The History of the 51st Highland Division, 1939–45* (Edinburgh: Blackwood, 1953), 155.
52. NAC, CP/8, 6-10-9, fs4-5, Crerar Memo of Conv with Crocker, 24 July 44, p. 2.
53. Ibid.; NAC, Mann Papers, Dirs, fl, FCA Dir, 22 July 44.
54. NAC, CP/8, 6-10-9, fs2-3, Memo of Visit to GOC IC, 24 July 44; f13, Crerar's Memo Mtng with CinC, 1500 25 July 44; fs15-16 Ltr BLM to Crerar, 26 July 44.
55. NAC, CP/2, 1-0-2-1, RFK3, Mess Keller to Crerar, 7 June 44.
56. IWM, BLM/119/7, Ltr Dempsey to BLM, 6 July 44, enclosing Ltr Crocker to Dempsey, 5 July 44.
57. NAC, CP/3, 5-0-3:VI, fs88-89, Ltr Simonds to Dempsey, 27 July 44.
58. English, Canadian, 306.
59. IWM, BLM/119/7-9, /13, various letters, July 44.
60. English, *Canadian*, 289–90.

61. NAC, CP/2, 1-0-4, f33, Note Phone Mess BLM to Crerar, 1130 12 Aug 44.
62. IWM, BLM/74, diary, 17 March 44; BLM/120/20, Ltr Sosnkowski to BLM, 20 March 44; NAC, CP/2, 1-0-2-1, Ltr Simonds to Crocker, 12 Oct 44. Keegan, *Six*, 270.
63. Hastings, *Overlord*, 55.
64. French, "Tommy," 165–66, 170–72.
65. NAC, CP/8, 6-10-9, fs4-5 Crerar Memo of Conv with Crocker, 1015 24 July 44.
66. IWM, BLM/119/9, M54, Mess BLM to CIGS, 15 July 44.
67. Salmud, 51st, 144, 149.
68. IWM, BLM/119/9, M54, Mess BLM to CIGS, 15 July 44; D'Este, *Decision*, 274.
69. Diary of Maj-Gen Verney, quoted D'Este, *Decision*, 272–74 ns. 1–2.
70. English, *Canadian*, 290. (Initial overconfidence): PRO, CABl06/1060, Hargest, entry 17 June 44.
71. (Tank superiority): PRO, WO205/422, GOC 7AD, Immediate Rpt 6, Impressions of Fighting in Normandy, 17 June 44; J. J. How, *The British Breakout* (London: Kimber, 1981), 86–87. (German 88mm guns): Wingfield, *Only*, 146.
72. E. Lefèvre, *Panzers in Normandy: Then and Now* (London: Battle of Britain Prints, 1983), 168–80. (Sackings): Michael Carver, *Out of Step: Memoirs of a Field Marshal* (London: Hutchinson, 1989), 196; Hastings, *Overlord*, 311, 345.
73. Carver, *Out*, 166–67.
74. D. Rissik, *The DLI at War* (Durham, England: DLI, 1953), 237; Maj E. W. Clay, *The Path of the 50th: The Story of the 50th (Northumbrian) Division in the Second World War* (Aldershot, England: Gale & Polden, 1950), 228.
75. Churchill lamented that only one in five "men who wear the King's uniform ever hear a bullet whistle" PRO, WO216/101, f16a, PM Minute M1159/4 to Grigg, 3 Dec 44.
76. PRO, CAB106/1060, Hargest, entry 21 June 44; WO163/162, Rpt Morale of the Army, Feb–Apr 44; French, "Tommy," 158.
77. Carver, Out, 176–77; D'Este, *Decision*, 271–72.
78. Verney diary, quoted D'Este, *Decision*, 273, How, *Breakout*, 86–87.
79. Maj-Gen. G. P. B. Roberts, *From the Desert to the Baltic* (London: Kimber, 1987), 168.
80. LHCMA, OCP/8, Comments on Senior Commanders [Snr Comds].
81. The Grossdeutschland Division suffered 250 percent casualties in three years: Bartov, Army, 48-58. During twelve months' combat in Northwest Europe, the twenty-four Canadian battalions involved suffered 152 percent casualties: NAC, CP/29, D449, Battle Casualties.
82. Holmes, *Firing*, 217.
83. (12SS): Paul Carell [pseud.], *Invasion—They're Coming!—The German Account of the Allied Landings and the 80 Days' Battle for France* (London: Harrap, 1962), 124–26, 225, 292; H. Meyer, *Kriegsgeschichte der 12SS-Panzerdivision "Hitlerjugend"* (Osnabruck: Munin Verlag, 1982), passim. (Lehr): Carell, *Invasion*, 147–52, 162. (1AB Div): R. J. Kershaw, *It Never Snows in September* (Marlborough: Crowood Press, 1990), passim.
84. PRO, WO205/5C, Ltr Weeks to de Guingand, 26 June 44.
85. LHCMA, OCP/1/5, Nairne's Qns; LHCMA, JNP/II/3/24 & /197a, Ltrs North to Belchem, 23 Jan 53, & to Liddell Hart, 10 Nov 53 & 26 March 52.
86. LHCMA, OCP/5/3/18, Memo re Rpt by Corps Psychiatrist; 5/4/103, Notes on Ryan's *A Bridge Too Far* [Ryan Notes].

87. The eight most reliable divisions in 21AG in Normandy were the 15th, 43rd, 49th, 50th, 53rd, 59th Inf, 6th AB and 11th Armd Divisions: LHCMA, OCP/5/3/14, Ltr O'Connor to Roberts, 8 July 44; /8, Snr Comds; Liddell Hart, *Tanks* 2:347; IWM, BLM/115/33, M137, Mess BLM to VCIGS, 1320 2 Sept 44.

88. CCA, Grigg papers, 9/8/12(B), Rpt on State of 6DWR as of 30 June, & /12(A) Ltr BLM to Grigg, 2 July 44; Hastings, *Overlord*, 177–79; French, "Tommy," 156–57.

89. PRO, WO171/855 & 856, (WDs 3 & 4CLY, 44).

90. PRO, CABl06/1060, Hargest, Opn for 20 June 44, & Notes on Attack on Fontenoy, 25 June 44.

91. (Meyer): English, *Canadian*, 209. (6 DWR): CCA, Grigg papers, 9/8/12(B), 6 DWR.

92. PRO, CAB 106/1060, Hargest, Actions to D+10.

93. CCA, Grigg papers, 9/8/24, Ltr BLM to Grigg, 15 Sept 44, p. 2.

94. CCA, RLEW/8/15, Notes for RUSI conf; Ltr Gavin to Lewin, 28 Feb 78; Kennedy, Business, 351.

95. LHCMA, OCP/5/4/103, Ryan Notes.

96. LHCMA, Turner Cain papers, Narrative, p. 33. Thompson noticed this at the time (Montgomery, 174).

97. LHCMA, OCP/5/4/103, Ryan Notes.

98. LHCMA, Leakey papers, draft autobiography *Nine Lives—A Soldier's Story*, 90.

99. NAC, CP/2, 1-0-2-1, f21, Ltr Simonds to Crocker (cc. Crerar), 12 Oct 44.

100. Ibid.

101. P. Simpkin, "North-West Europe," Lecture, Metropolitan Police History Society, 12 Oct 1994.

102. J. L. Granatstein, The Generals (Toronto: Stoddart, 1993), p.186.

103. All three quotes, Hasting, *Overlord*, 180, 372–73.

104. IWM, BLM/74/5, Minion, emphasis in original.

105. Hastings, *Overlord*, 372.

106. PRO, WO179/2579, (WD Cdn Planning Staff [CPS] 1944), Jan Diary, App 2, Headley Court Conference, 31 Jan 44 [Headley].

107. Moorehead, *Montgomery*, 189.

108. IWM, BLM/72, BLM Diary; Hastings, *Overlord*, 68–69; Thompson, *Montgomery*, 41.

109. IWM, BLM/104/4, Presentation of Plans before the King, 15 May 1944, para 20; PRO, WO163/162, Morale Rpt Feb–Apr 44. See Moorehead, *Montgomery*, 188.

110. LHCMA, AP/3/B/XI, Notes, entry 28 Feb 44, exclamation in original.

111. B. L. Montgomery, *The Path to Leadership* (London: Collins, 1961), 125–27.

112. LHCMA, AP/3/B/XII, Notes, entry 27 May 44.

113. IWM, BLM90/5, Euston; Hastings, *Overlord*, 69; Moorehead, *Montgomery*, 188.

114. LHCMA, AP/12/XI/4, /48 & /69, Interviews with Grigg & Paget respectively. In July 1943, Churchill told Brooke that he wanted him to command "Overlord," but later changed his mind: D'Este, *Decision*, 43.

115. IWM, BLM/41/5, Notes Morale, Aug 43. See also Grigg, *Prejudice*, 423.

116. Toronto Univ, Massey papers, Vol. 311, Diary, 12 March 43, quoted Granatstein, *Generals*, 102, n. 107.

117. Diary of Harry C. Butcher, app, Ltr Ike to Marshall, 5 Apr 43, quoted Hamilton, *Monty* 2:210–11, n. 1; This is not mentioned in Butcher, *Three*.

118. Thompson observed that BLM "blew Britain's trumpet as well as his own," Montgomery, 21.
119. R. Lewin, "Montgomery" in Michael Carver, ed., *The War Lords: Military Commanders of the Twentieth Century* (Boston: Little Brown, 1976), 503.
120. Thompson, *Montgomery*, 19.
121. Kershaw, "Lessons," *RUSI Jnl* 132, no. 3 (Sept 1987): 61.
122. IWM, MSC/20, Ltr BLM to Simpson, 20 June 44.
123. PRO, WO205/5B, M25, Mess BLM to de Guingand, 20 June 44.
124. IWM, MSC/20, Ltr BLM to Simpson, 20 June 44.
125. IWM, Lt-Gen G. C. Bucknall papers, various Ltrs, 4-17 Aug 44; LHCMA, OCP/5/3/25, Ltr O'Connor to Macmillan, 29 July 44.
126. Bradley, *Story*, 254.
127. These included Flail mine-clearers, AVsRE for engaging pillboxes, and Crocodile flame throwers: N. W. Duncan, *79th Armoured Division: Hobo's Funnies* (Windsor, England: Profile Books, 1972); D. Fletcher, *Vanguard of Victory: The 79th Armoured Division* (London: HMSO, 1984).
128. PRO, WO291/1169, AORG Rpt 17/52, Inf Rates of Advance.
129. See Korps Feldt's attacks on the eastern flank of "Market-Garden:" Kershaw, *Snows*, 189–91.
130. The importance of helping the ordinary soldier is evident in IWM, BLM/161, Morale.
131. LHCMA, AP/14/33, M344, Mess BLM to CIGS, 2220 23 Nov 44; IWM, BLM/78/1, Notes on the Campaign in NWE [Cmpgn NWE]; IWM, Brig D. F. A. T. Baines papers, Diary, 17, entry 5 Dec 44.
132. PRO, WO205/5B, Ltr de Guingand to BLM, 24 June 44.
133. PRO, CAB106/1060, Hargest, 17 June 44, Notes—Tanks.
134. Brig J. P. Kiszely has observed that the British army was—and still is—adverse to frank criticism, "Originality," in Reid, *Science*, 35–42.
135. BLM, IWM/90/9, Speech to Staff, 28 March 44.
136. Williams interview, Hastings, *Overlord*, 180, n. 30; "Pip" Roberts concurred: *Desert*, 214.
137. Paul Johnson, "What Makes a Great Commander," *Daily Mail*, 20 Nov 93, p. 8. A soldier in Normandy observed that "we had absolute confidence" in Monty's "ability to save our necks" (Wingfield, *Only*, 136).
138. R. F. Weigley, *Eisenhower's Lieutenants: The Campaigns of France and Germany 1944-45* (London: Sidgewick & Jackson, 1981), 329, 397; A. Kemp, *The Unknown Battle: Metz 1944* (London: F. Warne, 1981), passim.
139. CCA, Grigg papers, 9/8/12(B), Rpt on state of 6DWR as of 30 June 44.
140. CCA, Grigg papers, 9/8/12(A), Ltr BLM to Grigg, 2 July 44.

CHAPTER 3
1. Ellis, *Victory* 1:131–33, 308, 453n, and 2:141–42, 158–59; Stacey, *Victory*, 284–85, 385–86, 630–33.
2. D'Este, *Decision*, 258–59.
3. See Peaty, "Manpower."
4. Britain "has put in her body and soul . . . to win the battle of mankind . . . but she will come out of it poor in substance" (Smuts' Addrs to Empire Parliamentary Assoc, 25 Oct 43, quoted J. C. Smuts, *Jan Christian Smuts*, London: Cassell, 1952, 442–44).

5. Shelford Bidwell, "Indirect Artillery Fire as a Battle Winner/Loser," in Corelli Barnett, Shelford Bidwell, Brian Bond, John Harding, and John Terraine, *Old Battles New Defences: Can We Learn from Military History?* (London: Brassey's, 1985), 115, 133.

6. Shelford Bidwell, *Gunners at War* (London: Arms & Armour, 1970), 200.

7. H. M. D. Parker, *Manpower: A Study of Wartime Policy and Administration* (History of the Second World War: UK Civil Series), (London: HMSO, 1957), 226–28; D'Este, *Decision*, 252; Thompson, *Montgomery*, 21; (Disbandments): PRO, WO216/101, Estimates of Army Manpower Requirements.

8. D'Este, *Decision*, 254–55.

9. J. Peaty, Correspondence with Prof. D. Graham, "Decision in Normandy: The Manpower Dilemma (I)," 1993, p. 1. See also PRO, WO163/162, WO Comments on Morale Rpt, May–July 44.

10. PRO, WO199/1334, Memo, Maj-Gen Watson [DMP] to CinC HF, 28 Dec 43; and reply, 20 Oct 43.

11. PRO, WO285, (Dempsey papers) /2, Ltr BLM to Weeks, 19 March 44.

12. PRO, WO205/5C, Ltr de Guingand to Weeks, 20 March 44.

13. Howarth, *Monty*, 14.

14. LHCMA, AP/14/25/10, Ltr BLM to CIGS, 19 May 44.

15. Peter Earle Diary, quoted Horne and Montgomery, *Lonely*, 107.

16. Horne and Montgomery, *Lonely*, 107.

17. LHCMA, AP/14/25/10, Ltr BLM to CIGS, 19 May 44.

18. PRO, CAB78/21, Committee to Consider Transfer of Men from RAF Regt to Army, para 2. In late 1943 the British negotiated with the Canadians to obtain a loan of Canadian officers, ultimately 600 in number, under the Canloan scheme: W.I. Smith, *Code Word Canloan* (Oxford: Dundurn Press, 1992), 1–11.

19. IWM, BLM/120/32, Grigg Minute to PM on Manpower, 25 March 44.

20. PRO, WO216/101, Paper WP(43)464, 10 October 1943.

21. PRO, WO205/152, "Overlord:" British Casualty Projection.

22. Ibid.

23. IWM, BLM/120/32, Grigg's Minute to PM on Manpower, 25 March 44.

24. PRO, CAB78/21, Gen/36, Cab Mtng, 30 May 44.

25. IWM, BLM/120/32, Grigg Minute to PM on Manpower, 25 March 44.

26. On 18 April 1944 Churchill requested that 25,000 RAF Regiment personnel be transferred to the army as infantry, including 2,000 men immediately for the Guards (PRO, AIR8/809, various documents, April–June 44). The 2,000 were transferred by 27 June (Progress Rpt, 27 June 44), yet the bulk of the remainder were only gradually transferred in the winter of 1944–45 as the threat of air and V-weapon attacks on the U.K. receded (AIR2/8247). See also WO199/1334; Parker, *Manpower*, 230–31.

27. Gen. F. Morgan, *Overture to Overlord* (London: Hodder & Stoughton, 1950); G. Blake, *Mountain and Flood*, (Glasgow: Jackson and Son, 1950), 43.

28. PRO, WO199/1334, f16a, Memo, DA&QMG HF to DMP WO, 27 Feb 44.

29. An analysis of 28,099 Home Forces infantrymen revealed that 5,660 (20 percent) were undraftable (PRO, WO199/1334, f 9a Memo CinC HF to DSD WO, 15 Feb 44, App A, Tab B). Elsewhere this proportion was estimated at 25 percent (WO199/1334, Note DAAG HF to AA&QMG HF, 10 March 44).

30. PRO, WO199/1334, f16a, Memo DA&QMG HF to DMP WO, 27 Feb 44, Apps.

31. The Maj-Gen, RAC at 21AG [MGRAC] "stated that there was a marked shortage of O[ther]R[anks] reinforcements and that conservation of manpower

48. Maj-Gen. J. F. C. Fuller, "The Tactics of Penetration," *RUSI Jnl* 59 (1914): 378–79, quoted Brian Holden Reid, *J. F. C. Fuller: Military Thinker* (London: Macmillan, 1987), 27; Maj-Gen. J. F. C. Fuller, *Foundations of the Science of War* (London: Hutchinson, 1925), 109–10.

49. Luttwak, "Operational," 61–62; Reid, *Fuller*, 33, 42.

50. LHCMA, AP/14/31, M156, GUARD Mess BLM to CIGS, 0240 4 Sept 44.

51. Luttwak, "Operational," 61; T. N. Dupuy, *Understanding War: History and Theory of Combat* (London: Leo Cooper, 1992), 70–71.

52. MOD, Design, 4–11; U.S. Army, Field Manual 100-5: Operations (Washington, D.C.: Dept. of the Army, 1986), 10.

53. MOD, Design, 4–21 to 4-24; Luttwak, "Operational," 63.

54. Luttwak, "Operational," 62–63.

55. English, *Canadian*, 272; Reid, *Science*, 5.

56. U.S. Army, FM 100-5, passim.

57. The following discussion relies on Murray, "Historiography," unless otherwise stated; see also Powers, "Normandy," 455; Horne, *Lonely*, xxii–xxiii.

58. Dalgleish, *Planned*; J. D'Arcy-Dawson, *European Victory* (London: Macdonald, 1945); Lt-Gen. L. Brereton, *The Brereton Diaries* (New York: Wm. Morrow, 1946); P. J. Grigg, *Prejudice and Judgement* (London: Jonathon Cape, 1948).

59. R. S. Allen, *Lucky Forward: The History of General Patton's Third U.S. Army* (New York: Vanguard Press, 1947); H. C. Butcher, *My Three Years with Eisenhower* (London: Heinemann, 1946); R. Ingersoll, *Top Secret* (New York: Harcourt, Brace, 1946); George Patton, *War as I Knew It* (Boston: Houghton Mifflin, 1947).

60. Maj-Gen. F. de Guingand, *Operation Victory* (London: Hodder & Stoughton, 1947), 328–30; C. Richardson, *Send for Freddie: The Story of Monty's Chief of Staff* (London: Kimber, 1987), 161–63.

61. B. L. Montgomery, *Normandy to the Baltic* (London: Hutchinson, 1947); and "Twenty First (British) Army Group in the Campaign in North-West Europe 1944–45," *RUSI Jnl* 90, no. 560 (Nov 1945): 437–54.

62. R. A. Hart, "Learning Lessons; Military Adaptation and Innovation In the American, British, Canadian, and German Armies during the 1944 Normandy Campaign," Ph.D. Diss., Ohio State Univ., 1997, 4. (Paradigm): R. S. Kershaw, "Lessons to Be Derived from the Wehrmacht's Experience in the East," *RUSI Jnl* 132, no. 3 (Sept 1987): 61–68.

63. W. Beddell Smith, "Eisenhower's Six Great Decisions: Europe 1944–45," *Saturday Evening Post*, 8 June–13 July 1946, later published (New York: Longmans, Green, 1956); Dwight Eisenhower, *Crusade in Europe* (New York: Da Capo Press, 1948). See Richardson, *Freddie*, 198–201; Maj-Gen. F. de Guingand, *From Brass Hat to Bowler Hat* (London: Hamish Hamilton, 1979), 76–77.

64. B. L. Montgomery, *Memoirs* (London: Collins, 1958). See Richardson, *Freddie*, 202–5.

65. Wilmot, *Struggle*; North, *Europe* (1953); Belfield and Essame, *Normandy* (1965); H. Essame, *The Battle for Germany* (London: Batsford, 1969).

66. Ellis, *Victory*; J. Ehrman, *Grand Strategy*, vols. 5–6 (London: HMSO, 1956); Stacey, *Victory*; The American series (The U.S. Army in World War Two: European Theater of Operations), Washington, D.C.: Office of the Chief of Military History, Dept. of the Army, includes: G. A. Harrison, *Cross Channel Attack* (1951); F. C. Pogue, *The Supreme Command* (1954); R. G. Ruppenthal, *Logistical Support of the Armies*, 2 vols. (1953–59); M. Blumenson, *Breakout and Pursuit*

was most important"' (PRO, WO171/196, [WD G 8C July 44], Notes RAC Conf, 29 July 44).

32. PRO, WO 199/1334, f 17a, Memo DAQMG(Mov) HF to DQMG(Mov) WO, 26 Feb 44.

33. PRO, WO166/14174, (WD G GHQ HF, July–Dec 44), Memo CinC HF to WO, 7 Aug 44.

34. D'Este, *Decision*, 268; see also John Peaty, "Myth, Reality, and Carlo D'Este." *War Studies Jnl* 1, issue 2 (Spring 1996): 60–72, passim.

35. PRO, WO73/161, General Return of the Strength of the British Army, 30 June 44.

36. D'Este, *Decision*, 268–29.

37. Holmes, *Firing*, 36–37.

38. PRO, WO73/161, General Return, 30 June 44, puts this figure at 56,335.

39. The German army's replacement system was devastated when necessity forced it to dispatch entire training units to the front. See Kershaw, *Snows*, 115–17, 119–21.

40. PRO, WO73/161, General Return of the British Army, 30 June 44; WO199/1334, 1335; Home Forces Draft papers; WO166/14608, 15072, 15117–18, 15149–50, 15152, Various War Diaries. Abbreviations: Bn= Battalion; Coy = Company; Est = Establishment; Holdng = Holding; Res = Reserve. Caveats: {a} = unless decision made at chiefs of staff level. {b} = based on estimate that 75% were draftable. {c} Specialized "Mountaineer" troops.

41. See Table 3.2.

42. See Table 3.1.

43. PRO, WO205/152, "Overlord:" British Casualty Projection.

44. Stacey, *Victory*, 284.

45. PRO, WO162/116, NWE British Battle Casualties.

46. NAC, Papers of Lt-Gen K. Stuart, DND War Reinforcements File, Memo Montague [MGA CMHQ] to Minister of National Defense, "Strengths of Inf Bns," 14 Oct 44, enclosing Table of Inf Bns and their W/Es and Strengths 5 Aug-7 Oct 44, compiled by AG(Stats), 13 Oct 44.

47. BLM disbanded the 59th Division in August and the 50th Division in December 1944.

48. IWM, BLM/114/11, Ltr BLM to Grigg, 22 Jan 45.

49. Ltr BLM to Maud Montgomery, 8 Nov 1917, quoted Hamilton, *Monty* 1:121.

50. Steve Weiss, "Anglo-American Negotiations 1938–1944: Strategy and the Road to Anvil," Ph.D. Diss., Univ. of London, 1995, p. 10. Alexander was one of the few officers not "greatly affected by a disgust with the style of command adopted by First World War generals" B. H. Reid, "Alexander," in John Keegan, ed., *Churchill's Generals* (London: Weidenfeld & Nicholson, 1991), 109; Graham, *Coalitions*, 213.

51. O'Brien, in Howarth, *Monty*, 51.

52. Grigg, *Prejudice*, 377.

53. Graham, *Coalitions*, 209.

54. D'Este, *Decision*, 46–53; Hamilton, *Monty* 2:462–74.

55. Thompson, *Montgomery*, 20.

56. Montgomery, *Memoirs*, 332; Murray, "Historiography," 268.

57. Maj-Gen K. Strong, *Intelligence at the Top* (London: Cassell, 1968), 149–50.

58. IWM, BLM/73, BLM Diary, entry 15 May 44.

59. Ibid.

60. David Fraser, *Alanbrooke* (London: Hamlyn, 1983), 449.

61. PRO, PREM3/342/5, M786/3, PM's Personal Minute to Grigg & Brooke, 6 Nov 43.

62. PRO, WO216/101, f21, PM Mess to BLM, 12 Dec 44; Hamilton, *Monty* 3:158.

63. PRO, WO216/101, f16a, PM Personal Minute M1159/4 to Grigg, 3 Dec 44.

64. LHCMA, AP/14/34, M349, Mess BLM to CIGS, 2225 27 Nov 44; AP/14/35, M373 Mess BLM to Grigg, 1855 11 Dec 44; M375, Mess BLM to PM, 2025 12 Dec 44. See Major A. H. R. Baker and Major B. Rust, *A Short History of the 50th Northumbrian Division* (Yarmouth, England: 50th Division, 1966), 56; Clay, 50th, 305–6.

65. LHCMA, AP/3/B/XIII, Notes, commentary on 23 Aug 44 entry.

66. Strong, *Intelligence*, 149.

67. Montgomery, *Memoirs*, 270–71; Arthur Bryant, *Triumph in the West 1943–46* (London: Collins, 1959), 366.

68. Reid, "Italian," in Gooch, *Decisive*, 135; the Italian campaign demonstrated that "diplomacy was often more important than grip" (Ibid., 149).

69. Strong, *Intelligence*, 140.

70. Thompson, *Montgomery*, 182.

71. Fraser, *Alanbrooke*, 438, 453, 456–57.

72. Thompson, *Montgomery*, 86, n. 2, citing General Gehr von Schweppenburg, *The Spectator*, 5 June 64.

73. Ibid.

74. PRO, WO208/3193, MIRS Special Tactical Study 29 "German Views on Allied Combat Efficiency," 17 Nov 44, p. 2.

75. Col P. P. Rawlins, "Economy," in Reid, *Science*, 60.

76. LHCMA, AP/3/B/XII, Notes, 31 March 44; see Fraser, *Alanbrooke*, 403–4.

77. LHCMA, AP/3/B/XII, Notes, 1950s comment on 31 March 44 entry; see also English, *Canadian*, 188.

78. LHCMA, AP/3/B/XII, Notes, 1950s comment on 31 March 44 entry.

79. Rawlins, "Economy," in Reid, *Science*, 60.

80. This allocation infuriated Patton (Martin Blumenson, *The Patton Papers 1940–45*, 2 vols. [Boston: Houghton Mifflin, 1972–74], 2:472).

81. D. Irving, *The War between the Generals* (London: Allen Lane, 1981), 217; Strong, *Intelligence*, 140.

82. PRO, WO171/291, (WD, A 8C); IWM, Macmillan Papers; D'Este, *Decision*, 244–45.

83. Dawnay interview, in Hamilton, *Monty* 2:662.

84. LHCMA, AP/14/27, f12, M510, 21AG Dir, 10 July 44, emphasis in original.

85. Williams interview, in Hamilton, *Monty* 2:663.

86. Hamilton, *Monty* 2:732, Irving, *Generals*, 190–91.

87. Dempsey felt "Goodwood" was "desirable" as an attack "in which we could utilise that surplus of tanks, and economise infantry," LHCMA, LHP/1/230/22A; LHP/1/230/16, Dempsey's Notes Op Goodwood, 21 Feb 52; John Baynes, *The Forgotten Victor. General Sir Richard O'Connor* (London: Brassey's, 1989), 210.

88. PRO, WO179/2579, (WD CPS 44), Headley, 31 Jan 44.

89. Notes given verbally to DMO, 14 July 44, quoted Ellis, *Victory* 1:330, n. 8.

90. Butcher, *Three*, 622; also quoted D'Este, *Decision*, 265, n. 3.

91. LHCMA, AP/14/28, f"G," M514, Ltr BLM to Simpson, 24 July 44; expanding LHCMA, AP/14/28, f "F," M512, 21AG Dir, 21 July 44.

92. Liddell Hart's analysis of "Bluecoat" misleadingly calculated an Allied superiority of 30:1 (LHCMA, LHP/1/292/100, Ltr LH to C.S. Forrester, 18 Feb 52).
93. Clausewitz, *War*, 119–21.
94. Dupuy, *Understanding*, 146.
95. Kurt Meyer interview, quoted English, *Canadian*, 291–92.
96. LHCMA, AP/14/33 (& NAC, CP/2, 1-0:V1, fs99-101), M532, 21AG Dir, 16 Oct 44, para 16.
97. LHCMA, AP/14/6, M475, M481, Mess BLM to CIGS, 2330 12 Feb 45, & 2220 14 Feb 45, respectively.
98. English, *Canadian*, 125–26; Richardson, "Recollections," in Hamilton, *Legend*, 96; Broadhurst interview, in Hamilton, *Monty* 2:264; Eighth Army Brigade Major cited Johnson, "Great," 8–9.
99. D'Este, *Decision*, 258–59.
100. Ibid., 259.

CHAPTER 4
1. Bidwell, in Barnett, *Old*, 138–39; Mackenzie and Reid, *British*, 10.
2. War Office, Military Training Pamphlets [MTP], Nos. 2-90, (London: HMSO, 1938-45).
3. Ltr BLM to Vice CIGS [VCIGS], 21 Dec 43, cited Brooks, *Eighth*, 346; Lt-Gen Weeks, Deputy CIGS, felt that the contradiction of official policy in 21AG's RAC Liaison Ltr 1 was "not a sin" (PRO, WO205/5C, Weeks to de Guingand, 5 July 44).
4. English, *Canadian*, 160.
5. Ltrs BLM to VCIGS, 28 Aug, 7 Dec 43, & replies 7 Oct, 21 Dec 43; Comments by Director of Military Training [DMT], 17 Dec 43, quoted Brooks, Eighth, 274–75, 342–46; IWM, BLM/117/1, Memo BLM to GHQ Middle East Forces [MEF], 7 June 43; and 117/4, Ltr Weeks to BLM, Demi-Official [DO] 12/44, 16 Feb 44.
6. PRO, WO/179/2579, (WD CPS 44) Jan Diary, App 2, Headley, 31 Jan 44; LHCMA, de Guingand papers [DGP/]IV/2/9, Armoured Division in Battle (Dec 44) [Armoured]. IWM, BLM/117/7, Ltr DCIGS to BLM, 23 March 44, and 117/9, reply, 3 April 44.
7. Such as the Directors, Royal Artillery, and Royal Armoured Corps, [DRA, DRAC].
8. The British army is characterized by "innate and deeply ingrained conservatism," Kiszely, "Originality," in Reid, *Science*, 32–35.
9. BLM outlined these policies as an instructor at Quetta in 1934 (*Memoirs*, 80).
10. English, *Canadian*, 80, 108, 116–17, 125–37. (Africa): IWM, Belchem papers, Haifa, 21 Sept 42; Diary, quoted Brooks, *Eighth*, 30–33, 47–60, 79–82.
11. IWM, BLM/90/7, Address to Senior Officers, 2nd Army, 20 March 44 [SBA Addrs]; PRO, CAB106/1037, BLM Conference, 13 Jan 44, [BLM Conf]; WO179/2579, (WD CPS 44), Headley. (Leese): IWM, BLM/97/22, Ltr Leese to BLM, 11 June 44; G. Blaxland, *The Plain Cook and the Great Showman* (Abingdon, England: Purnell, 1977), 267; R. Ryder, *Oliver Leese* (London: Hamish Hamilton, 1987), 103.
12. LHCMA, DGP/IV/2/8, Some Notes on the Conduct of War (Nov 44); DGP/IV/2/10, Some Notes on the Use of Air Power (Dec 44) [Air]; DGP/IV/2/9, Armoured; IWM, BLM/159, High Command in War (June 45); BLM/160, Mod-

ern Administration in the Field in European Warfare (Oct 45); BLM/161, Morale. (Published works): See Montgomery, *Memoirs*, 80–90, 347–54; *Normandy*, 113–14.

13. Howard, "Price."

14. Keegan has argued that Montgomery was inconsistent both in what he said and did operationally, as typified by his flexibility during Second Alamein and his change of plan during the March 1943 Battle of Mareth: Carver, "Montgomery" in Keegan, *Generals*, 148–65, 156; Hamilton, *Monty* 2:183–195.

15. Picot, *Accidental*, 47. Montgomery did not invite de Guingand to the German surrender and hence monopolized the glory derived from the ceremony (Hamilton, *Monty* 3:511–18; Richardson, *Flashback*, 192).

16. Omar Bradley, and Clay Blair, *A General's Life* (London: Sidgewick & Jackson, 1983), 159, 190. (Ardennes): Hamilton, *Monty* 3:297–306.

17. LHCMA, LHP/1/230/22–23a, Liddell Hart and Dempsey's Notes on "Goodwood."

18. LHCMA, AP/14/28, f"D," BLM Notes on Second Army Ops 16-18 July, 15 July, paras 1, 8; [Notes SA Ops]; also quoted Ellis, Victory 1:327, n. 1. These were the only prior written operational orders BLM gave to Dempsey—his directives only confirmed in writing previous verbal decisions (CCA, RLEW/2/7, Notes, Talk with Monty, 28 Jan 69; RLEW/7/7 Notes, Talk with Dempsey, 4 Nov 68).

19. PRO, WO179/2579, (WD CPS 44), Headley, 31 Jan 44. WO171/193, (WD G(Ops) SBA June 44), IC 013, 19 June 44.

20. PRO, WO285/9, Dempsey Diary, entry 25 July 44.

21. PRO, WO205/19B, Mins CoS 21AG Mtng, 20 March 44; WO171/104, (WD G(Ops) 21AG May 44), App J, Dir Airfield Construction, 1 June 44.

22. Hamilton, *Monty* 2:662, interview with Dawnay, 1 Feb 83.

23. Montgomery, *Normandy*, 114.

24. Thompson, *Montgomery*, 315.

25. CCA, RLEW/7/8, Article on BLM by Edgar Williams, undated. Montgomery's Memoirs, Normandy, and "Twenty First," all display this distortion.

26. CCA, RLEW/7/8, Williams' BLM article, undated.

27. For Belchem's opinion of Williams, LHCMA, JNP/II/3/54; that Richardson "had an axe to grind," CCA, RLEW/2/13, Ltr Belchem to Lewin, 21 Aug 80. On fading memory see Lt-Gen. F. Morgan, LHCMA, JNP II/3/274; M. Howard reference CCA, RLEW/2/13, Ltr Belchem to Lewin, 6 Aug 79.

28. Maj-Gen. F. de Guingand, *Generals at War* (London: Hodder & Stoughton, 1964), 108; CCA, RLEW/2/13, passim. (Belchem): D'Este, *Decision*, 92–98; Maj-Gen D. Belchem, *All in the Day's March* (London: Collins, 1978), 191, and *Victory in Normandy* (London: Chatto & Windus, 1981), 92–96, 98.

29. War Office, Field Service Regulations, Vol. II (Operations—General), (London: HMSO, 1935), Ch 2, Sect 11, para 5; Reid, Fuller, 36.

30. IWM, BLM/159, Command; BLM/90/7, SBA Addrs.

31. The closest principle in modern British army doctrine is "Selection and Maintenance of the Aim" (MOD, Design, A-1).

32. Montgomery, *Memoirs*, 87.

33. Ibid., 81, 88, emphasis in original.

34. Ibid., 82.

35. Ibid., 82, 87–88.

36. 1WM, BLM/37/1, BLM Diary, 7 May–9 July 43, p. 2.

37. Morgan, *Overture*, 34, 114.

38. Bradley and Blair, *Life*, 226.

39. Some Americans claimed falsely that Montgomery originally intended to break out in the east, but then changed his plan; Beddell Smith, *Six*, 73; SHAEF, Report by the Supreme Commander on the Operations in Europe, 6 June 1944 to 8 May 1945 (Washington: U.S. Govt. Printing Office, 1946), 41. Bradley, however, refuted this (Bradley and Blair, *Life*, 264–65). For Eisenhower's misunderstanding, LHCMA, AP/14/27, f7, Ltr Eisenhower to BLM, 7 July 44. See Powers, "Normandy," passim; A. Harding Ganz, "Questionable Objective: The Brittany Ports, 1944," *Jmil.H* 59, no. 1 (Jan 1995): 82–83.

40. (21 Feb): PRO, CAB/44, Narrative, Overlord, pp. 116–19, SBA Outline Plan [SBA OP], 21 Feb 44. (Thunderclap): Belchem, *March*, 198; Bradley and Blair, *Life*, 232–35; D'Este, *Decision*, 75–79; Irving, *Generals*, 99, 177; (8 May Apprcn): PRO, WO205/118, G(Pl) 21AG, Possible Development of Ops to Secure Lodgement Area, [sic] 8 May 44 [Lodgement]; D'Este, *Decision*, 92–100; Belchem, *Victory*, 54. (15 May plans): PRO, AIR37/1057, Allied Expeditionary Air Force [AEAF] Record; AIR37/784, Leigh-Mallory Diary, pp. 106–8; D'Este, *Decision*, 82–92. WO205/5B, Mess M14, BLM to de Guingand, 0830 11 June 44. WO205/644, G(Pl) 21AG Apprcn, 7 July 44. For a correct appreciation of BLM's strategy, see Bradley and Blair, *Life*, 261, 264–65.

41. PRO, CAB44/242, pp. 116–19, SBA OP.

42. WO205/5B, Mess M14, BLM to de Guingand, 0830 11 June 44.

43. Montgomery, *Normandy*, 112; "Twenty First," 432.

44. D'Este, *Decision*, 164, 169–71.

45. Montgomery, *Memoirs*, 87.

46. PRO, WO106/5846 & /5845, British Army of the Rhine, Battlefield Tours "Veritable" & "Plunder," [BAOR BT "Verit" & "Plunder"].

47. PRO, WO205/247, M221, Mess BLM to Eisenhower, 22 Sept 44; & f23a, Notes for CoS, 21 Sept 44; IWM, BLM/107/25, M527, 21AG Dir, 27 Sept 44.

48. PRO, WO171/120, (WD G(Ops) HQ 21AG Oct 44), App J; WO171/210, (WD G(Ops) SBA Oct 44); WO285/16, Dempsey's Notes on SBA Autumn Dirs & Confs, Oct–Nov 44, [Autumn].

49. PRO, WO106/5846, BAOR BT "Verit," p. 63, Horrocks Lecture.

50. Ellis, *Victory* 2:160–61.

51. PRO, CAB44/255, The Opening of the Scheldt [Opening], pp. 81–87; PRO, CAB106/971, 21AG Rpt Clearing the Scheldt, [Clearing], p. 4; WO179/2770, (WD GS HQ 3rd Cdn Inf Div [3CID] Sept–Oct 44), Oct Diary narr; W. D. & S. Whitaker, *The Battle of the River Scheldt* (London: Souvenir Press, 1985), 263–78. (Simonds' idea): J. Williams, *Long Left Flank. The Hard Fought Way to the Reich, 1944–45* (London: Leo Cooper, 1988), 116.

52. CAB44/254, Arnhem, AL1200/96/C, p. 138; PRO, CAB106/1054, Horrocks, Arnhem, passim.

53. IWM, BLM/126/35, M535, Ltr BLM to CIGS, 17 Nov 44.

54. PRO, WO179/2579, (WD CPS 44), Headley, 31 Jan 44.

55. PRO, WO171/1, (WD 21AG July–Dec 43), Aug Diary, Lessons Tunisian Campaign.

56. PRO, WO171, Feb 45 WDs of: /4389, 129th Infantry Brigade [IB]; /4391, 130th IB; /4423, 158th IB; /4437, 214th IB; PRO, WO223, WD extracts of, /98, 44th IB; /101, 46th IB; /102, 71st IB; /107, 158th IB; /110, 160th IB; /112, 227th IB.

57. LHCMA, LHP/15/15, CWP/130, Discussion with Horrocks, 15 May 46.

58. LHCMA, Lt-Col D. Webster papers, Admin Hist Ops 21AG, p. 101; R. Gill and J. Groves (Comps.), Club Route in Europe (Hannover, Germany; 30 Corps, 1946), 130.

59. PRO, WO106/5848, BAOR BT "Verit," maps. Maximum troop density was 11,000 troops per square mile (PRO, CAB106/1020, Military Opt Research Unit [MORU] Rpt "Verit").

60. S. E. Ambrose, *The Supreme Commander* (London: Cassell, 1971), 573; Hamilton, Monty 3:221–23, 228–29, 236.

61. Baynes, *Victor*, 201.

62. ("Veritable"): PRO, WO106/4432, BLM's future intentions; WO106/5846, BAOR BT "Verit;" WO179/2609, (WD G(PL) FCA 44), Dec Diary; WO205/9, and /243-44, "Verit" Planning Papers; WO205/953, 21AG FR "Verit." ("Gatwick"): WO171/120, (WD G(Ops) 21AG Oct 44), App J; WO171/210, (WD G(Ops) SBA Oct 44); WO285/16, Dempsey's Autumn.

63. PRO, WO106/5846, BAOR BT "Verit," p. 63, Horrocks Lecture. (Cease): LHCMA, AP/14/6, M493, Mess BLM to CIGS, 20 Feb 45.

64. LHCMA, AP/14/1, Ltr CIGS to BLM, 28 July 44.

65. IWM, BLM/78/1, Notes Cmpgn NWE, para 11.

66. D'Este, Decision, 340, n. l, quoting Ltr Bradley to Eisenhower, 29 June 44.

67. LHCMA, AP/14/1, Ltr CIGS to BLM, 28 July 1944. Brooke told Eisenhower that due to the high German force density in Normandy and the relatively modest Allied numerical superiority, the Allies were not "in a position to launch an all out offensive along the whole front." See also Hamilton, *Monty* 3:138.

68. IWM, BLM/78/1, Notes Cmpgn NWE, para 11; also quoted Hamilton, *Monty*, 3:136, n. 1.

69. IWM, Maj-Gen. W. J. F. Eassie Papers lists daily rates of rounds fired by 21AG. BLM described the allocation of 100 rounds per gun per day for the American November 1944 Cologne offensive as "quite inadequate;" LHCMA, AP/14/33, M328, Mess, BLM to CIGS, 2225 13 Nov 44.

70. LHCMA, AP/14/33, M344, M328, Mess BLM to CIGS, 23 and 13 Nov 44. IWM, BLM/78/1, Notes Cmpgn NWE. PRO, WO205/18, Notes for CoS, 14 Nov 44.

71. Weigley, *Lieutenants*, 137–38; D'Este, *Decision*, 342–43.

72. English, *Canadian*, 271.

73. Maj. R. H. W. Dunn, "Reminiscences of a Regimental Soldier: S.P. Guns in Normandy," *Jnl. of the Royal Artillery* [*JRA*] 75 (Apr 1948): 89–95.

74. PRO, WO106/5846, BAOR BT "Verit," Horrocks Lecture, p. 63.

75. Reid, Fuller, 35.

76. Thompson, Montgomery, 315. Alamein restored "orthodox gunner doctrine" after an "extraordinary" period of "unorthodoxy" (Bidwell, *Gunners*, 180).

77. PRO, WO171/1, (WD 21AG Jul–Dec 43), Aug, Lessons Tunisian Campaign.

78. English, Canadian, 165–66.

79. S. Bidwell and D. Graham, *Firepower: British Army Weapons & Theories of War 1904–1945* (London: Allen & Unwin, 1982), 248–75 passim, 282, 288; Brian Horrocks, *A Full Life* (London: Collins Fontana, 1962), 169.

80. PRO, WO179/2579, (WD CPS 44), Headley; J. B. A. Bailey, *Field Artillery and Firepower* (Oxford: Military Press, 1989), 203. The guns of an AGRA, corps, and even an army fired respectively a "Yoke," "Victor," and "William," target.

To the author's knowledge, the only "William" fired was in Italy: NAC, CP/8 13-0-2, Cdn Ops Mediterranean, 29 June 44, Rpt CCRA ICC, 23 May 44; Maj-Gen G. Kitching, *Mud and Green Fields: The Memoirs of Major General Kitching* (Langley, B.C.: Battleline, 1986), 242–43.

81. Col A. G. Cole, "German Artillery Concentrations in World War Two," *JRA* 75 (July 1948): 196–99; P. Carell (pseud.), *Invasion—They're Coming!* (London: Harrap, 1962), 183–84, 191–93; Gen Karl Thoholte, "A German Reflects on Artillery," *Field Artillery Journal [FAJ]* 35 (Dec 1948): 709–14.

82. "Epsom" was supported by over 700 guns: Ellis, *Sharp*, 118-120; D'Este, *Decision*, 235. Operation "Windsor," 8th Canadian Infantry Brigade's attack on Carpiquet on 4 July, was supported by 760 guns (English, *Canadian*, 214).

83. LHCMA, LHP/15/15, CWP/43, Account of 2 Pz Div Ops 17 June–7 July, in 326 Inf Div Rpt Ops.

84. Some 376 guns supported the September "Market-Garden" operation, and 314 guns supported "Infatuate" in November, though the latter's original fire-plan envisaged 496 guns (PRO, WO179/2609, [WD, G(PL) FCA 44-45], Request for Certain Data, 14 Sept 44, App A, Arty Bombardment Program).

85. These guns fired 500,000 rounds equal to 8,377 tons (PRO, CAB106/1120, MORU Rpt "Verit"; WO205/408, f377a, Rpt Spectacular Examples of Massed Arty/Air Bombardment).

86. Bidwell, in Barnett, *New*, 134.

87. Maj-Gen. J. F. C. Fuller, *Thunderbolts* (London: Skeffington, 1946), 72.

88. D'Este, *Decision*, 484.

89. Brig C. N. Barclay, *The History of the 53rd (Welsh) Division in the Second World War* (London: Wm. Clowes, 1956), 117; IWM, BLM/97/22, Ltr Leese to BLM, 11 June 44, p. 3, para 5. LHCMA, Webster papers, Admin Hist Ops 21AG, p. 101.

90. D. Hist, 73/1302, Meyer interview, cited English, *Canadian*, 291–92, ns. 6, 9.

91. Carell, *Invasion*, 292.

92. PRO, WO205/5B, Ltr BLM to de Guingand, 23 June 44.

93. Richardson, *Flashback*, 174–78.

94. English, *Canadian*, 269.

95. D. Hist, 73/1302, Meyer Interview, cited English, *Canadian*, 291–92, ns. 6, 9.

96. Historians must treat both sides' intelligence with caution, as it often drew false conclusions; the Germans, for example, initially dismissed U.S. capabilities, and then overrated them after "Cobra," Pz. Lehr report, quoted Allan R. Millett and Williamson Murray, *Military Effectiveness*, 3 vols. (London: Allen & Unwin, 1988) 3:113; WO208/3193, MIRS Studies on the German Army, 29; WO171/223, (WD GS(I) SBA 44); /3957, (WD GS(I)a SBA 45); WO179/4072, (WD GS(I) FCA 45).

97. Reid, "Alexander," in Keegan, *Generals*, 120.

98. PRO, WO106/4348, Operational Research in North-West Europe [OR-NWE]; T. Copp, "Scientists and the Art of War: Operational Research in Twenty First Army Group," *RUSI Jnl* 136, no. 4 (Winter 1991): 65–70.

99. PRO, WO171/3957, (WD GS(1)a SBA Feb 45), IS 257, part II, 15 Feb 45.

100. F. Ruge, *Rommel in Normandy* (London: Macdonald & Jane's, 1979), 203.

101. 21AG's No, 2 OR Section [2ORS] worked hard to assess scientifically the impact of fire support: PRO, CAB106/1021, MORU Rpt 3 "Effects of Bombardment," March 46; CAB106/1033, Army O.R. Group [AORG] Rpt 292,

"Comparison of British and American Areas In Normandy In Terms of Fire Support and Its Effects;" WO291/262, AORG Rpt 282, "Study of Casualties and Damage to Personnel and Equipment Caused by some Air and Artillery Bombardments in European Operations;" WO106/4348, OR-NWE, various Rpts including 2ORS Memo 7, "Morale Effects of Artillery." Montgomery, "Twenty-First," 448–49.

102. PRO, DEFE2/230, MORU Rpt 23 "Goodwood;" WO205/953, 21AG FR "Verit," para 173.

103. The bombardment of Geilenkirchen was less effective than that on Bauchem even though it expended the same amount of shell tonnage, but at an incredible intensity for just half an hour. 2ORS scientists concluded that the optimum bombardment would have an intensity of 50–60 tons per square km per hour, and a duration of 3–4 hours (PRO, WO106/4348, OR-NWE, 184–85, 2ORS Memo 7, Morale Effects of Artillery).

104. ("Goodwood"): Luck, *Commander*, 152–56; ("Cobra"): Carell, *Invasion*, 259, 261. ("Veritable"): PRO, WO205/953, 21AG FR "Verit," para 173a; WO171/4076, (WD 30C Feb 45), App A to IS595, Interrogation Maj. Potratz.

105. PRO, WO106/4348, pp. 184–85, 2 ORS Memo 7, Morale Effects of Artillery.

106. LHCMA, LHP/1/153, Ltr Carver to Liddell Hart, 8 May 52.

107. English, *Canadian*, 290–91; LHCMA, LHP/1/153, Ltr Carver to Liddell Hart, 8 May 52.

108. Bailey, *Field*, 205; Bidwell, "Artillery," in Barnett, *New*, 136; WO205/951, 21AG FR "Verit"; the fire-plan reached a depth of 12 km, and had a "false end" to tempt German guns to fire and thus reveal their locations.

109. PRO, WO205/404, Ops Rpts 1, RA Notes on Recent Ops, 25 June 44. Maj-Gen Meade E. Dennis, the MGRA, was the army group's chief artillery officer.

110. English, *Canadian*, 282.

111. PRO, WO205/422, Combat Rpts, May 44–April 45, RA Notes on Recent Ops 2, 6 July 44, sheet 2, para 4a. ("Flo"): PRO, WO205/408, Op Rpts V, f307a, IR IN122, Account of Op "FLO," 22 Dec 44; f308, RA comment, 3 Jan 45.

112. LHCMA, Webster papers, Admin Hist Ops 21AG, p. 143.

113. A hull-down tank had only the turret exposed to view from the target (PRO, WO232/38, MTP 63, The Co-operation of Tanks with Infantry Divisions).

114. The troops failed to appreciate "how easily they could stop the German and destroy him with the weapons they possessed" (PRO; WO171/393, [WD G 1AB Div 1944], Sept Diary, 1 AB Div Rpt, Op "Market," p. 45, para 231).

115. Bradley and Blair, *Life*, 122, 146, 151, 254; D'Este, *Decision*, 222–24.

116. Mess BLM to CIGS, 29 July 44, quoted Hamilton, *Monty* 2:768–69.

117. Exploitation was a notable omission in a paper on tactical training a Capt. Montgomery sent to Liddell Hart in 1924: LHCMA, LHP/1/519/4, 24 July 24; Thompson, *Montgomery*, 312; Blumenson, "Over-rated"; CCA, RLEW/2/1, Maj-Gen. F. Tuker, 1958.

118. Dawnay's Notes, 14 July, quoted Ellis, *Victory* 1:330, n. 8.

119. PRO, WO205/5G, M518, 21 AG Dir, 11 Aug 44; Baynes, *Victor*, 211-12.

120. Roberts, *Desert*, 214. (German attack): FCA had prepared for this eventuality during the preinvasion planning: PRO, WO205/663, Op "Anubis;" WO179/2609, (WD G(PI) FCA 44), May Diary, App 4, Apprcn "Pintail," 18 May 44.

121. Thompson, *Montgomery*, 173–74; Luck, *Commander*, 165. R. Lewin, "Montgomery," in M. Carver, ad., *The War Lords: Military Commanders of the Twentieth Century* (Boston: Little Brown, 1976), 505.

122. LHCMA, AP/14/27, M508, Ltr BLM to CIGS, 7 July 1944.

123. Ellis, *Brute*, 375, 377, 380; Thompson, *Montgomery*, 173–74; Blumenson, "Overrated," 9.

124. D'Este, *Decision*, 174–98. ("Totalize"): English, *Canadian*, 279–82.

125. PRO, AIR37/784, Leigh-Mallory Diary, entry 27 June 44.

126. R. Hart, "Feeding Mars: The Role of German Logistics in the German Defeat in Normandy, 1944," *War in History* 3, no. 4 (1996): 418–35.

127. PRO, WO205/5G, M532, 21AG Dir, 16 Oct 44, para 3; CAB44/255, Opening, p. 19; J. L. Moulton, *Battle for Antwerp: the Liberation of the City & the Opening of the Scheldt, 1944* (London: Ian Allen, 1978), 98.

128. PRO, WO171/120, (WD G(Ops) 21AG Oct 44), App J, Mtng to Consider 2nd Army's Request for Extra Fmns for Gatwick, 27 Oct 44 [SBA Gatwick Request].

129. (Armor): Duncan, *79th*; Fletcher, *Vanguard*, both passim. (APCs): English, *Canadian*, 266. Before "Goodwood," Dempsey rejected O'Connor's request that obsolete AFVs be converted to APCs: LHCMA, OCP/1/5; 5/3/42, Ltr O'Connor to Dempsey, 24 Aug 44.

130. PRO, WO205/18, Notes for CoS 21AG, 22 Dec 44, quoting Hobart's views; WO171/120, (WD G(Ops) 21AG Oct 44), App J, SBA Gatwick Request.

131. Carell, *Invasion*; Kershaw, *Snows*, both passim; Luck, *Commander*, 148–192.

132. Allied Armies Italy [AAI] also behaved more like "a miscellaneous string of corps" than as an army group (Reid, "Italian," in Gooch, *Decisive*, 149).

133. Tedder, quoted Irving, *Generals*, 189. LHCMA, LHP/1/292/100, LH to Forrester, 18 Feb 52; Liddell Hart, "New Warfare—New Tactics," *Marine Corps Gazette* 39 (Oct 1955): 10–14.

134. Carver, "Montgomery," in Keegan, *Generals*, 156, citing Eighth Army Study Period, Feb 1943.

135. Ibid., 163.

136. LHCMA, AP/14/28, f"G," M514, Ltr BLM to Simpson, 24 July 44, (expanding AP/14/29, f"F," M512, 21AG Dir, 21 July 44).

137. LHCMA, AP/14/28, f"G," M514, Ltr BLM to Simpson, 24 July 44.

138. Ellis, *Victory* 2:160-61; Weigley, *Lieutenants*, 427-28; LHCMA, Papers of Lt-Gen H. E. Pyman, Account of Ops of SBA in Europe 1944–5, Vol. 1, Aug 45, p. 269.

139. This is how Michael Carver interprets the distinction, "Montgomery," in Keegan, *Generals*, 148, 155–56.

CHAPTER 5

1. IWM, BLM/90/1, Addrs Stf Coll, 7 Jan 44, point 3; Montgomery, *Memoirs*, 80–90; PRO, WO179/2579, (WD CPS 44), Headley.

2. Montgomery, *Memoirs*, 8.

3. LHCMA, AP/14/27, M508, BLM to CIGS, 7 July 44. (Instructions): LHCMA, AP/14/26, f19, M505, 21AG Dir, 30 June 44, para 6a; IWM, BLM/75, Notes Cmpgn NWE, /1, p. 2, para 8.

4. IWM, BLM/90/1, Addrs Stf Coll, 7 Jan 44, point 3.

5. IWM, BLM/74, Ping Cmpgn NWE.

6. PRO, WO205/5G, M515, 21AG Dir, 27 July 44, para 3.

7. IWM, MSC/17, Mess from BLM, 1130 14 June 44.

8. Blumenson, *Generals*, 98; Ellis, *Victory* 1:295–96.

9. IWM, BLM/75, Notes Cmpgn NWE, /1, p. 2.

10. IWM, BLM/75, Notes Cmpgn NWE, /1, p. 3. (Feints): NAC, CP/2, 1-0:V1, f38, Ltr Crerar to Crocker, 28 July 44; and f39, Crerar's Notes Mtng BLM, 29 July 44.

11. PRO, WO205/5G, M515, 21AG Dir, 27 July 44, para 4; NAC, CP/2, 1-0:V1, f42, Phone Conv BLM-Crerar, 0950 1 Aug 44; CP/15, D265, Crerar Diary, 1 Aug 44.

12. (Meijel): PRO, WO205/757, & /998, Imd Rpt IN 116, Action at Asten 28–30 Oct 44 by "X" Field Regt, 14 Nov 44; Ellis, *Victory* 2:159–60.

13. Bartov stressed "the demodernisation of the front" in the east, but this was also true of the *Westheer* in 1944–45 (*Army*, 12–29). This demodernisation involved increasing use of static, concrete defenses, for even poor-quality troops fought reasonably from such strong-points (PRO, CAB106/1090, AORG Rpt 299, The Westkapelle Assault on Walcheren; MacDonald, *Siegfried*, 46).

14. Int Sums in: PRO, WO171/3957, (WD GS(Int)a SBA 45); WO171/129, (WD GS 3ID 45); WO179/4148, (WD GS 2CC Feb 45); WO179/4199, (WD GS 2CID, Jan–Feb 45).

15. LHCMA, AP/14/27, fs7-8, Ltrs, M508, M50[9], BLM to CIGS and Eisenhower, 7 and 8 July 44, respectively; AP/14/4, Account by DMO of Visit, 30 Dec 44.

16. War Office, FSR II, Ch 2, Sect 11, para 5.

17. PRO, WO205/5G, M505, 21AG Dir, 30 June 44, para 6c; see North, *Europe*, 56.

18. PRO, WO285/21, Doctrine for the Army: The Principles of War, App A to The Problem of the Post-War Army, undated, [but summer 1945], [Doctrine—Principles].

19. SBA OP, 21 Feb 44; SBA OI 1, 21 April 44; both quoted PRO, CAB44/242, "Overlord" Prepns, pp. 116–19 and 122–24.

20. Montgomery, *Normandy*, 281; "Twenty-First," 435.

21. IWM, BLM/100/1, Op Neptune—Tentative Opt Framework, 20 Dec 43, App C; PRO, CAB44/242, p. 126, SBA 0I 1, 21 April 44, App G.

22. PRO, WO205/516, Overlord Planning: Orgn of Work, NJC 1003, 14 Dec 43.

23. R. Hart, "Mars," 420–25.

24. Thompson, *Montgomery*, 23–24, and *Legend*, 181.

25. R. Hart, "Mars," passim.

26. See, for example, Maj-Gen. Julian Thompson, *The Lifeblood of War: Logistics in Armed Conflict* (London: Brassey's, 1991).

27. LHCMA, LHP/1/519/4, Liddell Hart's Comments on Ltr from BLM, 24 July 1924.

28. Bradley and Blair, *Life*, 122, 146, 151.

29. R. Hart and S. Hart, "First Canadian Army's Operational Planning Process during the Autumn 1944 Scheldt Operations," unpublished paper, 1999, passim.

30. LHCMA, Webster papers, Admin History Ops 21AG, p. 36.

31. PRO, WO219/233, Air; WO285/21, Doctrine—Principles.

32. LHCMA, DGP/IV/2/10, Air.

33. MOD, Design, 4-22 to 4-31; Benjamin Franklin Cooling, *Case Studies in the Development of Close Air Support* (Washington, D.C.: Office of Air Force History, 1990), 491–555, passim.

34. Carell, *Invasion*, 115–17, 230, 237–38, 279, 304; Ruge, *Rommel*, 5 July 44.

35. Roberts, *Desert*, 176–78; NAC, CP/24, Mann's Analysis of Direct Air Support in NWE, 25 July 46; NAC, CP/3, 1-3-3, Air Support 84 Grp RAF; D. Hist, 86/544, Army HQ, Hist Sectn, Rpt 74, Offensive Air Support of FCA, 1955.

36. PRO, WO208/3118, 2ORS Rpt 15, Enemy Casualties in Vehicles and Equipment during the Retreat from Normandy; J. Lucas and J. Barker, *The Killing Ground: The Battle of the Falaise Pocket* (London: Batsford, 1978), 158–59.

37. IWM, BLM/110/2, M25, Mess BLM to CIGS, 2015 20 June 44.
38. Carell, *Invasion*, 304.
39. (HQ Layouts): NAC, RG24, V13620, (WD FCA June 44), mfs267, 276, 295. CP/5, 5-7-1, AVM L. O. Brown Lecture Composition and Orgn of the TAF, 26 May 44.
40. Montgomery, *Memoirs*, 81; LHCMA, AP/14/6, M1005, BLM to CIGS, 26 Feb 45.
41. Montgomery, *Memoirs*, 81–82.
42. Ibid., 81.
43. Thompson, *Montgomery*, 320.
44. On 11 June, Dempsey shifted 7th Armored Division's advance into a gap in the German front: D'Este, *Decision*, 172–73. (Simonds): English, *Canadian*, 313.
45. Montgomery, "Twenty-First," 435.
46. English, *Canadian*, map 275.
47. Kershaw, *Snows*, passim.
48. PRO, WO179/2579, (WD CPS 44), Headley, 31 Jan 44.
49. Col D. I. Strangeways' army group GS(R) section coordinated deception activities: PRO, WO171/142, (WD A 21AG Oct 44), App I/1/6, Fld Rtrn Ofrs; Strangeways performed "extremely well," WO205/5B, Ltr de Guingand to BLM, 12 June 44. WO205/97, f21a, Memo Strangeways to de Guingand, 3 May 44; WO205/5C, fs4035, 5108, Ltrs de Guingand to Crerar & Simpson, 21 Nov 44, & 16 Feb 45.
50. PRO, WO106/5846, BAOR BT "Verit," p. 9; CAB44/312, CMHQ Infm from German sources.
51. WO285/21, Doctrine—Principles. See also Grigg, Prejudice, 373.
52. PRO, WO179/2579, (WD CPS 1944), Headley, 31 Jan 44.
53. LHCMA, OCP/5/4/14, Maj-Gen MacMillan to O'Connor, 22 July 44.
54. NAG, CP/8, 1-0-7/11, v1, fs38-39, Dec Diary, App 12, Memo Mann to Crerar, 12 Dec 44. This was also true during "Overlord" (Clay, 50th, 235).
55. PRO, CAB106/1060, Hargest, Notes—Tanks, 17 June 44.
56. Allan Adair, *A Guard's General* (London: Hamish Hamilton, 1986), 152.
57. IWM, BLM/90/1, Addrs Stf Coll, 7 Jan 44, point 2.

CHAPTER 6

1. LHCMA, JNP/II/3/132a & /197a, Ltrs North to Hakewill Smith and Liddell Hart, 21 Sept 53, and 10 Nov 53, respectively.
2. Blumenson, *Battle*, 146; Bradley and Blair, *Life*, 267; Gelb, *Generals*, 324.
3. LHCMA, AP/14/26/17, Ltr BLM to CIGS, 27 June 44, para 4.
4. PRO, WO205/5G, M516, 21AG Dir, 4 Aug 44.
5. NAC, CP/7, 6-10-1, f29, Ltr Crerar to Simonds, 31 July 44; CP/2, 1-0-7/1, fs17-18, Crerar's Remarks to Snr Offrs FGA, 5 Aug 44, p. 2, para 6 ["Totalize" Rmrks]; CP/21, Ltr Crerar to Stacey, 7 June 52, quoted English, *Canadian*, 263, n. 1.
6. MOD, Design, 4-17 to 4-23.
7. LHCMA, Papers of Brigadier J. S. W, Stone, /5 Normandy Campaign, p. 38.
8. D'Este noted that "Dempsey would never admit" how "he had earned the nickname Bimbo,' and the question of his origin was said to make him blush," *Decision*, 60, n. 1. Patton felt Dempsey "to be a yes man" (Blumenson, *Patton*, 461).
9. Horrocks, *Corps*, 22; LHCMA, LHP/1/230, *The Times*, obituary, 7 June 69. The British Official History barely mentions Dempsey (Ellis, *Victory* 1:493).

10. Ritchie has a half-chapter in Keegan, *Generals*; Horrocks, O'Connor, and Simonds have full biographies: P. Warner, *Horrocks: The General Who Led from the Front* (London: Hamish Hamilton, 1984); Baynes, *Victor*; Dominick Graham, *The Price of Command: The Biography of General Guy G. Simonds* (Toronto: Stoddart, 1993).

11. Montgomery, *Normandy*, 163, 295, 346, 376, 400–401.

12. CCA, RLEW/7/6, Notes on Discussion with O'Connor, 2 July 68.

13. (Charming): Lord Lovat, *March Past: A Memoir* (London: Weidenfeld & Nicolson, 1978), 290. (Unflappable): LHCMA, LHP/1/230, *The Times*, obituary, 7 June 69; Richardson, *Flashback*, 181.

14. IWM, Whittaker papers, diary 12 May 45; Brereton, Diaries, 13 Sept 44; R. W. Thompson, *Men Under Fire* (London: Macdonald, 1945), 101.

15. CCA, RLEW/7/7, Dempsey's covering Ltr to his Comments, 15 Nov 68, on Lewin's Notes of Talk with Dempsey, 4 Nov 68.

16. CCA, RLEW/7/7, Dempsey's Comments on Lewin's Notes of Talk with Dempsey, 4 Nov 68, point 12; see also Richardson, *Freddie*, 153.

17. CCA, RLEW/2/7, Notes of Talk with BLM, 28 Jan 69.

18. Prof. Dominick Graham, interview with author, 1993.

19. PRO, WO285/9, Dempsey Diary, entry 1830 18 June 44; LHCMA, LHP/15/15, CWP/130, Notes on Dempsey's Diary—Mtng 27 June 46.

20. Ltr BLM to CIGS, 28 Dec 43, quoted Hamilton, *Monty* 3:475–76.

21. H. Pyman, *A Call to Arms* (London: Leo Cooper, 1971), 83.

22. IWM, BLM/1/101, Ltr Brooke to BLM, 11 July 44.

23. LHCMA, LHP/1/376/278-79, Ltrs LH to Hobart & reply, 15 & 18 Feb 44; OCP/8, Cmnts Snr Comds.

24. CCA, RLEW/7/7, Dempsey's covering Ltr to his Comments, 15 Nov 68, on Lewin's Notes of Talk with Dempsey, 4 Nov 68. Montgomery's self-aggrandizement also appalled Bill Williams (RLEW/7/8, Article on BLM by Williams, undated).

25. Chalfont, *Montgomery*, 280–81.

26. de Guingand, *Generals*, 166.

27. Ltr de Guingand to Eisenhower, 20 Jan 49, de Guingand Papers, Eisenhower Library, Abilene, USA, quoted Richardson, Freddie, 201–2.

28. CCA, RLEW/7/6, Notes on Discussion with O'Connor, 2 July 68, emphasis in original.

29. Horrocks, *Corps*, 23–24.

30. Belchem, *March*, 296.

31. PRO, WO285/9, Dempsey Diary, entry 1600 8 July 44.

32. CCA, RLEW/2/13, Ltr Belchem to Lewin, 21 Aug 80. For such rejections, see de Guingand, *Generals*, 168–71 (but this was less overt in his 1947 *Victory*); Richardson, *Freddie*, 165–66, citing de Guingand's Arnhem: Note for Posterity.

33. LHCMA, LHP/15/15, CWP/130, Notes on Conv with Dempsey, 4 June 46.

34. LHCMA, LHP/15/15, CWP/130, Notes on Dempsey's Diary—Mtng 27 June 46. See also Bill Williams' opinion in Howarth, *Monty*, 25.

35. LHCMA, OCP/5/3/16, DO395, Ltr O'Connor to BLM, 11 July 44.

36. O'Connor interview, quoted D'Este, *Decision*, 353, n. 1.

37. CCA, RLEW/7/6, Notes of Discussion with O'Connor, 2 July 68.

38. Horrocks, *Corps*, 30.

39. PRO, WO285/10, Dempsey Diary, entry 517, 1100 25 Sept 44.

40. LHCMA, OCP/5/3/16, DO395, Ltr O'Connor to BLM, 11 July 44.
41. LHCMA, OCP/5/4/9, Ltr BLM to O'Connor, 19 June 44; Baynes, Victor, 187–88.
42. LHCMA, LHP/15/15, CWP/130, Notes on Dempsey's Diary—Mtng 27 June 46, confirming PRO, WO285/9, Dempsey Diary, entry 18 June 1944.
43. Williams interview, 8 April 83, cited D'Este, *Decision*, 353, n. 2.
44. Terence Coverdale, one such LO, cited Horne and Montgomery, *Lonely*, 132.
45. Lamb, *Montgomery*, 16–17.
46. D'Este, *Decision*, 353.
47. NAC, RG24, V13711, (WD GS 2CC 44), June Diary, narr, mf705, entry 26 June 44.
48. LHCMA, LHP/1/230/16, Dempsey's Notes on Goodwood, 21 Feb 52, point 3; Chalfont, *Montgomery*, 242.
49. LHCMA, LHP/1/230/22A, Goodwood—Dempsey's expansion, 18 March 52, of his notes, 21 Feb 52, point 3; Irving, *Generals*, 193–94.
50. D'Este, *Decision*, 253–54.
51. PRO, WO205/5C, Op "Lucky Strike," July 44; Richardson, *Flashback*, 180.
52. PRO, W0285/9, Dempsey Diary, entries 1730 25 and 1730 26 July 44, respectively.
53. PRO, WO285/9-10, Dempsey Diary.
54. LHCMA, LHP/15/15, CWP/130, Notes on Conv with Dempsey, 4 June 46. See also Alexander McKee, *Caen: Anvil of Victory* (London: Pan, 1964), 108.
55. LHCMA, LHP/1/230/16, Dempsey's Notes on Goodwood, 21 Feb 52.
56. LHCMA, LHP/1/230/22A, Goodwood—Dempsey's expansion, 18 March 52, of his Notes, 21 Feb 52.
57. PRO, WO285/9, Dempsey Diary, entry 1730 29 July 44.
58. LHCMA, Stone Papers, /5, Normandy, p. 53.
59. PRO, WO285/9, Dempsey Diary, entry 1100 8 July 44.
60. LHCMA, LHP/15/15, CWP/130, Notes on Dempsey's Diary—Mtng 27 June 46.
61. PRO, WO285/9, Dempsey Diary, entry 1730 30 June 44.
62. PRO, WO285/10, Dempsey Diary, entry 504, 1930 22 Sept 44.
63. Pyman, Call, 79.
64. Ltr BLM to Leese, 24 July 44, c/o Mrs. F. Denby, cited Hamilton, *Monty*, 2:689; CCA, RLEW/2/7, Notes of Talk with BLM, 28 Jan 69.
65. LHCMA, AP/14/27, f16, M508, Ltr DLM to CIGS, 7 July 44.
66. Ltr BLM to de Guingand, 10 June 44, quoted Horne, *Lonely*, 137.
67. Ltr BLM to Leese, 24 July 44, quoted Hamilton, *Monty* 2:689.
68. PRO, WO285/16, Notes on Talk at Main Army, 27 Nov 44.
69. LHCMA, LHP/1/587, Ltr Pyman to Liddell Hart, 6 Dec 49.
70. Grigg, *Prejudice*, 424.
71. Stephen Badsey, "Faction in the British Army: Its Impact on 21st Army Group Operations in Autumn 1944," *War Studies Journal* 1, no. 1 (Autumn 1995): 13–28.
72. Baynes, Victor, 186. LHCMA, OCP/5/4/4, Ltr Dempsey to O'Connor, 19 Feb 44.
73. LHCMA, OCP/5/4/103, Ryan Notes.
74. LHCMA, JNP/II/3/24, Ltr North to Belchem, 23 Jan 53.
75. Adair, *General*, passim.; Badsey, "Faction," 24.

76. Baynes, *Victor*, 240.
77. LHCMA, OCP/5/4/62, DO544, Ltr O'Connor to Dempsey, 20 Oct 44.
78. LHCMA, AP/14/33, Ltr BLM to CIGS, 28 Sept 44.
79. Badsey, "Faction," passim.
80. LHCMA, OCP/1/5, Nairne's Qns.
81. Roberts, *Desert*, 221–22.
82. Carver, *Out*, 204.
83. LHCMA, OCP/5/3/28, DO430, Ltr O'Connor to Brig J. Combe, 10 Aug 44.
84. A. Brett-James, Conversations with Montgomery (London: Kimber, 1984), 70. For the distance that Dempsey studiously maintained from similar disputes concerning appointments, see LHCMA, Leakey papers, Nine Lives, p. 173.
85. CCA, RLEW/7/7, Notes of Talk with Dempsey, 4 Nov 68.
86. Pyman, Call, 74; LHCMA, LHP/15/15, CWP/130, Notes—Conv with Dempsey, 4 June 46.
87. LHCMA, Stone Papers /8, "Monty," p. 6.
88. PRO, WO285/16, Dempsey's Talk to COs, 7 Armd Div, 18 Oct 44.
89. PRO, CAB106/1061, Jackson's Interview with Dempsey, 8 March 51.
90. LHCMA, LHP/1/230, Ltr Selwyn Lloyd to *The Times*, 10 June 69; (Selwyn's role): LHCMA, Stone Papers, /5, Normandy, pp. 32–33.
91. Pyman, *Call*, 83.
92. PRO, CAB106/1061, Jackson's Interview with Dempsey, 8 March 51; LHCMA, LHP/1/230/22A, Goodwood—Dempsey's expansion, 18 March 52, of his notes, 21 Feb 52, part II, point 1.
93. PRO, WO285/9, Dempsey Diary, entry 1400 15 Aug 44.
94. Baynes, Victor, 239.
95. PRO, WO285/9, Dempsey Diary, entry 1230 17 July 44.
96. PRO, WO285/10, Dempsey Diary, entry 550, 4 Oct 44.
97. LHCMA, LHP/15/15, CWP/130, Notes on Conv with Dempsey, 4 June 46, & Notes on Dempsey's Diary—Mtng 27 June 46, re. entry 29 June 44; PRO, WO285/9, Dempsey Diary, entry 29 June 44.
98. Baynes, *Victor*, 193,
99. PRO, WO171/130, (WD G(Ops) 21AG Oct 44), App L; WO171/210, (WD G(Ops) SBA Oct 44); CAB44/255, Opening, pp. 189–95, Minutes of CoS SBA's Staff Conf, 2 Oct 44, dated 3 Oct, para 4.
100. PRO, WO285/14, Dempsey's Instructions to Comd 30 Corps, 1930 3 Aug 44.
101. LHCMA, LHP/15/15, CWP/130, Notes on Dempsey's Diary—Mtng 27 June 46.
102. LHCMA, LHP/15/15, CWP 130, Notes—Conv with Dempsey, 4 June 46; LHP/1/ 230/22A, Goodwood—Dempsey's expansion, 18 March 52, of his notes, 21 Feb 52.
103. Dempsey added that exaggerated demands should only be questioned later (LHCMA, Stone Papers, /5, Normandy, p. 2).
104. PRO, WO205/5C, f2290, Ltr Graham to de Guingand, 21 June 44.
105. PRO, WO205/318, 21AG Regrouping—SBA Requirements for Gatwick as Stated at Conf 27 Oct 44, dated 2 Nov 44.
106. LHCMA, LHP/1/230/22A, Goodwood—Dempsey's expansion, 18 March 52, of his notes, 21 Feb 52, part I, point 7.
107. LHCMA, AP/14/27, f6, M508, Ltr BLM to CIGS, 7 July 44, emphasis in original.
108. PRO, WO205/5B, Ltr de Guingand to BLM, 11 June 44; de Guingand's main role back in England was to liaise with the air commanders (WO205/5B, passim).

109. PRO, WO205/5B, Ltrs de Guingand to BLM, 11 and 9 June 44, respectively; de Guingand to Dempsey, 9 June 44.
110. Richardson, *Flashback*, 180–81.
111. LHCMA, LHP/1/587, Ltr Pyman to Liddell Hart, 4 Jan 55.
112. Reid, Brian Holden, "The Attack by Illumination: The Strange Case of Canal Defence Lights," *RUSI Jnl* 128, no. 4 (Dec 1983): 35–42.
113. LHCMA, OCP/1/5, Nairne's Qns; OCP/5/3/42(A), /45, DO460-61, Ltrs O'Connor to Dempsey & BLM, 24 Aug 44; Baynes, *Victor*, 205.
114. Irving, *Generals*, 245–46.
115. LHCMA, LHP/15/15, CWP/130, Notes on Conv with Dempsey, 4 June 46.
116. IWM, Bucknall Papers, Ltr Bucknall to Col Browne, 17 Aug 44.
117. The ability of many British senior commanders to conduct their formations effectively at the operational level of war fell well short of the abilities displayed by the best Soviet generals during the last eighteen months of the war.

CHAPTER 7

1. Kitching, Mud, 120. NAC, CP/2, 11-0-6, passim; P. D. Dickson, "Command Relations in the Northwest Europe Campaign, 1944–45," M.A. Thesis, Acadia University, 1985, 15–21.
2. NAC, CP/2, 1-0:V1, f81, Ltr Crerar to BLM, 13 Sept 44.
3. NAC, CP/3, 3-4, fs3-4, FCA Tact Dir, 22 July 44, para 1.
4. NAC, CP/2, 1-0-6, f16, Crerar Rpt to Ralston, 1 Sept 44.
5. Hart and Hart, "Scheldt," passim.
6. NAC, CP/3, 3-4, fs3-4, FCA Tact Dir, 22 July 44, para 1; fs1-2, Addrs by Comd FCA, 14 May 44.
7. Maj-Gen C. Vokes, *Vokes: My Story* (Ottawa: Gallery Books, 1985), 155–56.
8. LHCMA, AP/14/28, f"H," Ltr BLM to CIGS, 9 Aug 44, exclamation in original.
9. PRO, WO171/149, (WD Q 21AG 44), Sept Diary, App H, Notes of Conv Maj-Gen Walford—Col Poole, 24 Sept 44, para 7.
10. PRO, WO171/146, (WD Q 21AG 44), Sept Diary, App L, Admin Apprcn by Brig Feilden DQMG 21AG to MGA 21AG [Graham], 30 Sept 44.
11. NAC, CP/16, D265, Crerar's 1945 WD, Jan Diary, App 2, Addrs to Snr Offrs FCA on "Veritable," 22 Jan 45 ("Verit" Addrs).
12. ("Totalize"): NAC, CP/2, 1-0-7/l, fs17-18, "Totalize" Rmrks, 5 Aug 44. ("Veritable"): NAC, CP/16, D265, Crerar's 1945 WD, Jan Diary, App 2, "Verit" Addrs.
13. PRO, CAB44/255, Opening, p. 70, para 12, (and CAB44/301, HS/CMHQ/Rpt 188, The Clearing of the Scheldt Estuary [Clearing], p. 47, para 99), FCA OI, 2 Oct 44; CAB44/255, Opening, pp. 73-75, 2CC Outline Plan "Swbk," 2 Oct 44.
14. NAC, CP/2, 1-0-6, fs13-16, Crerar's Rpt to Ralston, 1 Sept 44. English, *Canadian*, 263, n. 1, quoting CP/21, Lit Crerar to Stacey, 7 June 52.
15. A. McKee, 30 Jan 45, cited Allen, *One More River* (London: Dent, 1980), 49.
16. PRO, WO106/5846, BAOR "Verit," p. 63.
17. Its ingenuity lay chiefly in its false end, which by prompting German batteries to fire exposed their positions to location (PRO, WO106/5846, BAOR BT "Verit," App F; WO205/953, 21AG FR "Verit").
18. English, *Canadian*, 291.
19. LHCMA, AP/14/27, f6, M508, Ltr BLM to CIGS, 7 July 44; Ltr BLM to CIGS, 28 Dec 43, quoted English, *Canadian*, 188, n. 23. Monty's opinion remained unchanged in 1970 (Williams, *Long*, 23, n. 12).

20. C. P. Stacey, *Arms, Men and Governments* (Ottawa: Queen's Printer, 1970), 224, n. 57, and *A Date with History* (Ottawa: Deneau, 1983), 236, n. 5, both citing NAC, Ralston Papers, Overseas Trip—Sept–Oct 44, Diary Notes 8 Oct 44.
21. Kitching, *Mud*, 229.
22. Granatstein, *Generals*, 115; see also Stacey, *Arms*, 219, 245; English, *Canadian*, 189, n. 26.
23. NAC, CP/8, 11-0-2(D167), f69, Ltr Crerar to Stuart, 12 Feb 44.
24. Dickson, "Command," 26; Kitching, *Mud*, 176–77.
25. Maj-Gen. Foster "never heard of Crerar coming up with an idea of his own" (T. Foster, *A Meeting of Generals* (Toronto: Methuen, 19861, 394).
26. NAC, CP/2, 1-0:V1, f81, Ltr Crerar to BLM, 13 Sept 44.
27. Beament interview. (Aloof): Interview with Lt-Gen. W. A. B Anderson, 15 May 1994. (Humorless): Vokes, *Story*, 152. (Uninspiring): Kitching, *Mud*, 178.
28. Granatstein, *Generals*, 107; Vokes, *Story*, 152.
29. Beament interview.
30. Anderson interview; Stacey, *Date*, 237; Graham, *Price*, 179.
31. LHCMA, AP/14/27, f6, M508, Ltr BLM to CIGS, 7 July 44.
32. LHCMA, AP/14/28, f"A," M511, Ltr BLM to CIGS, 14 July 44.
33. LHCMA, AP/14/1, Ltr BLM to CIGS, 24 July 44.
34. LHCMA, AP/14/28, f"H," Ltr BLM to CIGS, 9 Aug 44.
35. Anderson interview; Stacey, *Date*, 237.
36. Graham, *Price*, 139 n.4, 158.
37. NAC, CP/3, 5-0-2(D66) passim; CP/3, 5-0-2(D67), fs25-26, GS334, Mess Murchie to Stuart, 19 May 44; Stacey, *Arms*, 203, 207, 212.
38. Stacey, *Date*, 218.
39. NAC, CP/2, 11-0-3, Memo on Conv with BLM, 4 July 42; Dickson, "Command," 18, 21; Stacey, *Arms*, 217–18.
40. Stacey, *Date*, 236.
41. Stacey, *Arms*, 220–21.
42. NAC, CP/3, 5-0-2(D67), fs7, 34, 42–43, 55, Corresp between Crerar, Murchie, Stuart & Brooke, May 44; IWM, BLM/73, BLM's diary, entry 26 May 44.
43. CP/2, 11-0-3, Memo on Conv with BLM, 4 July 42.
44. NAC, CP/3, 5-0-2(D67), f34, Ltr Stuart to Crerar, 26 May 44.
45. NAC, CP/3, 5-0-2(D67), fs42–43, Ltr Crerar to Stuart, 30 May 44.
46. NAC, CP/2, 11-0-3, Memo on Conv with BLM, 4 July 42.
47. LHCMA, OCP/1/5, Nairne's Qns.
48. NAC, CP/3, 5-0-2(D67), f48, Ltr Crerar to Stuart, 10 June 44.
49. LHCMA, AP/3B/XII, Notes, entry 25 May 44.
50. Stacey, *Arms*, 222.
51. NAC, CP/3, 5-0-2(D66), fs72–73, Murchie's Instructions to Crerar, 19 May 44, para 9.
52. NAC, CP/3, 5-0-2(D67), f8, Ltr Crerar to Stuart, 15 May 44.
53. Hart and Hart, "Scheldt," p4.
54. Stacey, *Date*, 235.
55. Vokes, *Story*, 138.
56. Anderson interview; Stacey, *Arms*, 222–23.
57. Anderson interview; interview with Maj-Gen. N. Elliot Rodger, 27 April 1994; Stacey, *Arms*, 220, n.49.
58. Foster, *Meeting*, 390.
59. NAC, CP/3, 5-0-3:V1, fs26–27, Memo Crerar to Stuart, 2 July 44.

60. Ibid.; Stacey, *Arms*, 221.
61. Stacey, *Arms*, 215, 223.
62. NAC, CP/2, 11-0-6; English, *Canadian*, 125, 127, 136.
63. For Monty's sound judgment on appointments see CCA, Grigg Papers /14/4, Grigg's Sept 1949 article for BBC's BLM obituary file.
64. NAC, CP/2, 11-0-6, passim.
65. LHCMA, AP14/27, f6, M508, Ltr BLM to CIGS, 7 July 44; CCA, Grigg Papers, 9/8/34(a), BLM's Some Notes on the Present Situation, 6 Nov 44, para 4.
66. NAC, CP/3, 5-0-3:v1; CP/4, 5-0-2:v2 &v3.
67. Stacey, *Date*, 237.
68. Stacey, *Arms*, 207, 210.
69. See NAC, CP/15, D265, Crerar's 1944 WD, Aug & Sept diaries.
70. LHCMA, OCP/1/5, Nairne's Qns.
71. Lamb, *Montgomery*, 253.
72. PRO, CAB44/301, Clearing, pp. 27–29, paras 59–62, quoting Memo Simonds to Crerar, 21 Sept 44.
73. PRO, WO179/2609, (WD G(PI) FCA 44), Sept Diary, App 17, G(PI) Apprcn, 19 Sept 44; CAB44/301, Clearing, p. 24, para 53.
74. Only Stacey mentions "Siesta" (Victory, 434, 436 & 464).
75. NAC, Mann Papers, Directives Pile, fs107-8, Ltr Crerar to BLM, 28 Nov 44.
76. NAC, CP/2, 1-0-7/10; PRO, WO179/2609, (WD G(PI) FCA 44), Dec Diary, passim. See RG24, V13608, (WD G(PI) FCA 45), Jan Diary, App 2, Memo for CoS by G(PI) FCA, 6 Jan 45; Feb Diary, Ltr Simonds to Crerar, 19 Jan 45, and Crerar's Points arising from Comments of GOC 2CC, 22 Jan 45.
77. PRO, WO179/2579, (WD CPS 44), Headley, 31 Jan 44.
78. Anderson interview. PRO, WO179/2609, (WD G(PI) FCA 44), passim.
79. NAC, RG24, V13608, (WD G(PI) FCA 44-45), Nov Diary, mfs383-87, entry 11 Nov 44 on Schouwen plan; Jan 45 Diary, entries 4, 19, 26 Jan 45.
80. Interview with Prof. Graham, Sept 1993. Anderson's impression at the time was that Pangman felt frustrated that his recommendations were not being accepted (Anderson interview).
81. Stacey, *Date*, 236, n.5.
82. NAC, RG24, V13608, (WD G(PI) FCA 44-45), Jan 45 Diary, Minutes of Morning Joint Conf, Pt II, 6 Jan 45, point 20.
83. NAC, Mann Papers, Dirs, fs107-8, Ltr Crerar to BLM, 28 Nov 44.
84. NAC, CP/2, 1-0:vl, fs109–10, Ltr BLM to Crerar, 30 Nov 44.
85. English, *Canadian*, 274, 306; Graham, *Price*, 282. It seems unlikely that Simonds would have welcomed interference from Crerar, an army commander he believed to be less capable than himself.
86. LHCMA, AP/14/31, M120, Mess BLM to CIGS, 2200 27 Aug 44.
87. LHCMA, AP/14/31, M156, GUARD Mess BLM to CIGS, 4 Sept 44.
88. PRO, WO205/5C, Ltr Maj-Gen Steele (DSD WO) to de Guingand, 4 Sept 44; f3365, reply, 19 Sept.
89. Ibid. Though the War Office did not state that this procedure applied to the Canadians as well as the Americans, one can only assume that Montgomery used the GUARD classification here to prevent Canadian authorities from learning of his criticism.
90. NAC, CP/2, 1-0:V1, fs69-70, M141, Mess BLM to Crerar, 2 Sept 44; also quoted Terry Copp and R. Vogel, *Maple Leaf Route: Antwerp* (Alma, Ont.: Maple Leaf Route, 1983), 54; Graham, *Price*, 178, n. 2.

91. NAC, CP/2, 1-0:v1, f71, C73, Mess Crerar to BLM, 0010 3 Sept 44; also quoted Dickson, "Command," 67, n. 88.

92. Ibid.; Graham, *Price*, 178–79.

93. CP/7, 6-10A, fs1–5.

94. D. Hist, 86/544, Ltr Mann to Foulkes, 2 Apt 63, cited Granatstein, *Generals*, 113, n. 158. Simonds felt Crerar was fixated with Dieppe (Graham, *Price*, 177–78).

95. NAC, CP/7, 6-10A, fs6-9, (and CP/7, 6-10, f79), Notes on Situation 2–3 Sept 44.

96. NAC, CP/7, 6-10A, f10, Ltr BLM to Crerar, 7 Sept 44; RG24, V10651, Notes on Situation.

97. Copp, *Antwerp*, 54.

98. On the Dieppe dispute see Dickson "Command," 71, n. 103; Granatstein, *Generals*, 112-13; Copp argued that the 2 Sept clash was more important than Crerar's nonattendance on the Third (*Antwerp*, 54).

99. NAC, CP/8, 6-10-4, f60, Ltr Crerar to Stuart, 5 Sept 44.

100. Hart and Hart "Scheldt," passim.

101. CCA, RLEW/7/7, Dempsey's comments, 15 Nov 68, on Lewin's Talk with Dempsey, 4 Nov 68.

102. PRO, WO205/5B, Ltr de Guingand to BLM, 3 Sept 44.

103. Graham, *Price*, 177, 179.

104. Rodger interview.

105. NAC, Ralston Papers, Notes on Conv with BLM, 8 Oct 44; Rodger interview.

106. Stacey, *Date*, 236n.

107. NAC, CP/7, 6-10-2, f26, Ltr Crerar to Brooke, undated (probably 25 Sept 44); CP/15, D265, Crerar's 1944 WD, entry 25 Oct 44. Dickson, "Command," 115, n. 67, citing CP/7, 6-10-2, f26.

108. NAC, CP/8, D265, Crerar's 1944 WD.

109. Dickson, "Command," 34, n. 68.

110. Graham, *Price*, 188.

111. NAC, CP/2, 1-0-2, fs20, 31, Ltrs Crerar to Stuart, 25 April & 31 May 44; CP/7, 6-9/M, Ltr Crerar to McNaughton, 25 June 44.

112. NAC, CP/3, 3-4, fs3–4, FCA Tact Dir, 22 July 44; & f11, Ltr Crerar to Crocker, 28 Nov 44; see also PRO, WO208/3193, MIRS Special Tact Study, 29.

113. Montgomery believed that it was up to his army commanders to "train their armies" (IWM, BLM/90/3, BLM's Talk to Generals, 13 Jan 44).

114. Stacey, *Date*, 237.

115. LHCMA, AP/3B/XII, Notes, entry 29 March 44.

116. Vokes, *Story*, 155.

117. LHCMA, AP/12/XI/4/61, and /12/XII/5/5, Crerar & Grigg interviews, respectively; PRO, WO199/234, Lessons of Spartan; P. D. Dickson, "'The Hand That Wields the Dagger': Harry Crerar, First Canadian Army Command and National Autonomy," *War and Society* 13, no. 2 (Oct 1995): 113–41, passim.

118. Stacey, *Arms*, 231–47, passim. (Brooke's role): LHCMA, AP/3B/XII, Notes, entry 29 March 44; English, *Canadian*, 152–53; Fraser, *Alanbrooke*, 422.

119. NAC, CP/3, 5-0-3:v1, fs72–77, Notes by Stuart on his Trip to Italy, 9–15 July 44. (Burns' subordinates): Graham, *Price*, 210.

120. Vokes, *Story*, 159–60, 184. (Smiler): Kitching, *Mud*, 192. See also NAC, CP/4, 5-0-3:v2, corresp Burns, Crerar, Montague, Murchie, & Stuart, fs10–11, 19, 29–30, 58–59, Oct–Nov 44.

121. IWM, BLM/1/101, Brooke to BLM, 11 July 44.

122. NAC, Ralston Papers, Notes on Conv with BLM, 8 Oct 44.

123. CCA, RLEW/2/7, Notes of Talk with BLM, 28 Jan 69.

124. IWM, BLM/119/71, M482, Mess BLM to CIGS, 15 Feb 45.

125. Keegan, *Generals*, 213–14.

126. NAC, CP/3, 5-0-3:V1, f25, MA1467, Mess Alexander to CIGS, 1520, 29 June 44.

127. LHCMA, AP/14/27, f16, M508, Ltr BLM to CIGS, 7 July 44; Hamilton, Monty 2:689, n. 2, quoting Ltr BLM to Leese, 24 June 44.

128. IWM, BLM/1/101, Ltr Brooke to BLM, 11 July 44.

129. LHCMA, AP/14/28, f"A," M511, Ltr BLM to CIGS, 14 July 44.

130. English, *Canadian*, 305–6.

131. Anderson interview.

132. Kitching, *Mud*, 229. Kitching was Simonds' best friend, but that did not stop the latter sacking him.

133. Ibid., 229. On 19 August Simonds telephoned army HQ as he had not been given "a clear idea as to how he should operate during today." Discovering Crerar to be absent, Simonds asked that Brigadier Mann, Crerar's Chief of Staff, contact Montgomery to ascertain what action Simonds should undertake (PRO, WO179/2609, [WD G(Pl) FCA 44], Aug Diary, Memo, Mann to Crerar re Convs with Simonds & de Guingand, 1125–1140 19 Aug 44).

134. Beament interview.

135. LHCMA, LHP/1/56/1, Ltr Belchem to Liddell Hart, 28 July 50; Beament interview.

136. English, *Canadian*, 305; English interview.

137. NAC, CP/8, File Op "Axehead." FCA also planned measures to resist a German armored assault on the vulnerable eastern flank (PRO, WO205/663, Op "Anubis;" WO179/2609, [WD G(PI) FCA 44], May Diary, App 4, Apprcn "Pintail," 18 May 44).

138. NAC, CP/2, 1-0:V1, fs78–79, Ltr BLM to Crerar, 13 Sept 44.

139. PRO, CAB 106/1124, Ramsey Diary, entry 5 Oct 44.

140. LHCMA, AP/3B/XIII, Notes, entry 4 Oct 44; LHCMA, OCP/1/5, Nairne's Qns.

141. Montgomery, *Memoirs*, 297. On the opening of Antwerp, see Hamilton, *Monty*, 3:102–12; Montgomery, *Memoirs*, 283–85; and *Normandy*, 150–164; Hart and Hart, "Scheldt," passim.

142. PRO, WO179/2609, (WD G(PI) FCA 44), Dec Diary, Pangman's Note "Valediction," 7 Dec 44.

143. PRO, WO205/5G, M530, 21AG Dir, 9 Oct 44; IWM, BLM/107/25, M527, 21AG Dir, 27 Sept 44.

144. For this debate on whether SBA or FCA should undertake "Veritable," see NAC, RG24, V13608, (WD G(PI) FCA 44), Nov & Dec Diaries; CP/2, 1-0-7/11; Mann Papers, Dirs, FCA Dir, 14 Dec 44.

Select Bibliography

The author has consulted too many sources to list them all here. Although this bibliography lists all unpublished primary archival collections consulted, it in addition only includes those secondary sources directly referred to in this study, plus a few works not cited that have proved particularly useful in a general sense to the completion of this analysis.

PRIMARY SOURCES (UNPUBLISHED)
Government Records, Public Records Office, Kew
Royal Air Force Papers

    AIR2, Registered Correspondence

    AIR8, Chief of the Air Staff Papers

    AIR16, Fighter Command Papers

    AIR20, Air Ministry Unregistered Papers

    AIR37, Allied Expeditionary Air Force Papers

Cabinet Office Papers

    CAB44, Narratives for the Official Histories

    CAB78, War Cabinet Committees

    CAB101, Official War Histories (Second World War, Military)

    CAB103, Historical Section: Registered Files

    CAB106, Historical Section: Archivist and Librarian Files

Ministry of Defence Papers

    DEFE2, Combined Operations Headquarters: Reports

    Prime Minister's Papers

    PREM 3, Prime Minister's Private Office: Operational Papers

War Office Papers

    WO33, 'O' and 'A' Papers

    WO73, Monthly Returns

    WO106, Directorate of Military Operations and Intelligence

    WO162, Adjutant General's Papers

    WO163, War Office Council and Army Council Records

WO165, War Office Directorate War Diaries, 1939-45
WO166, U.K. Home Forces War Diaries
WO171, 21st Army Group War Diaries
WO179, War Diaries, Dominion Forces
WO193, Director of Military Operations: Collation Files
WO199, U.K. Home Forces Papers
WO205, Headquarters Papers, 21st Army Group
WO208, Directorate of Military Intelligence Papers
WO216, CIGS Papers
WO219, SHAEF Papers
WO223, Camberley 1947 Staff Course Papers: "Veritable"
WO231, Directorate of Military Training Papers
WO232, Directorate of Tactical Investigation Papers
WO277, Historical Monographs
WO285, Lieutenant-General M. C. Dempsey Papers
WO291, Military Operational Research Papers

Private Papers

Department of Documents, Imperial War Museum, London
Papers of Field Marshal Viscount Bernard Law Montgomery of Alamein
Papers of Brigadier D. F. A. T. Baines
Papers of General Sir Evelyn Barker
Papers of Major-General (David) Ronald F. K. Belchem
Papers of Major-General R. Bramwell Davis
Papers of Lieutenant-General A. T. A. Browne
Papers of Lieutenant-General Gerald Corfield Bucknall
Papers of Major-General J. C. D. D'A Dalton
Papers of Major-General Francis W. de Guingand
Papers of Major-General W. J. F. Eassie
Papers of Major-General L. O. Lyne
Papers of Major-General G. H. A. MacMillan
Papers of Lieutenant-Colonel G. Tilly
Papers of Major D. R. Vernon
Papers of Major N. Whittaker
Papers of Major R. H. D. Young
Enemy Document Series (EDS) Papers

Liddell Hart Centre For Military Archives, King's College London
Papers of Captain Basil Henry Liddell Hart
Papers of Field Marshal Viscount Alanbrooke
Papers of General Sir Ronald Forbes Adam

Papers of Major-General Francis W. de Guingand
Papers of Lieutenant-General Miles Christopher Dempsey
Papers of Major-General John Frederick Charles Fuller
Papers of Lieutenant-General Sir Humphrey (Middleton) Gale
Papers of General Sir John Windrop Hackett
Papers of General Sir Lionel Hastings Ismay
Papers of Major-General Arundel Rea Leakey
Papers of Major John North
Papers of Lieutenant-General Richard Nugent O'Connor
Papers of Lieutenant-General Harold English Pyman
Papers of Major-General Sir Digby Raeburn
Papers of Brigadier J. S. W. Stone
Papers of Major-General George Robert Turner-Cain
Papers of Major-General Gerald Lloyd Verney
Papers of Brigadier Richard Hearn Walker
Papers of Lieutenant-Colonel Derek Webster

Churchill College Archives, Cambridge University
Papers of Professor Arthur Davies
Papers of Lieutenant-General Sir Alex Galloway
Papers of Sir James Grigg
Papers of Ronald Lewin

National Army Museum, London
Papers of Major-General E. Hakewill Smith
Papers of Lieutenant-General Augustus Francis Andrew Nicol Thorne
Exhibition of Papers of Cornelius Ryan

National Archives of Canada, Ottawa, Ontario
Papers of General Henry Duncan Graham Crerar (MG30/E157)
Department of National Defense Papers (RG24)
Papers of Brigadier Churchill Mann (MG30/E384)
Papers of Colonel J. L. Ralston
Papers of Lieutenant-General Kenneth Stuart (MG30/E520)

Directorate of History, National Defense HQ, Ottawa, Ontario
Series 83 Papers
Series 87 Papers

Interviews and Correspondence with Participants
Lieutenant-General W. A. B. Anderson, May 1994
Brigadier G. E. Beament, May 1994

Major-General N. Elliott Rodger, April 1944
Correspondence with Major-General Turner-Cain, 1995

PRIMARY SOURCES (PUBLISHED)
Official Monographs
Ministry of Defence. *Design for Military Operations: The British Military Doctrine.* London: HMSO, 1996.

U.S. Army, *Field Manual 100-5: Operations.* Washington, D.C.: Department of the Army, 1986.

War Office. *Field Service Regulations I-III.* London: HMSO, 1930-35.

———. *Current Reports from Overseas.* 1941–45.

———. *Military Training Pamphlets.* 1938–45.

———. *Lessons from Theatres of War.* 1941–44.

Memoirs, Journals, and Accounts
Adair, Allan. *A Guard's General.* London: Hamish Hamilton, 1986.

Allen, Robert S. *Lucky Forward: The History of General Patton's Third U.S. Army.* New York: Vanguard Press, 1947.

Beddell Smith, Walter. *Eisenhower's Six Great Decisions: Europe 1944–45.* New York: Longmans, Green, 1956.

Belchem, Maj-Gen. David. *All in the Day's March.* London: Collins, 1978.

———. *Victory in Normandy.* London: Chatto and Windus, 1981.

Bradley, Omar N. *A Soldier's Story.* New York: Holt, 1951.

Bradley, Omar N., and Clay Blair. *A General's Life.* London: Sidgewick and Jackson, 1983.

Brereton, Lt-Gen. Lewis. *The Brereton Diaries.* New York: Wm. Morrow, 1946.

Burns, Lt-Gen. E. L. M. *General Mud: Memoirs of Two World Wars.* Toronto: Clarke and Irwin, 1956.

Butcher, Harry, C. *My Three Years with Eisenhower.* London: Heinemann, 1946.

Carell, Paul [pseud.]. *Invasion—They're Coming!—The German Account of the Allied Landings and the 80 Days' Battle for France.* London: Harrap, 1962.

Carver, Michael. *Out of Step: Memoirs of a Field Marshal.* London: Hutchinson, 1989.

Churchill, Winston S. *The Second World War.* 6 Vols. London: Cassell, 1948–54.

Dalgleish, John. *We Planned the Second Front.* London: Gollancz, 1945.

D'Arcy-Dawson, J. *European Victory.* London: Macdonald, 1945.

de Guingand, Maj-Gen. F. *Operation Victory.* London: Hodder and Stoughton, 1947.

———. *Generals at War.* London: Hodder and Stoughton, 1964.

———. *From Brass Hat to Bowler Hat.* London: Hamish Hamilton, 1979.

Eisenhower, Dwight D. *Crusade in Europe.* New York: Da Capo Press, 1948, 1983.

Gale, General Sir Richard. *With the 6th Airborne Division in Normandy.* London: Sampson Low, Marston, 1948.

———. *A Call to Arms: An Autobiography.* London: Hutchinson, 1968.

Grigg, P. J. *Prejudice and Judgement.* London: Jonathon Cape, 1948.

Horrocks, Sir Brian. *A Full Life.* London: Collins Fontana, 1960.

———. *Corps Commander,* London: Sidgewick and Jackson, 1977.

Kennedy, Maj-Gen. John. *The Business of War.* London: Hutchinson, 1957.

Kitching, Maj-Gen. George. *Mud and Green Fields: The Memoirs of Major General Kitching.* Langley, B.C.: Battleline, 1986.

Leeming, John F. *Always To-morrow.* London: Harrap, 1951.

Lovat, Lord. *March Past: A Memoir.* London: Weidenfeld and Nicolson, 1978.

Luck, Col. Hans von. *Panzer Commander.* London: Praeger, 1989.

Malone, Richard S. *Missing from the Record.* Toronto: Collins, 1946.

Meyer, Hubert. *Kriegsgeschichte der 12SS-Panzerdivision "Hitlerjugend."* Osnabruck: Munin Verlag, 1982.

Montgomery, B. L. *Normandy to the Baltic.* London: Hutchinson, 1947.

———. *El Alamein to the River Sangro.* London: Hutchinson, 1948.

———. *Memoirs.* London: Collins, 1958.

Morgan, General F. *Overture to Overlord.* London: Hodder and Stoughton, 1950.

———. *Peace and War.* London: Hodder and Stoughton, 1961.

Patton, George S. *War as I Knew It.* Boston: Houghton Mifflin, 1947.

Picot, Geoffrey. *Accidental Warrior: In the Front Line from Normandy till Victory.* Lewis, England: Book Guild, 1993.

Pyman, H. *A Call to Arms.* London: Leo Cooper, 1971.

Richardson, Charles. *Flashback: A Soldier's Story.* London: Kimber, 1985.

Roberts, Maj-Gen. G. P. B. *From the Desert to the Baltic.* London: Kimber, 1987.

Ruge, Friedrich. *Rommel in Normandy.* London: Macdonald and Jane's, 1979.

SHAEF. *Report by the Supreme Commander on the Operations in Europe, 6 June 1944 to 8 May 1945.* Washington, D.C.: U.S. Govt. Printing Office, 1946.

Smuts, J. C. *Jan Christian Smuts.* London: Cassell, 1952.

Stimson, Henry L. *On Active Service in Peace and War.* New York: Harper, 1949.

Strong, Kenneth. *Intelligence at the Top.* London: Cassell, 1968.

Thompson, R. W. *Men Under Fire.* London: Macdonald, 1945.

Vokes, Maj-Gen. Chris. *Vokes: My Story.* Ottawa: Gallery Books, 1985.

Wingfield, Rex. *The Only Way Out.* London: Hutchinson, 1955.

Articles

Dunn, Maj. R. H. W. "Reminiscences of a Regimental Soldier: S.P. Guns in Normandy." *Journal of the Royal Artillery* 75, no. 2 (April 1948): 89–95.

Montgomery, B. L. "The Major Tactics of the Encounter Battle." *Army Quarterly* 26, no. 2 (July 1938): 268–72.

———. "Twenty First (British) Army Group in the Campaign in North-West Europe 1944–45." *RUSI Journal* 90, no. 560 (November 1945): 430-54.

Parachute Sapper [pseud.]. "The Battle for Arnhem Bridge." *Blackwood's Magazine* 258 (July–Dec 1945): 234-50.

Schweppenburg, L. F. Gehr von. "An Old German War-Horse Reviews the British Army, Part II." *The Territorial Magazine* 31, no. 7 (July 1961): 9–11.

———. "Reflections on Soviet and Allied Generalship in World War Two." *An Cosantóir: The Irish Defence Journal* 23, no. 5 (May 1963): 267–82.

Thoholte, General Karl. "A German Reflects on Artillery." *Field Artillery Journal* 35, no. 12 (Dec 1948): 709–14.

SECONDARY SOURCES
Books and Monographs

Allen, Peter. *One More River: The Rhine Crossings of 1945.* London: Dent, 1980.

Ambrose, Stephen E. *The Supreme Commander.* London: Cassell, 1971.

Bailey, J. B. A. *Field Artillery and Firepower.* Oxford: Military Press Oxford, 1989.

Baker, Maj. A. H. R. and Maj. B. Rust. *A Short History of the 50th Northumbrian Division.* Yarmouth, England: 50th Division, 1966.

Barclay, C. N. *History of tire 53rd (Welsh) Division in the Second World War.* London: William Clowes and Sons, 1956.

Barnett, Correlli, Shelford Bidwell, Brian Bond, John Harding, and John Terraine. *Old Battles New Defences: Can We Learn from Military History?* London: Brassey's, 1985.

Bartov, Omer. *Hitler's Army: Soldiers, Nazis, and War in the Third Reich.* Oxford: Oxford University Press, 1991.

Baynes, John. *Morale.* London: Cassell, 1967.

———. *The Forgotten Victor: General Sir Richard O'Connor.* London: Brassey's, 1989.

Belfield, E., and H. Essame. *The Battle for Normandy.* London: Batsford, 1965.

Bennett, Ralph. *Ultra in the West: The Normandy Campaign 1944–45.* London: Hutchinson, 1979.

Bidwell, Shelford. *Gunners at War: A Tactical Study of the Royal Artillery in the Twentieth Century.* London: Arms and Armour Press, 1970.

Bidwell, Shelford, and Dominick Graham. *Firepower: British Army Weapons and Theories of War 1904–1945.* London: Allen and Unwin, 1982.

Blake, George. *Mountain and Flood: The History of the 52nd (Lowland) Division 1939–46.* Glasgow: Jackson and Son, 1950.

Blaxland, Gregory. *The Plain Cook and the Great Showman: The First and Eighth Armies in North Africa.* Abingdon, England: Purnell, 1977.

Blumenson, Martin. *Breakout and Pursuit. United States Army in World War II: European Theater of Operations.* Washington, D.C.: Office of the Chief of Military History, Department of the Army, 1961.

———. *The Patton Papers 1940–45.* 2 Vols. Boston: Houghton Mifflin, 1972–74.

———. *The Battle of the Generals.* New York: Wm. Morrow, 1993.

Brett-James, A. *Conversations with Montgomery.* London: Kimber, 1984.

Brooks, Stephen. Ed. *Montgomery and Eighth Army.* London: Bodley Head, 1991.

Bryant, Arthur. *Triumph in the West, 1943–46.* London: Collins, 1959.

Carver, Michael. *The War Lords: Military Commanders of the Twentieth Century.* Boston: Little Brown, 1976.

Chalfont, Alun. *Montgomery.* London: Weidenfeld and Nicolson, 1976.

Chandler, A. D., and Stephen Ambrose. Eds. *The Papers of Dwight David Eisenhower: The War Years.* 5 Vols. Baltimore: John Hopkins University Press, 1970.

Clark, Ronald W. *Montgomery of Alamein.* London: Phoenix House, 1960.

Clausewitz, Carl von. *On War.* (Michael Howard and Peter Paret. Eds), Princeton, N.J.: Princeton University Press, 1976, (orig. 1832).

Clay, E. W. *The Path of the 50th: The Story of the 50th (Northumbrian) Division in the Second World War.* London: Gale and Polden, 1950.

Cole, Hugh M. *The Ardennes: Battle of the Bulge. U.S. Army in World War II: European Theater of Operations.* Washington, D.C.: Office of the Chief of Military History, Department of the Army, 1965.

Cooling, Benjamin Franklin. Ed. *Case Studies in the Development of Close Air Support.* Washington D.C.: Office of Air Force History, 1990.

Copp, Terry, and R. Vogel. *Maple Leaf Route: Caen.* Alma, Ont.: Maple Leaf Route, 1983.

———. *Maple Leaf Route: Antwerp.* Alma, Ont.: Maple Leaf Route, 1984.

Creveld, Martin van. *Fighting Power: German & US Army Performances, 1939–45.* London: Arms and Armour Press, 1983.

Cruikshank, Charles. *Deception in World War Two.* Oxford: Oxford University Press, 1979.

Darby, H., and M. Cunliffe. *A Short History of 21 Army Group.* London: Gale and Polden, 1949.

D'Este, Carlo. *Decision in Normandy*. London: Collins, 1983.

Duncan, N. W. *79th Armoured Division: Hobo's Funnies*. Windsor, England: Profile, 1972.

Dupuy, Trevor N. *A Genius for War: The German Army & General Staff, 1807–1945*. London: Macdonald and Jane's, 1977.

———. *Understanding War: History and Theory of Combat*. London: Leo Cooper, 1992.

Ehrman, J. *Grand Strategy*. Vols. 5–6. History of the Second World War, UK Military Series. London: HMSO, 1956.

Eisenhower, David. *Eisenhower at War 1943–45*. New York: Random House, 1986.

Ellis, John. *The Sharp End: The Fighting Man in World War Two*. London: David and Charles, 1982.

———. *Brute Force: Allied Strategy and Tactics in the Second World War*. London: Deutsch, 1990.

Ellis, Maj. L. F. *Victory in the West*. 2 Vols. History of the Second World War, UK Military Series. London: HMSO, 1962–68.

English, John A. *The Canadian Army and the Normandy Campaign: A Study in the Failure of High Command*. London: Praeger, 1991.

Essame, Hubert. *The Battle for Germany*. London: Batsford, 1969.

———. *Patton: A Study in Command*. London: Batsford, 1974.

Essame, H., and E. Belfield. *The North-West Europe Campaign 1944–45*. Alderrthol, England: Gale and Polden, 1962.

Fletcher, David. *Vanguard of Victory: The 79th Armoured Division*. London HMSO, 1984.

Foster, Tony. *A Meeting of Generals*. Toronto: Methuen, 1986.

Fraser, David. *Alanbrooke*. London: Hamlyn, 1983.

Fuller, Maj-Gen J. F. C. *Foundations of the Science of War*. London: Hutchinson and Co., 1925.

———. *Thunderbolts*. London: Skeffington, 1946.

———. *The Second World War: A Strategical and Tactical History*. London: Eyre and Spottiswoode, 1948.

Gelb, Norman. *Ike and Monty: Generals at War*. London: Constable, 1994.

Gill, R., and J. Groves Comps. *Club Route in Europe: The Story of 30 Corps in the European Campaign*. Hannover, Germany: 30 Corps, 1946.

Gooch, John. Ed. *Decisive Campaigns of the Second World War*. London: Frank Cass, 1990.

Graham, Dominick. *The Price of Command: The Biography of General Guy G. Simonds*. Toronto: Stoddart, 1993.

Graham, Dominick, and Shelford Bidwell. *Coalitions, Politicians and Generals*. London: Brassey's, 1993.

Granatstein, J. L. *The Generals*. Toronto: Stoddart, 1993.

Hamilton, Nigel. *Monty*. Vol. 1. *The Making of a General 1887–1942*. London: Hamish Hamilton, 1982.

———. *Monty*. Vol. 2. *Master of the Battlefield 1942–1944*. London: Hamish Hamilton, 1983.

———. *Monty*. Vol. 3. *The Field Marshal 1944–1976*. London: Hamish Hamilton, 1986.

———. *Monty: The Man Behind the Legend*. London: Sphere, 1988.

Harrison, Gordon A. *Cross Channel Attack*. U.S. Army in World War II: European Theater of Operations. Washington, D.C.: Office of the Chief of Military History, Department of the Army, 1951.

Hastings, Max. *Overlord: D-Day and the Battle for Normandy*. London: M. Joseph, 1984.

Hinsley, F. H. *British Intelligence in World War Two*. 4 Vols. London: HMSO, 1982–88.

Holmes, Richard. *Firing Line.* London: Jonathon Cape, 1985.

Horne, Alistair, and Brian Montgomery. *The Lonely Leader: Monty 1944–1945.* London: Macmillan, 1994.

How, Major J. *The British Breakout.* London: Kimber, 1981.

Howarth, T. E. B. Ed. *Monty at Close Quarters.* London: Leo Cooper with Martin Secker and Warburg, 1985.

Ingersoll, Ralph. *Top Secret.* New York: Harcourt Brace, 1946.

Irving, David. *The War between the Generals.* London: Allen Lane, 1981.

Jackson, Lt-Col. G. S. *Operations of Eighth Corps: Normandy to the River Rhine.* London: St Clements Press, 1948.

Keegan, John. *The Face of Battle.* London: Jonathon Cape, 1976.

———. *Six Armies in Normandy.* London: Jonathon Cape, 1982.

———. Ed. *Churchill's Generals.* London: Weidenfeld and Nicholson, 1991.

Kemp, Anthony. *The Unknown Battle: Metz 1944.* London: F. Warne, 1981.

Kershaw, Robert J. *It Never Snows in September: The German View of Market Garden & the Battle of Arnhem, September 1944.* Marlborough, England: Crowood Press, 1990.

Lamb, Richard. *Montgomery in Europe 1943–45: Success or Failure.* London: Buchan and Enright, 1983.

Lewin, Ronald. *Montgomery as Military Commander.* London: Batsford, 1971.

———. *Ultra Goes to War: The First Account of World War: Its Greatest Secret Based on Official Documents.* New York: McGraw-Hill, 1978.

Lewis, Jon E. Ed. *Eye-Witness D-Day.* London: Robinson, 1994.

Liddell Hart, Capt B. H. *Great Captains Unveiled.* London: Blackwood, 1927.

———. *The Other Side of the Hill.* London: Cassell, 1951.

———. *The Tanks.* 2 Vols. London: Cassell, 1959.

———. *History of the Second World War.* London: Cassell, 1970.

Lucas, J., and J. Barker. *The Killing Ground. The Battle of the Falaise Pocket.* London: Batsford, 1978.

MacDonald, C. B. *The Siegfried Line Campaign.* U.S. Army in World War II: European Theater of Operations. Washington, D.C.: Office of the Chief of Military History, Department of the Army, 1963.

Mackenzie, J. J. G., and Brian Holden Reid. Eds. *The British Army and the Operational Level of War.* London: Tri Service Press, 1988.

Marshall, S.L.A. *Men against Fire: The Problem of Command in Future War.* New York; Wm. Morrow, 1947.

Maule, Henry. *Caen: The Brutal Battle and the Breakout from Normandy.* London: Purnell, 1976.

McKee, Alexander. *Caen: Anvil of Victory.* London: Pan, 1964.

———. *The Race to the Rhine Bridges 1940, 1944, 1945.* London: Souvenir, 1971.

McNish, Robin. *Iron Division: The History of the 3rd Division.* London: Ian Allen, 1978.

Miller, Russell. *Nothing Less than Victory: The Oral History of D-Day.* London: Penguin, 1994.

Millet, Allan R., and Williamson Murray. Eds. *Military Effectiveness.* 3 Vols. Boston: Allen and Unwin, 1988.

Montgomery, B. L. *The Path to Leadership.* London: Collins, 1961.

Montgomery, Brian. *A Field Marshal in the Family.* London: Javelin, 1973.

Moorehead, A. *Montgomery.* London: Hamish Hamilton, 1946.

Moulton, J. L. *Battle for Antwerp: The Liberation of the City & the Opening of the Scheldt, 1944.* London: Ian Allen, 1978.

Murray, G. E. Patrick. *Eisenhower versus Montgomery: The Continuing Debate.* New York: Praeger, 1996.

North, John. *Northwest Europe.* London: HMSO, 1977.

O'Neill, H. C. [Strategicus, pseud.]. *The Victory Campaign, May 1944–August 1945.* London: Faber and Faber, 1947.

Orenstein, Harold S. Trans. *The Evolution of Soviet Operational Art, 1927–1991.* 2 Vols. London: Frank Cass, 1995.

Parker, H. M. D. *Manpower: A Study of Wartime.* Policy and Administration. History of the Second World War: UK Civil Series. London: HMSO, 1957.

Pemberton, A. L. *The Development of Artillery Tactics and Equipment.* The Second World War, 1939–45: Army. London: War Office, 1951.

Perry, F. W. *The Commonwealth Armies: Manpower and Organisation in Two World Wars.* Manchester, England: Manchester University Press, 1988.

Pogue, Forest C. *The Supreme Command.* U.S. Army in WW2; ETO. Washington, D.C.: Office of the Chief of Military History, Department of the Army, 1954.

Powell, G. *The Devil's Birthday: The Bridges to Arnhem, 1944.* New York: Franklin Watts, 1984.

Reid, Brian Holden. *J. F. C. Fuller: Military Thinker.* London: Macmillan, 1987.

———. Ed. *The Science of War: Back to First Principles.* London: Routledge, 1993.

Richardson, Charles. *Send for Freddie: The Story of Monty's Chief of Staff.* London: Kimber, 1987.

Rissik, David. *The D. L. I. at War.* Durham, England: DLI, 1953.

Ruppenthal, Roland G. *Logistical Support of the Armies.* 2 Vols. U.S. Army in World War II: European Theater of Operations. Washington, D.C.: Office of the Chief of Military History, Department of the Army, 1953–59.

Ryan, Cornelius. *A Bridge Too Far.* London: Hamish Hamilton, 1974.

Ryder, Roland. *Oliver Leese.* London: Hamish Hamilton, 1987.

Salmud, J. B. *The History of the 51st Highland Division.* Edinburgh, Scotland: Wm. Blackwood, 1953.

Schulman, Milton. *Defeat in the West.* London: Secker and Warburg, 1947; Revised Ed., London: Ballantine, 1968.

Smith, W. I. *Code Word Canloan.* Oxford: Dundurn Press, 1992.

Snoke, E. R. *The Operational Level of War.* Fort Leavenworth, Kans.: Combat Studies Institute, 1985.

Snowie, J. Allan. *Bloody Buron: The Battle of Buron, Caen—08 July 1944.* Erin: Boston Mills, 1984.

Sparrow, Lt-Col. J. H. A. *Morale.* The Second World War, 1939–1945: Army. London: War Office, 1949.

Stacey, C. P. *Official History of the Canadian Army in the Second World War.* Vol. 3. *The Victory Campaign.* Ottawa: The Queen's Printer, 1960.

———. *Arms, Men and Governments: The War Policies of Canada.* Ottawa: Queen's Printer, 1970.

———. *A Date with History.* Ottawa: Deneau, 1983.

Thompson, Maj-Gen. Julian. *The Lifeblood of War: Logistics in Armed Conflict.* London: Brassey's, 1991.

Thompson, R. W. *The Eighty Five Days: The Story of the Battle of the Scheldt.* London: Hutchinson, 1957.

———. *The Montgomery Legend.* London: Allen and Unwin, 1967.

————. *Montgomery the Field Marshal: A Critical Study.* London: Allen and Unwin, 1969.

————. *The Battle for the Rhineland.* London: Hutchinson, 1985.

Warner, Philip. *Horrocks: The General Who Led from the Front.* London: Hamish Hamilton, 1984.

Weigley, Russell F. *Eisenhower's Lieutenants: The Campaigns of France and Germany 1944–45.* London: Sidgewick and Jackson, 1981.

Whitaker, W. Denis, and Shelagh Whitaker. *The Battle of the River Scheldt.* London: Souvenir Press, 1985.

————. *Rhineland: The Battle to End the War.* London: Leo Cooper, 1989.

Whiting, Charles. *Poor Bloody Infantry 1939–45.* London: Arrow Books, 1989.

Williams, Jeffrey. *The Long Left Flank: The Hard Fought Way to the Reich, 1944–45.* London: Leo Cooper, 1988.

Wilmot, Chester. *The Struggle for Europe.* London: Collins, 1952.

Winterbottom, F. W. *The Ultra Secret.* London: Weidenfeld and Nicolson, 1974.

Articles, Theses, Dissertations, and Unpublished Monographs

Badsey, Stephen. "Faction in the British Army: Its Impact on 21st Army Group Operations in Autumn 1944." *War Studies Journal* 1 no. 1 (Autumn 1995): 13–28.

Bartov, Omer. "Indoctrination and Motivation in the Wehrmacht: The Importance of the Unquantifiable." *Journal of Strategic Studies* (March 1986): 16–34.

Blumenson, Martin. "The Most Over-rated General of World War Two." *Armor* (May–June 1962): 4–10.

Cole, Col A. G. "German Artillery Concentrations in World War Two." *Journal of the Royal Artillery* 75, no. 3 (July 1948): 196–99.

Copp, Terry. "Scientists and the Art of War: Operational Research in Twenty First Army Group." *RUSI Journal* 136, no. 4 (Winter 1991): 65–70.

Copp, Terry, and R. Vogel. "'No Lack of Rational Speed': First Canadian Army Operations, September 1944." *Journal of Canadian Studies* 16 (Fall–Winter 1981): 145–55.

Corkhill, Lt-Col W. G. R. "The Effectiveness of Conventional Field Branch Artillery in General War in North-West Europe." *Journal of the Royal Artillery* 94, no. 2 (September 1967): 117–23.

Dick, Charles J. "The Goodwood Concept—Situating the Appreciation." *RUSI Journal* 127, no.1 (March 1982): 22–26

Dickson, Paul D. "'The Hand that Wields the Dagger': Harry Crerar, First Canadian Army Command and National Autonomy." *War and Society* 13, no. 2 (Oct 1995): 113–41.

————. "The Politics of Army Expansion: General H. D. G. Crerar and the Creation of First Canadian Army, 1940–41." *Journal of Military History* 60, no. 2 (April 1996): 271–98.

————. "Command Relations in the Northwest Europe Campaign 1944–45." M.A. Thesis, Acadia University, 1985. (Unpublished).

Franz, Col W. P. "Operational Concepts." *Military Review* 64 (July 1984): 2–15.

French, David. "'Tommy Is No Soldier:' The Morale of Second British Army in Normandy, June–August 1944." *Journal of Strategic Studies* 19, no. 4 (December 1996): 154–78.

Harding Ganz, A. "Questionable Objective: The Brittany Ports, 1944." *Journal of Military History* 59, no. 1 (January 1995): 77–95.

Harington, General C., and Major D. L. Waterworth. "The Battle of 's-Hertogen-bosch, October 1944." *British Army Review* 80 (August 1985): 35–42.

Hart, Russell. "Feeding Mars: The Role of Logistics in the German Defeat in Normandy, 1944." *War in History* 3, no. 4 (1996): 418–35.

———. "Learning Lessons: Military Adaptation and Innovation in the American, British, Canadian, and German Armies during the 1944 Normandy Campaign." Ph.D. Diss., Ohio State University, 1997.

Hart, Russell, and Stephen Hart. "First Canadian Army's Operational Planning Process during the Autumn 1944 Scheldt Operations." Unpublished Paper, 1999.

Hart, Stephen. "Corps Command in North-West Europe." Unpublished Paper, 1999.

Howard, Michael. "How Will History Judge Montgomery's Generalship?," *The Times* (25 March 1976).

———. "Monty and the Price of Victory." *The Sunday Times* (16 October 1983).

Johnson, Paul. "What Makes a Great Commander?" *The Daily Mail* (20 November 1993).

Kohn, Richard R. Ed. "The Scholarship on World War II: Its Present Condition and Future Possibilities." *Journal of Military History* 55, no. 3 (July 1991): 365–94.

Liddell Hart, Capt B. H. "New Warfare—New Tactics." *Marine Corps Gazette* 39, no. 10 (October 1955):10–14.

Lossow, Lt-Col W. von. "Mission-Type Tactics versus Order-Type Tactics." *Military Review* 57 (June 1977): 877–91.

Luttwak, E. N. "The Operational Level of War." *International Security* 5, no. 3 (Winter 1980-81): 61–79.

Madej, W. V. "Effectiveness and Cohesion of the German Ground Forces in World War II," *Journal of Political and Military Sociology* 6 (1978): 233–48.

McAndrew, William. "Fire or Movement? Canadian Tactical Doctrine, Sicily." *Military Affairs* 51 (July 1987): 140–45.

Murray, G. E. Patrick. "Eisenhower and Montgomery, Broad Front versus Single Thrust: The Historiography of the Debate Over Strategy and Command, August 1944 to April 1945." Ph.D. Diss., Temple University, 1991.

Peaty, John. "Myth, Reality, and Carlo D'Este." *War Studies Journal* 1, no. 2 (Spring 1996): 60–72.

———. "Manpower and the 21st Army Group." Working Drafts for M.Phil/Ph.D. Diss, University of London, in progress.

Powers, S. T. "The Battle of Normandy: The Lingering Controversy." *Journal of Military History* 56 (July 1992): 455–71.

Reid, Brian Holden, "The Attack by Illumination: The Strange Case of Canal Defence Lights." *RUSI Journal* 128, no. 4 (Dec 1983): 35–42.

Rippe, Maj. S. T. "Leadership, Firepower and Manoeuvre: The British and the Germans." *Military Review* (October 1985): 32–39.

Samuels, Martin. "Operation Goodwood: The Caen Carve-Up.'" *British Army Review* 96 (December 1990): 4–13.

Scott, Major G. L. "British and German Operational Styles in World War Two." *Military Review* 65 (October 1985): 37–41.

Shils, E., and M. Janowitz. "Cohesion and Disintegration in the Wehrmacht in World War Two." *Public Opinion Quarterly* 12 (1948): 280–315.

Review Articles

Granatstein, J. L. "Granatstein on Montgomery." *Canadian Military History* 1, no. 1–2 (Autumn 1992): 95–96.

————. "Researching Guy Simonds." *Canadian Military History* 1, no. 1–2 (Autumn 1993): 32.
Lamb, Richard. "Rude but Effective." *The Spectator* (28 May 1994): 40–41.

Lectures
Simpkin, Peter. "North-West Europe, 1944–45." Metropolitan Police History Society (12 October 1994).

Index

Page numbers in italics indicate illustrations

Stackpole Military History Series

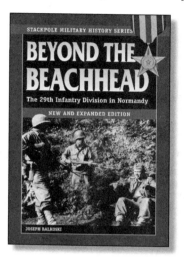

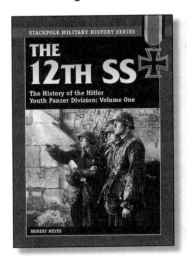 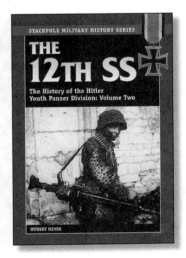

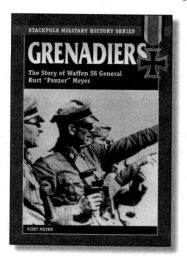

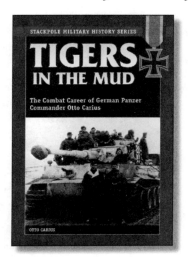

Stackpole Military History Series

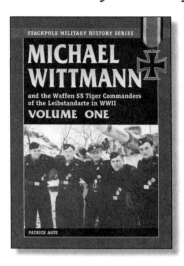

MICHAEL WITTMANN AND THE WAFFEN SS TIGER COMMANDERS OF THE LEIBSTANDARTE IN WORLD WAR II

VOLUME ONE

Patrick Agte

By far the most famous tank commander on any side in
World War II, German Tiger ace Michael Wittmann destroyed 138
enemy tanks and 132 anti-tank guns in a career that embodies the
panzer legend: meticulous in planning, lethal in execution, and
always cool under fire. Most of those kills came in the snow and mud
of the Eastern Front, where Wittmann and the Leibstandarte's
armored company spent more than a year in 1943–44 battling the
Soviets at places like Kharkov, Kursk, and the Cherkassy Pocket.

$19.95 • Paperback • 6 x 9 • 432 pages • 383 photos • 19 maps • 10 charts

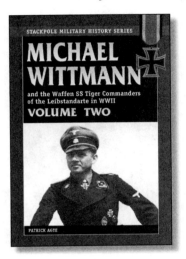

Stackpole Military History Series

ARMOR BATTLES
OF THE WAFFEN-SS
1943–45

Will Fey, translated by Henri Henschler

The Waffen-SS were considered the elite of the
German armed forces in the Second World War and
were involved in almost continuous combat. From
the sweeping tank battle of Kursk on the Russian
front to the bitter fighting among the hedgerows
of Normandy and the offensive in the Ardennes,
these men and their tanks made history.

$19.95 • Paperback • 6 x 9 • 384 pages
32 photos • 15 drawings • 4 maps

WWW.STACKPOLEBOOKS.COM
1-800-732-3669